Meet at the Schools

Meet at the Schools

A History of Education in Bream

Ian Hendy

Douglas McLean Publishing
Coleford, Gloucestershire

Published by
Douglas McLean
8 St John Street
Coleford
Gloucestershire
England
GL16 8AR

Typeset in Garamond 12 pt on 13.5 pt

British Library Cataloguing in Publication Data

A CIP catalogue record of this book is available from the British Library

ISBN 978-0-946252-67-1

Printed and Bound in England by
The Cromwell Press Ltd., Trowbridge, Wiltshire

Dedication

This book is dedicated to all those who have come through the gates –
pupils, teachers and parents. Past, present and future.

Contents

A Note on Money

Decimal currency was introduced into Britain in 1971. Prior to that date money values were based on pounds, shillings and pence (£. s. d.), i.e. 12 pence (12d.) to the shilling (1/- or 1s.) and 20 shillings (240 pence) to the pound.

Most money figures given in this book are expressed in pre-decimal currency. Obviously, the purchasing power of the pound has changed over time. On some of the past figures I have, for the sake of comparison, provided a modern value equivalent.

A Summary of Key Dates

1700	Mary Gough's will provided funding for a charity school.
1819	Revd Henry Poole affiliated Bream charity school to The National Society.
1830	Revd Henry Poole built the Tufts school.
1862	Cornelius Witherby completed the Eaves school.
1873	Extension completed by Reverend John Gosling.
1900	Further extension completed by Reverend Ernest F Eales.
1905-7	Temporary council school housed in the Primitive Methodist chapel schoolroom.
1907	Bream infants council school built.
1927	Bream girls' council school built.
1948	Bream Church/boys' school accepted voluntary controlled status.
1951	Bream girls' school became a secondary modern school for both boys and girls.
	Bream Church/boys' school became a junior mixed school.
1973	Secondary modern school closed.
1973-6	Bream junior school transferred to secondary modern school site.
1979	Bream Church/junior school site purchased by Gloucestershire County Council for use as library and youth and community centre.
1986	Bream infant and junior schools amalgamated to form Bream primary school.
2000	Glos. CC agreed to sale of youth and community centre to WDPC.
2004	David Milliband opened primary school extension.
2005	WDPC open parish office in community centre.
2007	Celebration of centenary of 1907 council school.

Acknowledgements

Thanks are due to the staff of *The Forester*, Forest Enterprise and Gloucestershire Archives for their support for this project and their permissions to reproduce a number of sources. Thanks go to my fellow governors, the staff of the school and the pupils for much appreciated support and practical contributions. Thanks go to Geoff Davies for his assistance in acquiring a number of photographs and the loan of some published but rare local material.

My thanks also go to Sue for word-processing a difficult manuscript, to Karen for checking the same and to Ella for her cartoons to enliven chapter five. Thanks also to Doug, Lyn and the publishing team for their enthusiasm and hard work.

Finally my thanks, as always, go to Catherine, my long-suffering wife. Without her support over the last three years this project would never have been completed. Alas, I shall now have to re-learn the delights of cleaning, ironing, cooking and gardening.

Foreword

I plead guilty for suggesting that Ian write a history of Bream School. But I have no regrets, simply because his achievement is amazing; a scrupulously researched celebration, not merely of the school's centenary, but a complete picture of education in the village, and in the context of local, national and international events.

As governors of Bream School, we share a concern for its present and future development, but its foundations and values are deep-rooted in a colourful and sometimes dramatic past, brought vividly to life through anecdotes relating to characters and events, and the fascinating collection of old photographs.

We are both 'foreigners' who have an affection and respect for the Forest, Bream and its school where I worked for sixteen years with Cath, Ian's wife, who has made her own contribution to this book as have the twenty-first century pupils.

Personally, I was very touched by the comment of the late Mrs Cecily Leach, a dear friend and head teacher of the infant's school in 1955. 'I loved my school' she confided to Ian, and to me she expressed her admiration for him and for his talents.

Ian's love of his subject, his affection for the many characters and his thorough dedication to his subject exemplify the best qualities of a good teacher – the ability to impart knowledge and inspire genuine interest through his enthusiasm and power of communication.

Elizabeth Cann 2007

Introduction

Meet at the Schools has taken over three years to research and write. Had I known at the time how much work was involved I am not sure that I would have taken it on! It came about when the governors became aware in 2004 that the school building was approaching its centenary. I was asked if I would produce a history of the school to help commemorate the anniversary. Like a fool I said yes. I am not sure which governor to 'blame' for the idea. It could have been Caroline Alty, Liz Cann or Alistair Kendall or a conspiracy of all three. Since Liz is the only governor still serving I have had a little revenge in asking her to write the foreword to this book. Thank you Liz.

In 2004 I was naïve in my assessment of the scale of educational records available for this project. Having been in education for most of my adult life, I assumed – falsely as it turned out – that being buried under a mountain of paper on educational initiatives was a comparatively recent phenomenon. I thought the paper mountain had started when the Comprehensive debate made education a political football in the 1960s. In fact there has always been a political agenda in education and on several different levels – nationally, at county level and in the immediate locality. Likewise there has always been a faith agenda as different groups have sought to develop or maintain their control of schools. Similarly, there has always been an economic agenda and the accountants of 1862 were as influential in the introduction of the Revised Code for Education (1862) as any are in today's performance management and national curriculum. Vested interests are powerful and the thought of an educational agenda uncluttered by any other interest is a pipedream.

Originally it was my intention to cover the history of the present school over the last 100 years. In fact, to understand how the 1907 building came about it became necessary to go back well before 1907. It soon became apparent that to focus only on 1907–2007 would result in a very incomplete story. Education in Bream goes back over 300 years and embraces a number of different schools in different locations and at different times. The original '100 year idea' consequently evolved into a 300 year epic.

Meet at the Schools, the title of this book, is from a phrase I first heard when I moved into the village nearly thirty years ago. The football club played all their home games in Bathurst Park, Lydney at the time and, whether playing home or away, they would always 'meet at the schools' before matches. I think people have been 'meeting at the schools' for nigh on 150 years. Even in the 1860s when the boys school and the girls school were separate departments, I think people would have referred to 'the schools.' And the schools were the centre of village life. The buildings have always been used for various community events, even for club photographs. It is appropriate now that the 1862 school is a parish office and a community centre. In a sense it has always been that.

If one were asked to define the key components that make up a Forest village community, different people would respond in different ways. Some would argue that the church and/or chapel is essential. Others would highlight sports clubs, pubs, shops or a post office. Most would agree that the school is a major part of the village community. In Bream we are fortunate that all of these elements are present. When village schools close because of lack of numbers something very precious disappears from that community.

Change and continuity are central to any history of education. The practicalities of the teaching and learning processes change. The technology now available is very different, even over a comparatively short period of time. Yet at heart much remains the same. For a new teacher to brave a class of children for the first time is surely as daunting in 2007 as it was in 1862 when the Eaves School was built. Then, as now, inspectors' visits were dreaded by staff. Then, as now, inspectors could damn with faint praise. Then, as now, teachers could take issue with inspectors' findings. *Plus ça change, plus la même chose!* In February 1959, the new head of Bream Secondary Modern, Mr Stokes, expressed concern at the lack of facilities in the area for children and young people. A head today might make the same point.

History can be written around famous people. I have deliberately avoided any name dropping of the subsequent careers of past pupils over the last fifty years. No doubt some have gone on to fame and prominence but I certainly am not in a position to judge whether to include them or not. In this case the democratic option is safer. None are called and none are chosen.

I have spoken to many people in the village and beyond during my research. A few are named in the text. The rest are too many to list but, believe me, they have my sincere thanks. As with *Retrieving Wenty's Sturty Bird'* [1] this book is a community effort and many have contributed to the final outcome.

---

[1] *Retrieving Wenty's Sturty Bird,* the stories behind the names on Bream Cenotaph by Ian Hendy. Published by Black Dwarf Publications, Lydney, 2001.

Memory can be a strange thing. It is not always reliable. Talk to two children about a teacher and they may have completely different views. Childhood memories can be particularly vulnerable. 'When we are young we think as a child.' As adults we 'see through a glass darkly' and are less black and white in our assessments. Some of the stories in this book are based on very young memories – sincerely held but so distant they may be difficult to confirm with absolute certainty.

Even the written record can be open to doubt. Heads are upright and honest citizens but when they describe an incident in the log book it may be the version the head wants posterity to accept. If there is another side to the story it may never have been told. No matter how full the record is, it can never be complete. That said, if my description of events here is, in any way, in error, my apologies. Similarly, if anything written causes offence I apologise unreservedly.

Back in 2004, I was curious as to what had happened to the school bell. When the school was built in 1907 the bell was in a small tower on the roof, similar to the bell on St James Church. It performed a similar function. As the church bell summoned people to church, so the school bell told children and parents it was time for school. Any number of people still ask me if I know what happened to the bell. My answer is both yes and no.

The bell was operated by a rope inside the school entrance hall. In 1966 a young teacher named Hilary Wood (née Wildin) was ringing the bell and the mechanism broke or jammed. Possibly, Hilary didn't know her own strength.

Hilary would be mortified if that was the end of the story. It was not. I have been reassured by Mrs Maisie Kear that, prior to Hilary 'breaking' it, the bell was already defective. It was apparently cracked and you had to know exactly how to ring it to get it to work at all. The bell probably needed a considerable amount of money spending on it to return it to its former glory. The Local Educational Authority (LEA) seemed to have decided that it was not worth it. The bell–rope was removed the following year. Later, as the 1907 roof deteriorated, structural repairs were necessary and the non-functioning bell was taken down, probably for safety reasons. By now it had outlived its original function. Every home had clocks and watches that could tell parents and children when it was time to go to school. In the school itself there was also an old air-raid warden's handbell that could be heard all over the site.

Sadly the bell went into outside storage. I suspect it disappeared completely when County Supplies collected surplus furniture and stock from the infant school before it amalgamated with the junior school in

1986. In its heyday, I suspect that bell could have been heard as far away as Clements End and Brockhollands. It was part of the history of the school. Along with any other item that gives us a significant connection with the school's past it should, in my opinion, have been retained.

People today sometimes voice regret at the passing of childhood. We bemoan the fact that our consumer society makes children grow up before their time. Research for this book gives a different view on this argument. Where was childhood in Bream 150 years ago when probably all the village schoolchildren were in full-time employment by the age of twelve? It is likely that some never went to school at all and were at work by six years of age.

It may be that each generation has a different perspective on how to treat children and on how they should be educated. Today any trips involving children are very bureaucratic and every eventuality has to be risk-assessed. The difference can be illustrated by two specific events, one in 1966 and the other in 1879.

On 8 September 1966 the present Queen opened the Severn Bridge between Aust and Beachley. Most staff in the schools in Bream at the time took the 'easy' option. Courtesy of the new technology of black-and-white television the children watched the event at school on TV. Some however in the secondary modern school went as a party with Peter Saysell, the pottery teacher, to witness the event at first hand. Who had the better experience – the TV watchers or the trippers?

When the railway bridge across the Severn at Purton was opened on 15 September 1879, there was of course no television to record the event. Nor was there a school party organised to go there. Yet most of the schoolchildren of Bream went. They simply made their own way. Probably they went in groups or – if parents could afford time off work – with families. A different world.

The centenary of the school building is a matter of celebration. Indeed 300 years of education in the village should be a matter of enormous pride for the whole community.

I am delighted that the children of the school are responsible for chapter nine. This illustrates what a joy we have in our midst.

Chapter nine shows how far education has come since the Reverend Francis Close, an eminent early nineteenth century Cheltenham clergyman, wrote 'peaceful and hopeful death beds are the real end and object of education'!

Ian Hendy
Hang Hill
2007

CHAPTER ONE

1907:
'A very handsome pile of buildings'

The current Bream school that we all know and, I hope, love was erected in 1907. That fact is self-evident even to a stranger visiting the school for the first time since the date is prominent at the top of the down-spout to the left of the main entrance door. Likewise the original function of the school is not in doubt since in capital letters a foot high the name BREAM INFANTS SCHOOL is inscribed over the main door. Now of course it is no longer specifically an infant school and in fact, such was the rate of change 100 years ago, it was no longer just an infant school within five years of it being built.

The building of the school was in response to a local educational crisis that very much mirrored a national malaise of underfunding and lack of organisation in education. Nationally, the late nineteenth century had seen a tremendous increase in the number of pupils – nearly two million in 1870 had risen to four and a half million by 1886. This pressure on accommodation was exacerbated by the raising of the school leaving age – to eleven in 1893, twelve in 1899 and a staggering fourteen in 1900. The organisational system complicated matters further because in some areas there were board schools funded from local rates as well as a grant from Central Government but in many areas schools were controlled by voluntary societies, principally The National Society of the Church of England and the British Society of the Nonconformist Chapels. The voluntary schools were funded locally by the churches or chapels and by an inadequate central grant. Money was scarce and the steady increase in pupil numbers caused serious problems.

Bream, in common with many rural villages at the beginning of the twentieth century, had a National School which was run by Bream Church and located at the present parish office and community centre. The

National School – or schools since there was a mixed school and a separate infants school – educated all Bream children, other than those in private education, up to the age of fourteen. The school was not only suffering pressure from a national trend of increasing pupil numbers, but also from the economic growth of Bream as an industrial village with families moving in because of the prospect of employment in the Forest coalfield. For these reasons, Bream National School was bursting at the seams. Led by the vicar of the time, Ernest F Eales, a major fund-raising exercise was undertaken and the school was considerably extended in 1900. Yet within twelve months of this the accommodation was being described as 'insufficient' by the inspectorate. By 1903 the inspectors were advising that the infants be housed in a separate new school.

Clearly this would have been beyond the financial capability of Bream Church and The National Society but salvation was to hand. 1902 saw the passing of the Balfour Education Act, one of the greatest constructive measures of the twentieth century. The act abolished the school boards and gave county councils a statutory and financial responsibility for schools in their area.

In 1903 Gloucestershire County Council Education Committee began its long and illustrious career. No doubt much to the relief of the treasurer of Bream church, the maintenance and running expenses of Bream National School were now met by the county council out of the rates. Any new school would be completely funded by the county council. Because the overcrowding situation in Bream was so dire, the new infants school, as suggested by the inspectors in 1903, became a county council priority. Thus Bream infants school built in 1907 was one of the first council schools in Gloucestershire. Ironically it was not, however, the first council school in Bream.

Bream Temporary Council School

That honour goes to Bream temporary council school which existed from 1905–7. A decision to build a new infants school had been taken by the County Council Education Committee shortly after they came into existence in the spring of 1903 but building a new school involved acquiring a suitable site, organising, funding and tendering, carrying out public consultation and notice. All this could be a protracted process. In Bream, courtesy of the Office of Woods, it became a very protracted process and Bream infants school took four years from conception to completion.

16

Meanwhile the overcrowding at Bream National School was desperate and requiring urgent action. The solution was to educate some of the children in a temporary council school until such time as the new school would be built. The temporary school was located in the schoolroom of the Primitive Methodist Chapel, now known as the Eaves Centre. The chapel itself had been built in 1858 and had just built a commodious Sunday school room in 1903.

There are two documents in the Public Record Office (PRO) that relate to this temporary school, ED21/6048 and ED7/35/347A, that tell us the school opened on 9 January 1905 with 102 junior mixed standard I children and closed on 31 October, 1907. The council paid an annual rental of £30 to the chapel trustees. Being standard I, the children would already have left the infants department of Bream National School and would be aged seven and eight.

It is staggering to know now that there were only two teachers for the 102 children on roll. They were Mrs Annie M Hine (née Morse) a trained certificated teacher who was the head and Miss Mary W Smith supplementary teacher. Both came from the National School. And was everything perfect in the temporary school on day one? Of course not. Work was still going on in the cloakroom and toilets so they could not be used. Four days later the girls had access to two WCs but the school had been working for a week before the boys had access to their toilets. By this stage the cloakroom was ready except that the workmen had no pegs for hats and coats; they used eighty-eight nails instead. It was not till February that the pegs were installed – ninety-six of them and each one numbered. It goes without saying that there was no school clock until the beginning of March and the new desks, ordered in February, did not arrive till 31 March.

Staffing at the temporary school had a high turnover; possibly the head of the mixed school, Mr W F Mullan, saw it as an opportunity to give different staff some responsibility and independence. Mrs Hine served as head for one year only and was replaced by Miss Sara Ann Wrighton in January 1906. The assistant teacher, Miss Smith, was replaced by Miss Kezia A Fox in September 1905, who was in turn replaced by Miss Lucy Amy Barrington in March, 1907. Miss Barrington herself left in June and was replaced by Miss Jennie Ethel Jones. In September she in turn was replaced by Miss E J Hatch. Thus in less than three years the two classes of standard I children had been taught by two different heads and five different assistant teachers. Rarely has the staff of any Bream school had such a rapid turnover.

As far as the children themselves were concerned the temporary school was a place of transition. Children came up from the infants school in May 1905, June 1906 and September 1907 and at the same time children left the temporary school to go up to standard II in the mixed school. The transition seemed to operate with the minimum of disruption. The log book tells us that on 11 June 1906 Mr Baker 'marched down' sixty-one children (twenty-six boys and thirty-five girls) for standard I and took back seventy-four (forty boys and thirty-four girls) for standard II. Those were the days when pupil teacher ratios really were pupil teacher ratios. The fact of the transfer in 1907 being in September rather than May or June reflects a different end to the school year and one that we currently still employ.

Moving up a standard at this point in time at Bream seems to have been done according to age rather than ability. Miss Wrighton bemoans the fact that of the seventy-four she sent up to standard II in June 1906, some twenty were 'backward' and 'not fit to work a standard II syllabus.' She also stated that most of the twenty were 'weak and delicate' children. Whether progression should be by age or ability or both has always been (and, still is) an issue in education, elsewhere as well as at Bream, and there were certainly times at Bream when the school was castigated by the inspectorate for straying too far one way or the other.

The behaviour of the children in the temporary school seems for the most part to have been good and there are few recorded incidents of misbehaviour. A special lesson was given in June 1905 on the great use that birds are in destroying insects. By doing this the staff were hoping to discourage the children from 'bird-nesting'. In February 1906, one of the managers complained that a board had been taken out of the harmonium and that the seat round the room had been scratched, but this may well have been the head's fault because, on her own confession, she allowed the children to stand on this seat so they could see properly for object lessons. Hob-nailed boots are not particularly kind to furniture. Another incident that occurred was when the boys' toilet seat (their only one) was broken. This was reported at the end of May 1906 but was not finally repaired or replaced till 23 July. This particular problem ended up being reported to the vicar, the Reverend Cass, not probably because he was in charge of toilets but (and more likely) because it was a serious matter and he as a manager would have had a commissioning role in the repair.

The children's routine school life was occasionally interrupted by special events. On 29 June, 1905 a whole holiday was given for a Band of Hope festival at Cinderford. A similar closure occurred in June 1907, and the log book records the interesting fact that many children from Bream were attending. Special half-day holidays were also given whenever church or chapel organised their respective Sunday school treats and in July these came rather thick and fast. For example in 1906 half-holidays occurred on 5, 10, 11 and 19 July. Presumably the children attended all of these treats irrespective of whether they attended chapel or church or not (though non-attendance would have been rare at the time). July 1906 must have been a special time for the children. As well as attending their four treats they also were privileged to hear – probably for the first time – a gramophone. This event was clearly special to merit entry in the school log book. The gramophone – no doubt a wind-up one – was specially brought in by the vicar 'for the children to hear.' The machine had only been invented some twenty years previously. It is possible the vicar was one of the first in the village to acquire one and it is highly likely that none of the children had heard one before. I find it difficult to speculate how they would have felt on hearing a gramophone for the first time and whether our current seven and eight-year-olds, living as they do in a technological age, could possibly have a comparable experience. If so, what might it be? It would also be interesting to know what type of record the vicar first played to them – band music, a song, opera? No doubt whatever it was, it would have crackled and had a variable speed.

Apart from closing for holidays the school also could easily be closed on medical grounds. We are reminded of how fragile young life could be by a log book entry for 18 January 1907 which records that 'many children were away ill, some with measles, Gordon Camm with diphtheria.' The vicar, Reverend Cass, visited that afternoon and probably with the consent of other managers authorised the immediate closure of the school and the nearby Church of England school. The vicar's action was challenged on a technicality in that he acted without the previous authority of the Sanitary Authority, the medical officer of health (MOH), who was based in Cinderford. Cass himself asked the Board of Education for a ruling as to whether his prompt action had been justified. I am confident that the community would have fully supported the vicar irrespective of the ruling; had the school stayed open until the MOH had arrived and a child had subsequently died, the vicar would have found himself in a difficult position.

In any set of regulations primacy should always be given to common sense and while the vicar may have had difficulty justifying closure to the Board of Education, I am sure he would have had no such difficulty in respect of the local community.

The school stayed closed for six weeks, re-opening on 4 March. Even so the crisis was not yet over – late in March three more children were ill with diphtheria and one with scarlet fever. However I am pleased to record that no school children died in Bream in 1907. The vicar's action was therefore fully justified.

In terms of what these seven and eight-year-olds studied at school we are fortunate that the Scheme of Instruction for 1906–7 has survived. The timetable consisted of:

Arithmetic
Reading
Writing
Geography
History
Recitation
Drawing (Boys)
Needlework (Girls)
Elementary Science
Nature Study
Singing
Drawing for Boys and Girls

It would be interesting to compare the details of what was taught and how it was taught in 1907 and 2007. To take one subject as an example, the details of the geography syllabus were as follows:

Geography:
    Definitions of wood, forest, hill, mountain, valley, village, town,
    illustrated from scenery seen from school yard
    Meaning and use of plans and maps
    Cardinal points
    Descriptive lessons on people of far off lands

Much of the teaching on a ratio of one teacher to fifty pupils would be by chalk-and-talk and slate but clearly there was an emphasis on using the environment, for instance the school yard, as a teaching resource. The school log book for 15 May 1906 informs us 'Geography lesson taken outside the school on places seen from school yard.' Of course at that time there would have been an uninterrupted view from the yard. What a practical and delightful way of learning definitions of wood, forest, hill and valley.

It is important to remember that throughout the existence of this temporary council school, work was underway with the planning and building of the new council infants school at the crossroads and opposite the Church school. It is also important to remember that the children in the temporary school were not infants but seven and eight-year-olds. Thus when the infants school was finally completed in October 1907 and the temporary school was no longer required the infants vacated the infants school in what is now Bream library to move across the road and the seven and eight-year-olds were then moved into the Church school. Thus the children from the temporary school missed out completely on the new infants school. There is a famous postcard photograph of Bream school-girls taken in the car park of the present sports club and with the schools in the background. The photo was taken in 1908 and I like to think it may have been compensation for those girls who 'missed out' on the new school.[2]

Difficulties over the site

Building a new school nowadays is an immensely costly and consequently very rare event. It is also time consuming. In the late nineteenth and early twentieth centuries however, new schools were regularly being built and though of usually solid materials – stone and/or brick – they were in comparative terms cheaper to build than now because unit labour costs were lower. They did though, as now, take time to plan and to build. This was certainly true of Bream infants council school which took some four years from start to finish.

Discussions as to the site of the proposed school began in the spring of 1904. As required by law the Education Department of Gloucestershire County Council, usually now known as the LEA, issued a public notice of their intention to build a new public elementary school for about 250 infants at a site to be selected at Bream and serving the parishes or townships of West Dean, Newland, Lydney and St Briavels. The notice was dated 9 May 1904 and published in the local press once a month for three months. By now the decision to go ahead had already been taken and negotiations could begin with the Office of Woods and Forests as to where the building should be.

At this point negotiations became difficult since the Office of Woods had a different view to that of the LEA and the local community. For once the local community were in complete accord with what the county council were trying to achieve – there does, I suppose, have to be a first

---

[2] See cover picture and page 31

time for everything. The principal protagonists in the negotiations were Mr P Bayliss, Deputy Surveyor of Woods in the Forest of Dean, and Mr Horace W Household, secretary of the Gloucestershire Education Committee.

Five possible sites were under discussion and, as it happened, the site the County and the community wanted was the one the deputy surveyor least wished to sell. Throughout the discussions he threw up objection after objection to the site Horace Household wanted to purchase on behalf of the County but Household conducted a shrewd and tough negotiation. He countered every objection that was raised and ultimately ground down the deputy surveyor to achieve the best possible site for the school. Horace West Household served Gloucestershire Education Committee for over thirty years from 1903 till his retirement in 1936. His contribution to education in Gloucestershire in the twentieth century was huge and bears comparison with that of Robert Raikes in the eighteenth century, the founder of the Sunday School movement. Insofar as any one person deserves all the credit for building Bream School in 1907 that person was Horace Household. It was literally the case of the hero being a household name.

The five possible sites under discussion for the new school were known by the labels A, B, C, D and E. (See plan on page 32) The county council held local consultations and very much preferred site E. The Office of Woods however, preferred to sell sites A and/or B. Site A can now be accessed from Lansdowne Walk or Blue Rock Crescent and currently consists of four properties – Floradin, Holly Cottage, Overdale and Cornerways. Site B consisted of the land on which The Keys Pub and Snippets is built through to Hang Hill Road. In 1906 this was used as a playground for the school. Site C was the land at the top of Whitecroft Road which later housed the Co-op. Site D was the land opposite the present chemist's shop and site E is the current site of the school. All five sites were technically Forest waste, but from the Office of Woods' point of view they were of varying value as sites for growing and harvesting timber.

Initially, in July 1904 Deputy Surveyor Philip Bayliss was reluctant to sell B and C because those sites adjoined land already alienated (sold) and therefore they would be easy for the Office of Woods to sell. He definitely did not want to sell D and E because they did not adjoin any land which was not the property of the Crown and they were both covered in timber.

He raised a further strong objection to D and E on grounds of safety because they bordered on the High Street and were opposite the Church of England or National School i.e. the school children used the road as a playground and when he had visited Bream to check on the sites he had found over 150 children from the Church school 'playing in the road' (what a different world!) His suggestion was that the LEA should build on the present playground (site B) and use site A as a playground because it had 'a beautiful view.' Mr Household said no to this suggestion and asked directly if the Crown would sell site E. The Office of Woods in London in turn said no to this and, as an inducement, they were prepared to offer B or C at the cheap price of 30/- per perch.

In October 1904 Horace Household detailed the LEA reasons for favouring site E. It was exactly opposite the existing school and thus the older children could take the younger ones to and from the infant school. It was level ground and easy to build on. The local community favoured this site. Household dismissed site A as being small, an awkward shape, 100 yards from a metalled road and only accessed by 'narrow dirty cart roads', and finally for the fact that the overflow from the cesspool at the mixed school ran out over this land. This last point really punched home and within two weeks the Office of Woods in London had instructed Bayliss to give formal notice to the mixed school managers to stop their cesspit overflowing.

By May 1905 Household was winning the argument. He wrote again to Whitehall to ask whether the Crown would sell site E. Reluctantly Whitehall agreed in principle provided there were safeguards not to allow the children to play on the road. Bayliss however still had a few cards to play. He offered to sell site E in June 1905 but at the increased price of 35/- per perch and on condition that there was no gate in the fence on the south-east side i.e. facing the mixed school. He went even further by suggesting that the county council should build a tunnel under the High Street to safely connect the two schools. Later Bayliss wrote to Whitehall that the price 'since they persist (in site E)' is to be £2 per perch *and* they would have to pay for all the timber on site as a growing crop. At this point Household wrote to Bayliss that he (Household) had had a letter from London agreeing a price of 35/- per perch and was his (Bayliss') price of £2 an error? The Office of Woods did eventually rule on a price of 35/- per perch since this was a sale 'for a public matter.'

By the beginning of 1906 an out-manoeuvred Bayliss had conceded. It had taken Household eighteen months of tough negotiation but he had achieved what he, the county council and the local community wanted. A lesser man would not have succeeded. In a document dated 24 February 1906 the Office of Woods consented to sell three roods, 37¾ perches at

35/- per perch in Parkend Walk[3]. The length of the boundaries were to be on the south-east side 410 links, south-west side 364 links, north-east side 311 and north-west side 224. In February the trees were counted, numbered and measured according to their girth. The girth established the value. There were sixty-six trees, the biggest was valued at 19s. 3d. and their total value was assessed at £30. 19s. 6d. Of course not all of them were cut down, many were retained and a few have survived even to this day and that is so appropriate in a Forest school.

The bill of sale did specify there was to be no opening in the fence on the High Street side of the school so in one sense Mr Bayliss did not leave the negotiations empty-handed. Thus the Oakwood Road entrance to Bream school was a legal requirement. Some of you may point out that there is a side gate on the south-east side opposite Blue Rock Crescent but this was a later gate for a later and different school and belongs in another chapter. The bill of sale also specified that the local wells or springs would need to be safeguarded from pollution.

The total cost of the land conveyed by the Office of Woods on 30 May 1906 was £307. 1s. This figure consisted of three roods at 35/- per perch (£210), 37¾ perches at 35/- (£66. 1s. 3d.) and timber (66 trees at £30. 19s. 6d.). The total was rounded up to the nearest shilling.

The Building Itself

Plans had been drawn up by the LEA at the beginning of 1906 but had to be revised on recommendations from the Board of Education in London. The Board was particularly concerned that there should be 'adequate provision for marching' with a corridor, now the entrance hall, 12 feet wide, that the soil drains should be laid in concrete, that the infant urinal should be at least 10 feet long and that the classrooms should be arranged so that the greater part of them face south or south-east because 'it is important to get all the sun possible into the rooms in cases of schools for young children.' The plans were revised and approved by the Board of Education on 17 July 1906.

Building could now go out to tender. Remarkably eighteen tenders were received ranging from £2,763 to £4,640. The Education Committee

---

[3] Historical footnote on imperial measurements:

1 perch = 30¼ square yards

1 rood = 40 perches = over 10 acres

1 link = 7.92 inches

(The link was one link in a surveyors chain which consisted of 100 links. 100 links = 1 chain = 22 yards = the length of a cricket pitch).

accepted the lowest which was from Messrs Orchard and Peer of Stroud. Remarkably the school was to have a 'heating apparatus' – one is tempted to use the adjective new-fangled – which was to have radiators, certainly something that was not to exist in the Church school for many years yet. The heating apparatus was to be installed by Messrs Bevan and Sons of Gloucester at a price of £59. 10*s*.

And how was all this to be funded? Gloucestershire County Council took out two loans in December 1906 for a total of £3,350 to cover land and building works to be repaid over thirty years and a further loan of £200 for furnishing which was to be repaid over ten years – the total cost of the entire project therefore being £3,550 (though the printed Education Committee minutes dated 27 April 1907 has the loan total as being slightly higher at £3,650) . It is interesting to compare building costs in 1907 with those of 1998 when the new hall and accompanying two classrooms were built. The building cost of 1906-7 would equate to some £255,000 in 2005. The building grant of 1998 was £400,000 which would be £472,000 in 2005. How building costs change; the original school of four classrooms and an entrance hall was comparably nearly half the price of its 1998 extension.

Building work began early in 1907. As Horace Household had pointed out the site was level and therefore should be easy to build on. It was not however completely straightforward. For one thing, there was a pond in the middle of it as illustrated on the site plan. When I first saw the site plan I remembered a conversation I had with Alice Cook. Alice remembers her mother telling her that the land on which the school had been built was wet – clearly Alice's mother remembered the pond. Presumably the pond would have to be drained (in fact it was not). Also some of the trees would need to be felled. A further problem which had been raised by Philip Bayliss was the need to safeguard local wells and springs from pollution. The site diagram shows a dry well to be built in the corner of the site by the present day double gates with an overflow going under Oakwood Road and feeding into the ditch that ultimately runs down the side of Bream cricket and football pitch.

Early in October, Horace Household wrote a letter to the Forest of Dean Group of Council Schools Managers who met at Cinderford to advise that the Education Committee had decided that the new school would be entrusted to their care and that the building would be ready in a few weeks. He asked that they agree a date for opening and organise a celebratory event. The Forest of Dean managers in turn agreed that the West Dean managers should decide these issues and they also recommended that one or two people from Bream should be asked to become members of the council schools group. That honour went to the Reverend George William Leonard Cass, vicar of Bream, and John Edwin Hirst of Bream Eaves, grocer and draper.

The delegation of the opening event to West Dean managers was an interesting example of co-operation between East and West Dean. It was customary that both contributed to each other's schools (ref. *Dean Forest Guardian* 10 June 10 1904). However, the same newspaper article reported that a Mr Nicholls (no doubt from West Dean) stated that West Dean had contributed 'wonderfully' to East Dean's schools but wanted to ask what help East Dean had given to West Dean's schools? Fortunately the chair ruled the question out of order and open warfare between East and West Dean was averted.

The West Dean managers decided the opening of the school should take place on Thursday evening 30 October 1907. This was very much a local news item and we are fortunate that a full description of the building is contained in the *Dean Forest Guardian* on Friday 18 October 1907. This description is here produced in full:

'Operations were commenced very early in the present year, and having regard to the bad hay-making weather, which is therefore equally hindering in regard to building operations, the contractors are to be congratulated on having got the work out of hand well within the specified time. It is satisfactory to be able to note that as far as practicable the builders have engaged local labour – they could not well do otherwise than use local material as far at least as the shell of the building is concerned, and it is a pleasant reflection that the operations have been carried through without accident or untoward event of any kind. The main block consists of one large room, and two smaller ones. Arrangements are provided so that the large room can, if necessary, be divided into halves, making them four classrooms in all. This large apartment measures 50 feet by 25 feet, the classrooms proper being 18 feet square. As regards these latter, they rise 11 inches from the floor to the wall plate, or 14 feet to the level of the ceiling. There is a marching hall 30 feet by 13 feet whilst the cloakroom is 16 feet square. The lavatories measure 12 feet by 4 feet, and there are six basins in them. An abundant supply of water is provided by a tank fixed in the roof, the tank being supplied from a large underground reservoir, capable of holding several thousand gallons, and is fed with a pump which raises the water from the underground store. The heating chamber, also underground is 16 feet square. It is provided with a sectional boiler, of the

Rose Marie type, and the heating pipes are carried from two radiators to each of the rooms above described. It should be pointed out that the heating arrangements are carried out by Messrs. Bevan and Sons, of Westgate Street, Gloucester, a firm of high repute and renown, and who always do their work well. As we have already said the building is of grey Forest stone, supplied by the Forest of Dean Stone Firms, whilst the Wilderness red dressings are supplied by the same firm. The roof is covered with Broseley tiles, and in the centre of the main covering is a good sized bell turret and bell, which lends added beauty and pretty effect to the establishment. It will readily be noticed by anyone on seeing it that the contrast set up by the grey stone and the red dressings, is very pretty, and has quite a charming effect. The interior of the rooms is stained green, and varnished. There is, of course, a spacious playground – it contains about an acre, and the whole of the property is surrounded by iron fencing, 5 feet 6 inches high, supplied and fixed by Messrs. Chew and Sons, King Street, Stroud. It is painted a dark Holland green. It should be added that an excellent play shed is provided and that the children's offices are up-to-date, and that careful regard is had for all those considerations which would naturally occur in arranging all these things.'

Some parts of this article need explanation. What is referred to as 'the lavatories' would today be called washbasins and what are referred to as 'the children's offices' means their toilets. These were outside. Sadly the fence, provided by Messrs Chew & Sons of Stroud, unlike the building, did not make its century. It had to be replaced in 2006, aged ninety-nine.

It is not difficult to see the 1907 layout in the present school. The entrance hall of the school now accommodating the junior library was the original marching hall which measured 34 feet by 12 feet.

The present secretary's office and the head's office were the two smaller classrooms being 18 feet square. The 1907 large classroom sometimes called the schoolroom measured 50 feet by 25 feet but could be partitioned into two rooms of approximately 25 feet square. This room was the furthest away from the school entrance (see photo page 34) and ran the entire width of the school and approximately parallel to Oakwood Road. It has the weather vane on top and currently is Mrs Wathen's classroom and the infant library. Off to the left of the marching hall was the washroom and cloakroom.

The toilets, measuring 26 feet by 8 feet, were outside. A separate description in the *Gloucester Journal* for 2 November informs us that the architect was Mr R S Phillips who was the official architect and surveyor for the LEA. The Journal also informs us of a detail that some of us will well remember that all the rooms and corridors had glazed brick dados. A further fact recorded in the Journal that is of interest is that 'half of the site was allowed to remain in its original state' and 'very few' of the sixty-six trees were removed. The natural state of much of the site is actually visible in the A J Batten 1907 post card of the school even to the fact that the pond had not been drained. Now of course school grounds are very much more managed in terms of risk and even environmental areas are carefully designed.

The school was intended to accommodate 200 children, forty each in the two 18 feet square classrooms and sixty each in the two parts of the schoolroom. Of course nobody is now alive who attended the school in 1907 but an ex-Bream pupil who was at the school during the First World War, Margaret Addis, did tell me a lovely story concerning the marching hall. In 1917 America came into the war on the side of the allies against Germany. It was hoped this would help to break the stalemate on the Western Front and was a cause of much celebration in this country. The infants of Bream School, to celebrate the event, were made to march from the marching hall into the schoolroom and then out of the other school-room door back into the marching hall singing 'Yankee Doodle came to town a riding on a pony . . .' A delightful image.

The Grand Opening, 30 October 1907

The public meeting to commemorate the handing over of the school to the County Education Committee took place in the schoolroom on Thursday 30 October 1907. Unfortunately the man who had done the most to build the school, Horace Household, could not attend. He sent his apologies. Chairman for the evening and one of the principle speakers was Mr Sidney J Elsom JP who was chair of the Forest of Dean Group of Council Schools. Mr Elsom praised the building as a 'very handsome pile of buildings.' He also referred to the 'not a few' people who had opposed the building of the school on grounds of expenditure but he felt that 'money judiciously spent . . . for the training of the young was well spent' and that he 'could not conceive of money being better employed than in educating the children of the working class.' He then went on to say that 'the value of education consisted not merely in making clever men and women but in teaching them the value of good citizenship.' Who could argue?

The following speaker, the Reverend G W L Cass, in his opening remarks also referred to those who had opposed the building of the school when he asked whether congratulations or condolences were more appropriate for the people of Bream on their brand new school.

It is interesting to speculate on the possible reasons for local opposition to the school. Earlier in this chapter, I described the Balfour Education Act of 1902 as 'one of the greatest constructive measures of the twentieth century.' In 1902 however it faced significant nonconformist opposition in that it gave financial Local Government support to Church schools such as Bream National School. Many nonconformists resented the virtual stranglehold the Church of England had on education and were hopeful that lack of money would gradually result in Church schools 'withering on the vine.'

The 1902 Act, because it subsidised Church schools out of the County rates, ensured that this would not happen. No doubt there were some in the village who shared this disgruntlement with the act. If they were nonconformists why should they have to pay rates to Gloucestershire County Council which were then used to subsidise a Church school in the village which their children had little or no option but to attend.

A probably far more significant reason for opposition to the new school would be financial. Not only would people be paying a county council rate for education but there would also be a levy on East and West Dean and the parishes of Newland (then stretching to parts of Bream) and possibly Lydney (if pupils came up from the town) to help pay for the school. We know there was a lot of financial hardship in Bream in the early twentieth century and any rate increase would understandably be resented.

Of course there is another possible reason for opposing the building of the new school and that is because it was simply 'new.' It is entirely possible that some parents felt that they had been educated as infants in the National School and what was good enough for them was good enough for their children.

Despite the opposition to the school felt by some members of the community the Reverend Cass was optimistic that the school would be a great success. He voiced the opinion to general cries of 'hear hear!' from his audience that they ought to feel most grateful for 'the presence of this splendid school right in their very midst.'

Before the meeting finally dispersed there were calls for a speech from the headteacher. This was Miss Annie M Williams who had been head of the infants school since 1902. Miss Williams said she really could not make a speech (a rare modesty in a head) but could say they would all, staff and pupils, be very pleased to take possession of and work in this 'nice new school.' Touchingly she also thanked the parents who had kindly sent flowers to adorn the windows. After this the formal meeting closed.

The school finally opened its doors for its first full day on Monday 4 November. There were 119 children on roll and three teachers. The other two, apart from Miss Annie M Williams, the headmistress, were Miss Elsom and Miss Morris[4]. The future development of the school will be detailed in a later chapter.

I have spent a long time describing the events surrounding the building of the 1907 school but, in a centenary year, it is right and proper to do so. It is now time to look at educational developments in Bream prior to 1907.

---

[4] To avoid confusion at this point it is important to point out that there were two Annie Williams teaching in Bream schools at the same time. Both were spinsters. Differentiation was by one being known as Miss Annie M Williams, the other simply as Miss Annie Williams. Miss Annie M Williams was the modest head of the infants school 1902-13 who refused to make a speech in 1907. The other Miss Annie Williams who began teaching at the National School in 1893 and transferred to the infants in 1923 would probably have had no such problem. She was nicknamed Annie Parrot by the children because she talked so much, and is still remembered today by many of Bream's older residents.

Post card by A J Batten of Bream schoolgirls in the sports club car park. At the time this was their playground. *Courtesy of the Neil Parkhouse Collection*

EDUCATION ACT, 1902

Section 8 (1).

GLOUCESTERSHIRE COUNTY COUNCIL.

LOCAL EDUCATION AUTHORITY.

NOTICE IS HEREBY GIVEN in accordance with the provisions of Section 8 (1) of the Education Act, 1902, that the County Council of the Administrative County of Gloucester, being the Local Education Authority for the purposes of Part III of that Act, propose to provide

A NEW PUBLIC ELEMENTARY SCHOOL

for about 250 Infants at a site to be selected at **BREAM**, in the **PARISH OR TOWNSHIP OF WEST DEAN**. The School will be available for the following area, vizt.:--The Parishes or Townships of

WEST DEAN, NEWLAND, LYDNEY, AND ST. BRIAVELS.

H. W. HOUSEHOLD

County Education Office.
College Court, Gloucester.

Secretary to the Education Committee of the above-mentioned
Local Education Authority.

DATED 9th MAY, 1904.

Section 8 (1) of the Education Act, 1902, provides as follows :--

" (1) Where the Local Education Authority or any other persons propose to provide a new " Public Elementary School, they shall give public notice of their intention to do so, and the " Managers of any existing School, or the Local Education Authority where they are not them- " selves the persons proposing to provide the School), or any ten rat-payers in the area for which " it is proposed to provide the School, may, within three months after the notice is given, appeal " to the Board of Education on the ground that the proposed School is not required, or that a " School provided by the Local Education Authority, or not so provided, as the case may be, is " better suited to meet the wants of the District than the School proposed to be provided, and " any School built in contravention of the decision of the Board of Education on such appeal " shall be treated as unnecessary."

CHANCE AND BLAND, PRINTERS, GLOUCESTER.

The public notice of 1904 advertising the building of a new school in Bream. *Courtesy of Dean Forest Guardian (The Forester)*

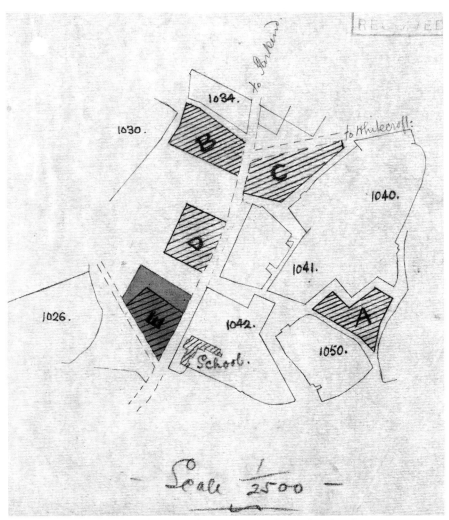

The five sites under consideration for the new infant school 1904-6.
Courtesy of Forest Enterprise

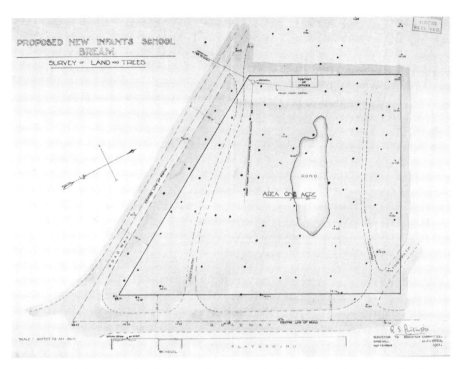

The plan of the 1907 site. The pond was not drained when the new school was built. This may well have been the pond that Mr Williams' pigs were driven onto in 1880.
Courtesy of Forest Enterprise

H. W. Household.

Horace Household, secretary of the Gloucestershire Education Committee 1903-36, who played a key role in building the 1907 and 1927 schools in Bream.
Courtesy of Gloucestershire Archives

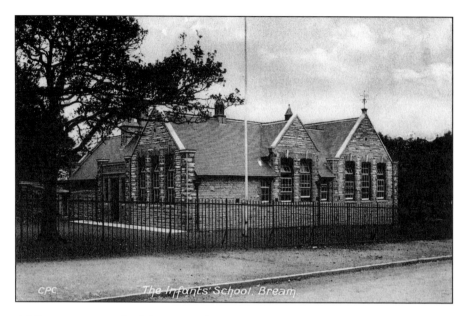

A J Batten post card of the new infants school. The large pond can clearly be seen on the right of the building. *Courtesy of the Neil Parkhouse Collection*

F Norman postcard showing the crossroads soon after the building of the infant school. Children can be seen in the playground. Could the lady on right of camera possibly be the Hoppin Potter of chapter six?

Courtesy of 'Buster' Batten

CHAPTER TWO

1700–1862: A £50 Acorn and an 'Indefatigable Clergyman'

In the seventeenth and eighteenth centuries education was largely the preserve of the rich. Most children of the time had no formal schooling; life itself was their teacher. They learnt their religion from church or chapel – assuming they attended. They learnt about family life in their own home and about working life by instruction and imitation. They had no need to be literate or numerate. Consequently they weren't. It was not until the late eighteenth and early nineteenth centuries, as Britain's commercial and industrial supremacy grew, that there was a growing demand for a more educated population.

Even then there were those who argued that education was dangerous to the social well being of the nation and its productivity. These views are well expressed in Bernard Mandeville's *An Essay on Charity and Charity Schools* in 1732 when he wrote 'to make society happy . . . it is requisite that great numbers should be ignorant as well as poor. Knowledge both enlarges and multiplies our desires, and the fewer things a man wishes for, the more easily his necessities may be supplied . . . reading, writing and arithmetic are very necessary to those whose business requires such qualifications but . . . they are very pernicious to the poor . . . Few children make any progress at school . . . every hour they spend at their book is time lost to society. Going to school in comparison to working is idleness . . .'

Similar thoughts were voiced in the House of Commons as late as 1807 when David Giddy argued that to educate the poor was either mischievous or unnecessary. Education was 'prejudicial to their morals and happiness' in that it would teach them to 'despise their lot in life.'

But the tide was beginning to turn. The Select Committee on the Education of the Lower Orders in 1816 accepted that to educate the poor could be socially cohesive in that, rather than lead to radical thought and rebellion, it could lead to 'submission, contentment and humility.' This would be particularly so if the Church were to be the driving force in the process. This was very much the state of affairs in the early nineteenth century and the State as such did not become involved in education until 1833 and then reluctantly. Prior to that date elementary education had largely been led by two voluntary education societies – the National Society and the British and Foreign Schools Society, the former representing the Anglican Church and the latter the nonconformist chapels.

Despite the dearth of elementary education in the seventeenth and eighteenth centuries some tentative local provision had begun to appear because of the benefaction of a few well-to-do individuals. This would usually be by endowment in a will. The earliest such in Gloucestershire was in 1616 when a Chepstow widow, Margaret Clayton, left £2 per annum to the church wardens of Woolaston for schooling four poor boys.

By the end of the seventeenth century some twenty such charity schools existed in Gloucestershire, all the result of endowments.

The Charity School movement in Gloucestershire was further boosted by the Society for the Promotion of Christian Knowledge (SPCK) founded in 1698. One of the founders was Colonel Maynard Chichester (1665–1715) of Westbury Court. He was one of the pioneers of local and national education and may well have been known personally to the benefactor who endowed Bream's first charity school and advised on the endowment and what the school actually taught.

'Breeme' Charity School

The endowment of Bream charity school was contained in the will of Mary Gough dated 1699. Mary was the widow of James Gough of Pastors Hill Estate. Both were very generous in their support of the Church and community. James, who died in 1691, bequeathed land at Stroat to the poor of the tithing of Bream and to provide for a preacher in Bream chapel. This became Gough's Charity. He and his wife had also provided communion plate for the church in 1680.

Mary outlived her husband by some nine years. By her will written in 1699 and proved in January 1700 she created Bream charity school, the first educational establishment in the village. Her will provided 'the sume of fyftye pounds of lawful English money . . . for the teaching of poore peoples children of the sayd township or tything of Breeme to reade and for placing out yearly if it may be one or more of them apprentice to some trader or burgess . . .'

The £50 of the endowment, worth now over £5,000, was used to buy land which the trustees then rented out to pay for a teacher. A survey of Gloucestershire charity schools for 1712, listed in *Gloucester Notes and Queries* (Vol. 1 pp 292–3), informs us that another benefaction 'by a neighbouring gentleman' had been added to Mary's endowment and that the charity school was then, in 1712, teaching twenty three children.

Needless to say there are no records of the charity school and we can only hazard an informed guess as to what went on in the classroom. If the SPCK were involved in the establishment of Bream charity school, and I think it is a distinct possibility that it was, the basic education for the children would be reading and writing, learning the Catechism by heart and being taught 'their station in life.'

Mary Gough's charity later became the subject of correspondence in 1905–7 that is now in the Public Record Office. These letters include one from the vicar of Bream in 1905 stating that the annual income from Mrs Gough's charity had not been paid for some fifty years, that the present clerk and sexton George Batten understood from his father, Thomas Batten, that the money had been paid in the early nineteenth century to his grandmother, Elizabeth Batten, for keeping the charity school. The endowment itself, which seems to have been on fields 'just outside Bream' seems to have disappeared. The PRO correspondence also includes a Charity Commissioners Report of 1827–8 about the lost endowment. It states that the endowment realised £2. 10s. per annum for 'the teaching of twelve poor children' and though no documentation of the endowment existed the money was paid out of property belonging to Lord Dunraven of Clearwell Estate to the Clerk of the Chapelry of Bream. His Lordship supposed that this was Mrs Gough's charity but had no documents to confirm this.

In respect of Thomas Batten's recollection of his grandmother keeping the charity school, a separate piece of evidence confirms this. The Batten Memorial alongside the church entrance records that Elizabeth Batten 'kept the village charity school for fifty-five years.' Elizabeth died in 1839 at the stated age of eighty-nine, which gives us some idea of when she was in charge of the school.

There is a further reference to Elizabeth's teaching at the charity school in a document written by the dynamic curate of Bream, the Reverend Henry Poole, in 1828. The curate was determined to build a purpose-built school as part of his ministry in the village. His funding application to the National Society is dated 27 June 1828 and contains details of the existing educational provision. The current school only caters for six boys and six girls (the number of pupils seems to have become fixed at twelve since the heady days of 1712 when twenty-three were recorded). Poole also states that the twelve 'were very imperfectly taught by an old woman.' Clearly as well as wanting to build a new school Henry Poole wanted to employ a new teacher as well. The new school was finally built in 1830 and, given Henry Poole's remarks, it would be reasonable to assume that Elizabeth Batten's charge of Bream school ceased in 1830 if not a couple of years earlier.

The new school, because it was funded partly by donation and subscription, also marked the end of Bream charity school which had provided free education.

In summary, Bream charity school existed from c.1700 to c.1830; the highest recorded number of pupils was twenty-three and the teacher probably earned from Gough's Charity £2. 10s. per annum for her labours.

To be fair to Elizabeth Batten, who served the school for fifty-five years, she would have been some seventy-eight years of age at the time of Henry Poole's remarks. He also would not have expected anyone in the village to have seen what he wrote. Further he was making a funding bid for a new school and may well therefore have had a motive in painting the existing picture worse than it was. Finally, in defence of Elizabeth, one should perhaps ask a member of today's teaching profession how they would feel about the job after fifty-five years in it. It gives a whole new perception of teaching being a job for life.

In the few references to the charity school that have survived there is no record as to its location. Almost certainly it took place in the church with its one Dame schoolmistress and its twelve poor children.

Bream's present educational system grew from this tiny acorn.

The Inhabitants of Bream . . . 'a horde of free-booting banditti'

Consideration of Bream charity school in the eighteenth and early nineteenth centuries prompts the realisation of how different things were at that time. Reading some contemporary descriptions of Foresters reinforces that view. The Reverend Payler Proctor, appointed vicar of Newland in 1803, was appalled 'by the heathendom of the Foresters, their lawlessness and laxity of morals.' In 1819 he was more specific in commenting on Foresters' 'habitual profanation of the Sabbath-day, drunkenness, rioting, immodest dancing, revellings, fightings, an improper state of females on their marriages and an absence and ignorance of Holy Scriptures.'

Thoughts on a similar vein were expressed by the Bible Christian, John Moxley, who described Bream as 'a dark place of the earth, inhabited by a people little better than a horde of free-booting banditti.'

Life in Bream is very different now. Isn't it?

Actually both Proctor and Moxley may have seen the Foresters in rather black and white terms. Both were ardent evangelicals who possibly saw a dark world full of sinners. It is conceivable that there were also decent and God-fearing folk in the early nineteenth century. Certainly the curate of Bream 1819–54, the Reverend Henry Poole, made comment on the stark poverty in the village at that time but he never made public written pronouncement about the moral shortcomings of the people. In fact he devoted his life and most of his fortune to the service of this community.

Reverend Henry Poole and Bream National School

Henry Poole became curate at Bream in 1819 and held that position till the Reverend John Beverstock became Bream's first vicar in 1854. During his ministry in the Forest he was also curate of Coleford and vicar of Parkend. Henry Poole was a man of enormous energy, vision and capacity for leadership. By 1830 he had been instrumental in rebuilding Bream church and building Coleford and Parkend churches and Bream and Parkend schools. He also designed the tower of Christchurch at Berry Hill, rebuilt the Parkend school when it was undermined and helped build the Viney Hill (1850) and Blakeney (1851) schools.

He spent much of his own fortune on his building enterprises, £1,000 by 1829, to the extent that he was £300 in debt and having difficulty meeting the demands of building a parsonage at Parkend. Poole's expenditure of his private fortune on public works clearly led to criticism from within his own family. In 1829 he confessed 'I dare not apply to my own family for aid, for they are greatly displeased at my sinking my own property – not being able to enter into my motives for so doing.'

Henry Poole died aged 72 in 1857 leaving what little he had left (less than £300) to his sister Alice Powell Poole. There is a nice story arising out of his will. Alice was his sole beneficiary and having spent his fortune on good works during his lifetime he was concerned about her welfare after his death. His will specifies that such as remains of all his worldly goods should be sold at public auction. This I think was deliberate in that it would enable his friends and admirers to provide for Alice and thus counteract his lifetimes' generosity which had impoverished him and could thus have jeopardised her future financial security. He is buried in his peaceful churchyard at the east end of the idyllic Parkend church that he built. Parkend, Coleford and Bream owe a huge debt to this man. On any set of criteria in any generation Henry Poole's achievements were truly remarkable.

As soon as he became curate of Bream, Henry Poole decided to do something about the school. In the first year of his ministry he enrolled the school in the National Society. The full name of the National Society was the National Society for Promoting the Education of the Poor in the Principles of the Established Church. It was founded in 1811 by a Doctor Bell. The Society used the Bible as a textbook and gave instruction in reading, writing and arithmetic with a smattering of geography or general knowledge. It may be that Henry Poole's 1828 dissatisfaction with the teaching of Elizabeth Batten dates from his enrolment of Bream as a National School in 1819, especially if the curate was hoping the school would have a modern national curriculum (please forgive the pun). Elizabeth was still teaching as she had taught for the last forty years and could not adapt to new-fangled gimmicks such as arithmetic and geography. One new idea she certainly would have found difficult was the method of instruction favoured by the National Society. This was the monitorial system. By this system the teacher gave the information for each lesson to senior pupils called monitors who then in turn conveyed it to their appointed groups. The monitorial system became common place in Bream National School throughout the nineteenth century. A relic of it today is our prefect system in secondary education.

Having enrolled Bream as a National School in 1819 Henry Poole was entitled to apply for a grant from the Society for a capital building project, a new purpose-built school to avoid using the church. His application, made in 1819, was to build a Sunday and day school for fifty boys and seventy girls. The population for which the school was intended he estimated as being 600. He stated that the current school building (the church) was 'very contracted and in a dreadful state of repair.' He estimated it would cost £120 to build a schoolroom 40 feet long, 15 feet wide and 12 feet high and he was hopeful he would build it on waste land belonging to the Crown. In answer to the question as to what present means existed to meet this cost his answer was an honest one 'too trifling to be mentioned from the poverty of the district.' And as to how the school would be financially supported he answered 'voluntary subscriptions and small payments from the children.'

The Bishop of Gloucester recommended the application but the scheme proposed was rather tenuous and I do not feel that Henry Poole himself was very confident of its success. It was probably no big surprise that the Society did not accept the application – their judgement on it was that it should be 'suspended.'

Henry Poole however did not know the meaning of the word failure. For the next few years after 1819 he had a few churches to build – Coleford, Parkend and Bream to name but three – but he returned to his Bream school project in 1828. This time there was far more flesh on the bones and his application was successful.

The population of the area the school was intended to serve had increased considerably between the 1819 and 1828 applications. In 1818 Poole had estimated an area population of 600, by 1828 he had raised that figure to 817 – 400 in the tything of Bream and 417 living within one mile of the intended school. The 1819 application had specified only one room but the 1828 scheme specified two rooms, each to house some fifty boys and fifty girls. Poole had calculated the space each pupil needed as being 6 square feet and had planned for each of the two rooms to internally measure 20 feet long, 15 feet wide and 8 feet high to the eaves or wall plate. The building was to be of stone and covered with stone tile. Interestingly Poole wanted to build small apartments at the back of the schoolrooms as a residence for a master or mistress. It appears that employers normally provided housing as part of the teacher's salary at that time and Henry Poole believed it would, in the long run, be cheaper to provide a residence as part of the school site, rather than have to provide lodgings or a small cottage nearby. That same thought was to be a consideration when Bream built its next National School in 1860–2.

Poole estimated the cost of his 1828 school as being £195. The building would cost £180, the fittings £15. Enclosing the land was included in the estimate. He stated that the ground would be 'granted free by the Commissioners of Woods etc.' Presumably by the time of his application in June, 1828 he had done a deal on the land hence his statement that the land was 'free.' In time the details of his deal were to come back and cause him some considerable difficulty at the end of his ministry in Bream. More of that later.

The estimated annual cost for a master/mistress would be £50 per annum and if accommodation had to be provided elsewhere it would be an additional £5 per annum. To offset the costs, Poole had already organised a house to house collection, seventy individuals had contributed and the sum of £20 had been raised. In addition to that was the £2. 10s. coming annually from Mary Gough's charity. Henry Poole wanted the education provided by the school to be free '*if possible* as the population is extremely poor' but recognised that it would probably be necessary to demand a small weekly payment of 1d. or 2d. from the parents of the children. Finally the aid application form gives us an interesting insight into how tough life was in this district at that time. The aid form itself asks the question how many children there were in the district between seven and thirteen years old. In the National School system these were the expected start and finish dates for education. Henry Poole, however, had crossed out the start date of seven years and replaced it with six. His explanation for the alteration was 'because the children are taken to work earlier than in towns and cities.' It is entirely possible that all children in Bream at the time were at work before thirteen years of age.

The grim reality of the harshness of child labour is borne out by Elijah Waring's 1842 Report on the Employment of Children and Young Persons in the Dean. Pressure from the philanthropist Lord Shaftesbury had led the Government to set up a Mines Commission in 1840 to investigate child labour in Britain's mines. The report was issued in 1842 and its findings created a reaction of widespread horror. Children in Britain were working underground as young as five years old and both boys and girls under ten were filling, hauling or pushing trucks full of coal. The resultant Mines Act of 1842 forbade the employment of women and girls and of boys under ten years old in underground workings.

Elijah Waring was one of the commissioners appointed in 1840 as part of the Mines Commission. His specific responsibility was mines in the Dean and his report gives a fascinating insight into working conditions in the Forest. It also provides some information on Henry Poole's National School since Waring's remit also included moral and educational opportunities for young people as well as their employment conditions.

In comparison with the South Wales coalfield Waring commends the Forest mines for the fact that there were virtually no females working underground. He also noted that most boys in the Forest went into either the coal or iron mines; 'that three fourths of the males in the Forest worked underground and only one fourth worked in the woods and quarries.' The easiest and least well paid of the underground jobs was 'trapping' – opening and closing the trap doors in the pit to control the flow of fresh air. Waring observed that there were one or two boys in the Forest pits working as trappers who were only six or seven years old. Most of the trappers however were aged eight to ten and earned 3s. per week. Boys over ten years old would be 'hodding' or 'carting' to help get the coal out of the pit. This earned between 7*s*. and 18*s*. per week. In the iron mines he found boys from eight to ten years old employed in picking stones out of the ore before it left the mine. It was also common for a boy of thirteen to carry a 'billie' of a hundredweight of iron ore out of the mine at a wage of 1*s*. per day. As part of his investigation Waring visited the Scowles near Bream where he found some boys at work as young as six.

Waring was aware of the grinding poverty that drove families to the necessity of child labour but he also pointed out the fact that 'many parents do not attach due value to the advantages of education whilst aversion to restraint, natural in all children, gladly seconds the indifference of the parents . . . ' No surprises there! Also as a 'foreigner'– he was from Bristol – Waring had some interesting observations on Foresters' reactions to outsiders. He states they possess 'a cherished jealousy of all foreigners' . . . and . . . 'a hearty contempt for all practices and opinions differing from their own' . . . leading to 'a rugged and untractable character.' I could not possibly comment on whether this is still the case. On the other side of the coin Waring also paid tribute to Foresters being 'a brave and generous race' and that 'they were no strangers, even to the finer affections of our common nature.' In this respect he was particularly impressed by the local custom of decking family graves with flowers on Palm Sunday.

As part of his report Waring interviewed children and one particular paragraph of his report is fascinating. 'Certainly the uncouth speech and behaviour of the most untaught boys, is very characteristic of a semi-barbarous condition. I could not induce some of them to come near me, others replied to my questions, however good humouredly put, with sullen abruptness and now and then a very wild one fairly took to his heels, as though afraid I was going to kidnap him. The better taught class, on the contrary were at once frank and respectful, though perfectly rustic, in their replies, and seemed pleased that 'a gentleman' should take so much interest in their affairs.' A convincing argument for the civilising effect of education.

In general Waring acknowledges that progress was being made in the Forest and gives much of the credit for it to the work of the National Schools and Sunday Schools in their attempts to teach the children who attended them.

As previously indicated Waring wrote a brief report on 'Breme' school. He states that the school was established in 1830 and that the master and mistress were William Webb aged thirty-five and his wife. The 1830 date is an interesting one since Henry Poole, when asked the same question in

1854, stated that he thought the school had been built around 1834. There is a reason why he was not sure – he was relying entirely on his memory and not on any written record. Elijah Waring tried to interview Henry Poole for his report but the 'indefatigable clergyman' was not at home. Thus it is likely that the 1830 building date came from the Webbs and I think it is probable that they started work in the newly built school as a new master and mistress in that year when they replaced Elizabeth Batten. The 1830 date of the new building is all but confirmed by a separate record – the minutes of Gough's and Paulett's[5] Charity Trust. The trustees met usually annually and in the late 1820s their venue was 'The New Inn, Breem.' The minute entry of the meeting on 20 January 1831 states that their venue was the 'New School Room Breem.' Waring's 1830 date appears confirmed. Henry Poole's new school was thus built and was operative in 1830.

Other nuggets that come from Waring inform us that the Webbs were 'not trained to the work of instruction' but they 'appear to take a warm interest in it.' There were about thirty boys and thirty girls on the books (not as many as Poole had anticipated in 1828) and attendance was regular. The old endowment (Gough's charity) of £2. 10s. helped maintain the school. The fixed salary was £24 per annum for the two teachers and the parents paid a penny subscription – 1d. per child per week. Waring also refers to the old school and the fact that Elizabeth Batten kept it for fifty-five years and that there were twelve scholars, nominated by the vicar. He also points out that the Webbs followed the 'usual course of teaching.' In practical terms this would mean that they would use the monitorial system and that William Webb would take the boys in the boys' room and his wife, Sophia, would take the girls in the girls' room. The National School system which the Webbs no doubt followed, catered for six year classes. Every child did reading, writing, arithmetic and tables every day. The older children studied geography, grammar, spelling, catechism and scripture. The little ones were the only ones to do 'exercise' and a subject called 'prayers and graces.' Inevitably the girls learnt needlework and knitting.

National Schools in the nineteenth century, as previously stated, often had accommodation on the school site for a master or mistress. This being so it was often the case that a husband and wife team occupied the accommodation, such as the Webbs – and they were not the only ones to do so in Bream School in the nineteenth century. Others were to follow

---

[5] Please note that Paulett has different spellings in this book to reflect contemporary use of the name. In the *Victoria County History* the name is spelled Powlett.

later in the century, for clearly teachers married other teachers then as now.

We can track the Webbs as schoolmaster and mistress of Bream through the census. William came from Abingdon in Berkshire and was born in c.1804. Sophia was a year or so older and had been born in Gloucester. In the 1841 Census they were listed as living at the school house at the end of New Road with their five sons. All seems well with the Webbs and with their school at the time of Elijah Waring's report c.1840. It seems as though they were enjoying their teaching at Bream and, though the salary may not have been very much, we do know from Henry Poole that William Webb supplemented his income by letter writing and making wills for a few shillings. This comfortable existence for the Webbs came to an abrupt and dramatic end at some point during the winter of 1853–4. William Webb and/or his wife were dismissed by Henry Poole for 'grossly improper conduct'. As a result he lost his job and his home – as did his wife, because it would have been a case of one out, both out. With nobody there to teach the children the school was suspended.

We do not know what offence was committed or whether it was one or both of them. To my knowledge there are only two references to the situation; the first in a letter from Henry Poole to the Office of Woods in Whitehall, dated 10 January 1854 and stating that the school is at present 'stopped until a new master and mistress are appointed (the former having been dismissed for grossly improper conduct).' A similar comment appears in an education form that Poole completed on 13th February 1854 when he wrote that the school 'was taught by William Webb and his wife but now removed for bad conduct.'

Life thereafter went dramatically downhill for the Webbs. The 1861 Census has the Webbs living at Colliers Beech but taking in lodgers. Their occupations are still listed as schoolmaster and schoolmistress but that may have been a case of living on a former reputation – or they may have established a private school together. The Gough and Paulette Charity accounts have a very sad reference to the Webbs from Colliers Beech in 1868. Sophia was now a pauper and applied for charity money, she could not maintain herself because her husband was in an asylum. Sophia's charity money was £3 per annum and was discontinued in 1870 when she started to receive Parish Relief. William Webb died on New Year's Eve 1871 in Wooton Lunatic Asylum. His occupation was listed as a 'labourer.' The cause of death was 'softening of the brain and senile decay.' His given age was sixty-eight. Sophia ended her days in Bream and was buried in Bream churchyard on 17 February 1880, aged eighty-one. Henry

Poole was perpetual curate of Bream from 1819 to 1854. During that time he had known three teachers at Bream School; Elizabeth Batten, William Webb and Sophia Webb. He certainly dismissed one of them, possibly two of them and conceivably all three.

The problem of a suspended school in 1853–4 prompted a fresh initiative on the part of Henry Poole. He decided to increase the salary of the master 'in order to secure a person of superior school attainments to the former.' To do this he needed to increase the grant income for the school. One potential source of funding was the Office of Woods, which did contribute already, but the major source would be the Lords of the Committee of the Privy Council on Education which was the forerunner of the present day Department for Education and Science (DFES). Poole's application for funding gives us a snapshot of the school and its finances in the year 1853.

It was a National *and* Sunday school and was open every day of the week except Saturday. The site covered half an acre. Apart from the two separate schoolrooms each with a closet for clothes and books, the masters' residence consisted of a combined parlour and kitchen measuring 14 feet by 12 feet and a scullery 9 feet by 7 feet 6 inches. The principal bedroom was 12 feet by 11 feet and the second bedroom 9 feet by 7 feet 7 inches. (Interesting that the Webbs had five sons at that address in 1841). The floors of the school were paved, though Poole was hopeful of funding to allow wooden floors to be installed. The school had one manager – himself. He listed the annual expenditure for 1853 as follows:

	£	s.	d.
Salary for Masters and Mistress	25	10	0
Books and Apparatus	1	5	9
Fuel and Lights	2	7	0
Repairs	2	5	9
Total	£31	8	6

Income for the year was as follows:

	£	s.	d.
Endowments:	12	15	0
(Church, Office of Woods and Gough's Charity)			
Voluntary Contributions:	6	10	0
School Pence 30 boys @ 1*d.* per week	5	10	0

School Pence 20 girls @ 1*d*. per week		3	15	0
No infants				
	Total	£27	10	0

The deficit for 1853 was £4. 8*s*. 6*d*. and was covered by Henry Poole – as had no doubt been the case since he became curate in 1819.

Poole's grant application (technically called a Preliminary Statement) includes the fact that he had been *verbally* granted the land in 1833 and the school had been built in 1834. It was the verbal nature of the arrangements of 1828 (yes it was 1828, – possibly he had built so many schools and churches he had forgotten the exact chronology) that now created considerable difficulty. A gentleman's agreement and a handshake is a legally binding contract if it can be proved. When Poole asked for an increased grant in 1854 from the Lords of the Committee of the Privy Council to improve his school they, in reply, would consider the application only if Poole sent the Deed of Conveyance of the site as proof of ownership. Poole of course had no such thing.

Never one to panic he wrote to the Office of Woods in Whitehall explaining that about thirty years ago the Commissioners of the Forest had given verbal consent to build Bream School but 'no legal grant of the land was ever made.' He requested, therefore, that a conveyance be speedily executed 'for the present benefit and future prosperity of the school.' Henry Poole's letter was dated 10 January 1854 and stirred up quite a legal problem that took nearly a year to resolve and cost him some money. Correspondence took place between Whitehall and Edward Machen, Deputy Commissioner in the Dean, who had possibly been involved in the verbal agreement. Machen confirmed that the land had been appropriated and enclosed and he thought a plan of it had been sent up to London (was this a blame shifting exercise?) but there was no grant as such.

This was a complex matter requiring legal opinion. It would be a retrospective conveyance. Could this be done? Legal opinion came from John Gardner, solicitor to the Office of Woods in Whitehall, who magisterially replied in a way that only a lawyer could. His answer was that the Office of Woods could not grant a conveyance. The statute enabling the Office of Woods to make free grants for sites for schools was reserved by 'section 45 of 10 Geo 4 Cap 50' and was limited to *ground* only. The fact that the site was now ground *and* buildings meant that a conveyance would not be legal within the act.

At this point it looked as though Henry Poole's verbal agreement of 1828, which was no doubt gratifying at the time, was turning into a nightmare. How could Bream School develop if the minister of Bream could not gain legal title to the land?

As is often the case in such situations there was an answer to hand. This was for the Committee of the Privy Council for Education to use their executive power to warrant a conveyance in the peculiar situation that had arisen. The cost of this deed would be £10. Henry Poole attempted to get the Office of Woods to foot this bill on the grounds that 'the deed ought to have emanated from your office at the time of granting the land.' His argument would not wash and the Office of Woods said no. They had no 'interest' in the transaction, for the two parties were Henry Poole, minister of Bream and the Committee of the Privy Council for Education. Thus Henry Poole paid the full £10 for his conveyance in 1854 on land he had 'owned' as a school site for over twenty-five years. This matter was finally concluded in December 1854 and was just about Henry Poole's last service to Bream School. By way of consolation Henry Poole was not the only minister of Bream church to encounter difficulties over a Deed of Conveyance; a subsequent incumbent actually lost an 1860 deed and, to this day, there is consequently not an enrolled copy in the Public Record office as by law there should be.

When Henry Poole arrived in Bream in 1819, Bream charity school catered for twelve children and met in a dilapidated church. When he handed over the ministry of Bream to John Beverstock in December 1854 the school was purpose-built in half an acre of land and could house fifty boys and fifty girls. It was now time to pass on the baton to another minister to move the school forward with the next stage of its development.

John Beverstock and the Wooden Floors

Bream became a parish in its own right in 1854 and the Reverend John Beverstock BA became the first vicar of Bream in December 1854. An improvement that was in progress that John Beverstock inherited from Henry Poole was the installation of wooden flooring in the school. In February 1854 Henry Poole had written 'I am convinced of the great benefit of *board floors* but when this school was built almost all such rooms were paved.' He also added, in the words of an honest man who had literally spent his fortune on his ministry in West Dean, 'I have <u>no means</u> to floor the rooms with wood.' The underlining is Henry Poole's. The only way to proceed was to apply for a building grant from the Committee of the Privy Council for Education. Henry Poole made the application in March 1854. His estimate for 'flooring with wood' was £25 and he thought that the community could only raise £8 towards this even with the 'utmost exertion' because of 'the poverty of the people.'

The Certificate of Completion duly signed by John Beverstock was sent, with a final balance sheet, to London in April 1856. In its final form the job included not just the flooring but some desks and seats and masonry work. The subsequent alterations were the subject of a plan (see page 53) which give us a full layout of how the school was before and after the 1855 alterations.

The balance sheet for the work tells us the following:

Income:		£	s.	d.
Private subscriptions		13	0	0
Sale of old materials (paving slabs?)		1	1	0
Grant from Committee of Privy Council		28	0	0
	Total	£42	1	0

Expenditure:		£	s.	d.
Legal expenses on account		14	0	0
Balance of legal expenses		1	19	0
To John Dobbs for masonry and flooring		20	10	0
To John Dobbs for 8 desks and seats @ 14/- each		5	2	0
	Total	£42	1	0

Like Henry Poole before him, John Beverstock was sole manager of what he referred to as 'Breem school.' Keen to develop the school further, as well as the 1855 improvements listed above he wrote to the Commissioners of Woods and Forests in June 1855 to see if they would pay for a master's salary. Traditionally the Office of Woods had made an annual donation to the Forest schools and in Bream's case the sum involved was five guineas (£5. 5s.). The commissioners wrote to James Campbell at Whitemead Park to get a local opinion on what would be a suitable annual donation. Sir James recommended that Bream receive a donation of £15. This was approved with effect from 1856.

Beverstock's letter to the commissioners contains an interesting comment to the effect that the school would be open for scholars in August 1855. Presumably it had been closed for flooring and building work, although it is also possible it was still closed following the Webbs' dismissal.

The letter is also of interest in stressing that salary was the major cost facing the school at the time. It would be interesting to compare the differences, if there are any, on the then and now principle as to what proportion of school expenditure is salary. Beverstock, after the floors had been completed, sent a balance sheet to the Committee of the Privy Council. Salaries comprised some 75 per cent of expenditure in 1856. As follows:

	£	s.	d.
Salary	35	0	0
Books and apparatus	2	2	0
Fuel and lights	5	1	0
Repairs	4	13	0
Other expenses	1	1	0
Total	£47	17	0

The income for that year was as follows:	£	s.	d.
Endowments Mary Gough and Bettons Church Charity	7	10	0
Voluntary Contributions (inc. Office of Woods £15)	21	4	0
School Pence	19	2	6
Sale of Copy Books	1	4	3
Total	£49	0	9

In 1855 John Beverstock had written 'since becoming vicar . . . I have been trying to establish the school on a more efficient footing.' He had certainly done so financially if we compare his 1856 balance sheet with Henry Poole's of three years earlier. Henry Poole ran a deficit budget in 1853 and made good from his own pocket. John Beverstock not only ran a surplus budget but considerably increased the school income of five guineas from the Office of Woods up to £15 and the 'school pence' contribution, set in concrete and reluctantly under Henry Poole at 1d. per child per week, was raised to 2d. Under Beverstock children also bought their own copy books.

With this kind of income it was possible to pay a higher salary for a teacher who was more qualified than the Webbs were. We sometimes judge someone's qualifications by saying 'he's got letters after his name.' In March 1857 John Beverstock appointed a teacher who not only had letters after his name but plenty in his name as well. His name was Joseph

Augustus Lewis Littlewood. He held a teaching Certificate of Merit. He had been privately educated and had taught at St Columba's School Edinburgh from 1853 to 1857, a school which had been subject to the latest innovation – inspection. He and his wife Margaret assisted by a pupil boy teacher took charge as master and mistress of Bream School on 2 March 1857. There were some sixty pupils in the school at the time.

It is interesting to speculate how, in 1857, 'Breem School' recruited a teacher who was working in Edinburgh. Presumably an advertisement was in a national newspaper and appointment was on the basis of recommendation/reference.

Such was the state of the school when Cornelius Witherby replaced John Beverstock as vicar in 1858.

Cornelius Witherby was to leave his mark on Bream Village every bit as much as Henry Poole. It was he who built what is without doubt the finest Victorian building in the village and employed an architect of national renown to do it. The building was Bream National School now the parish office and community centre and the architect was William White of Wimpole Street, London.

The £50 endowment in Mary Gough's will, proved in 1700, that began 'Breeme' charity school. *Courtesy of Gloucestershire Archives. Wills 1699/29*

'An Indefatigable Clergyman . . .'
Revd. Henry Poole, perpetual curate of Bream, 1819-54.
Courtesy of the vicar of Parkend Church

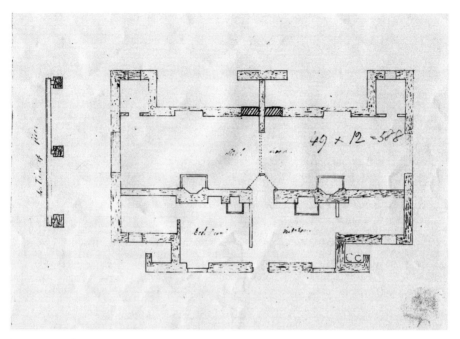

Drawing of Henry Poole's school at the Tufts before it was modified under John Beverstock in 1855.

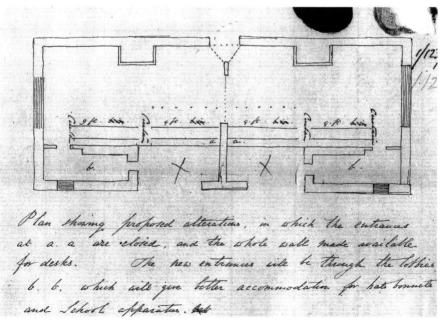

The proposed modification of the Tufts school in 1855. *Courtesy of Gloucestershire Archives D2186/94*

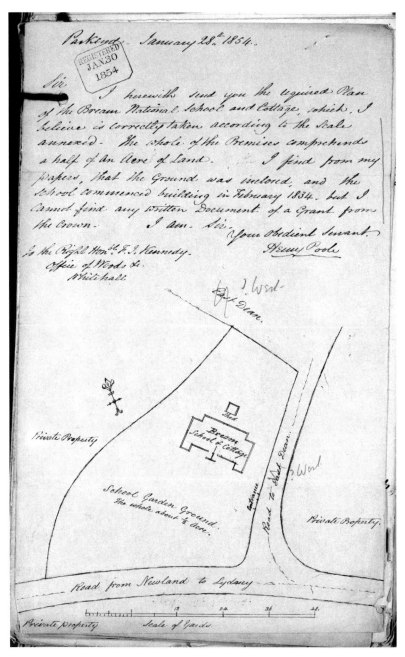

Plan of Bream Tufts National School and cottage sent by Henry Poole in January 1854 to the Office of Woods in Whitehall, London. At the time of this letter Bream church's title to this land was in dispute. Interestingly, whoever drew up the plan confused East Dean with West Dean.

CHAPTER THREE

1862: The Wonderful Work of Witherby and White:
The Vision

Despite the considerable increase in population that had occurred in their ministries in Bream, both Henry Poole and John Beverstock seemed content with the size of the building used by the National School and its location on the Tufts. Indeed both of them had been involved in the 1855 improvements to bring the building up to standard. However, the new vicar, Cornelius Witherby, who replaced Beverstock in 1858, was clearly dissatisfied with the school building in terms of both its size and location.

Within a few months of becoming vicar, Witherby was writing to the Lords Commissioners of Woods and Forests to set in train the process that would lead to a new and larger school in a different location. His letter, dated 6 December 1858, stated the population of the parish had increased rapidly and that the existing school accommodation was built when the population was a mere 500, whereas now it was 2,000. Witherby thought the building could cater for about sixty children but at present (1858) it was housing over 100 on a weekday and 140 on a Sunday. Furthermore, regarding the suitability of the existing site, it was far away from those parts of the village from which most of the children now came. This was because the centre of the village, traditionally around the Maypole and the Newland Road, had moved by 1858 beyond the Rising Sun to Bream Eaves.

Within a week of this letter, Sir James Campbell, Deputy Surveyor of the Dean who lived at Whitemead Park, gave his support to a new grant for a new school site. He emphasised the Office of Woods' continuing support for Bream Parish, as recently evidenced in a grant of £200 towards a parsonage house and the £15 annual grant paid to the school.

It seems to have been Sir James Campbell who chose the one acre site. In February 1859 he wrote to the Office of Woods in Whitehall and enclosed a tracing showing the piece of land 'which I think would be most suitable for the site of a school at Bream. The Reverend Mr Witherby concurs with my opinion as to it being in a most central and convenient situation.' Bream would soon, literally, be 'meeting at the schools.'

Witherby was trying to plan for a larger school. He believed that if it were more central in the village more children would attend. In January 1859, he wrote that there were now eighty in the day school and 155 in the Sunday school. When the school was more central he anticipated these numbers would be 150 and 200 respectively. Inevitably there were obstacles with the project but Cornelius Witherby swept aside any difficulties with the able support of James Campbell. A formidable team. One difficulty initially was that the Commissioners of Woods and Forests in Whitehall would not agree to a site until they knew that the Committee of the Privy Council for Education were committed to funding a new school. Inevitably the Committee would not commit themselves until the site was actually granted.

Eventually on 31 May 1860, the Commissioners of Woods and Forests wrote to Cornelius Witherby with good and bad news. The good news was that the site would be granted. The bad news was their demand that, at the school site at the Tufts, the 'present buildings be removed, ground levelled and land to become Forest waste from which it was enclosed by the Reverend Poole in 1827 without authority from the officers of the Crown.' Henry Poole had been dead for two and a half years and thus could not reply to this slur.

Witherby however did react angrily by questioning why the Commissioners had not made their demand about the Tufts site twelve months before? In fact he had already sold the Tufts site by public auction for c.£225 but possession was not to be given for a year – presumably to allow the school to continue, while the new building, funded in part from the proceeds of the sale of the Tufts site, was constructed.

This situation now became uglier since the Commissioners investigated whether they could appropriate the £225 sale money, since Witherby had, in effect, sold off Forest waste and taken the proceeds. Witherby on the other hand needed the money to build his new school.

Light could possibly be thrown on this issue by an examination of the Deed of May 4 1855 from the Lords Commissioners allowing (somewhat belatedly) a school on the Tufts site. Unfortunately I have not seen the deed but it may contain a covenant specifying the Crown's rights to the land if it ceased to be a school. The 1860 Deed for the Eaves school certainly did contain such a clause.

Fortunately for Witherby, legal opinion decided that the Crown had no entitlement to the sale proceeds so the new school project could now continue. On 21 June 1860 the Commissioners wrote to the vicar stating they were prepared to grant the land and asking how many children the school was for. Witherby replied that there were 160 boys, girls and infants. He pointed out that he had already raised £457. 9s. 11d. for the project not including any grant from the Committee of the Privy Council on Education.

It is ironic that Henry Poole's school at the Tufts, which only existed for some thirty years, had created two serious legal wrangles – one at its beginning over a verbal conveyance in c.1828 and one at its end in 1859 when it was sold into private ownership.

The Much Debated Deed

The deed, granting an acre of land at Bream Eaves that Cornelius Witherby had been so anxious to acquire, was eventually signed and sealed on 14 December 1860. The deed itself has been such a subject of local debate over the last twenty years because of the controversy over the future of the site that it is worth looking in detail at what the deed actually states and examining its subsequent history as a legal document.

The grant of one acre of land was made by the Lords Commissioners of Her Majesty's Treasury to the archdeacon of Gloucester and the incumbent (the vicar) of St James Church Bream. The site was granted very specifically 'for a school or schools for the education of children and adults or children only of the labouring [sic] mining, manufacturing and other poorer classes in the said Chapelry District of Bream and for no other purpose.' The deed further stipulated the school(s) had to be open to the school inspectors and conducted according to the principles of the National Society. The vicar of Bream was to have the 'superintendence of the religious and moral instruction of all the scholars attending.' The vicar also had exclusive control and direction of the building if it were to be used as a Sunday school.

In the more secular aspects of the management of the school the vicar was to be assisted by a committee consisting of – at the invitation of the vicar – his curate or curates and his chapel wardens. There were also to be 'four other persons' who had to meet certain specified criteria.

The first four were named; Sir James Campbell, Baronet of Whitemead Park, Thomas Allaway Esquire of Highfield near Lydney, William Savage Poole Esquire of Pastor's Hill Bream and Kenilworth, Warwickshire and Robert Poole Esquire of the same addresses. Presumably the latter two were both relatives of Henry Poole and guaranteed a 'Poole connection' in the new National School. The criteria applying to these four and all future managers of this Church school were that they were to be communicants of the Church of England, resident or have property in St James or an adjoining parish and be a 'contributor' to school funds to the tune of at least £1 per annum. Any vacancy caused by the death, resignation, incapacity or otherwise of a manager was to be filled by the others electing a nominee. Each of the current managers had the right to exercise up to six votes in the ballot for a new manager, each vote costing a donation of 10/- to school funds (An interesting fund-raising idea and I wonder how it would be received by today's governing body). The committee were further, every January, to appoint up to four Anglican ladies who were specifically to assist with the management of the girls' and infants' schools.

Crucially, the deed does specify a restrictive covenant – if the site ceased to be a school or schools the grant then became void and the Commissioners of Woods and Forests or their successors could 're-enter and repossess free from all claims and demands of John Timbrill and Cornelius Witherby and their respective successors as archdeacons of Gloucester and vicars of Bream.'

This restrictive covenant was the cause of much speculation when there was a recent possibility that the site, controlled at the time by the county council, could be used for housing development. A similar scenario had occurred in 1941 when legal opinion had been sought on the matter. The correspondence is in Lambeth Palace Library. In 1941 the Church School on the site was in a woeful state of repair, local reorganisation of schools was under consideration (the 1944 Butler Education Act was approaching) and the site may have closed as a school though it could have continued as a Sunday school. The legal question was then put as to whether the 1860 grant could be varied or modified to allow the buildings to be used as a Sunday school and 'for other parish purposes.'

The legal answer to this in 1941 was that it was not possible to modify the 1860 deed. In the 1860 grant any Sunday school use had been ancillary to the use of the site as a day school. The plain fact was that if the buildings ceased to be used as a school the site reverted automatically to the Crown. The Crown was also incapable of modifying the 1860 grant because it was of land only, not land and buildings, and anyway the power to make grants of land (and vary the same) for educational and ecclesiastical purposes had been withdrawn many years previously. The suggestion made in 1941 was that the 1860 Deed be left alone and if the site ceased to be a school the Commissioners of Woods and Forests should consider renting it out at a nominal rent to the ecclesiastical authorities. In the event this did not happen because the site continued as a school.

The 1860 Deed was again discussed in 1979 when the building finally did cease to be a school and was under consideration as a youth and community centre. At this time though the legal position was clearer and the Commissioners had power under the Crown Estate Act of 1961 to release the restrictive covenant of 1860. They did this by a Deed of Release dated May 1 1979 and signed by the successors of the parties involved in the 1860 deed. The 1860 Lord Commissioners of Her Majesty's Treasury were replaced by the 1979 Crown Estate Commissioners. The other parties to the transaction were the 1979 archdeacon of Gloucester and the vicar of St James, Walter Thomas Wardle and John Philip Walford Rees, respectively. The fee paid to the Crown Estate Commissioners to release the restrictive covenant was £17,500. This was paid by Gloucestershire County Council and the way was then clear for them to acquire the site. This was duly done by a deed of conveyance dated 5 June 1979 whereby the archdeacon and vicar conveyed 'The Old Church of England School, Bream Eaves to the (county) council free of monetary consideration.'

As a footnote to the saga of the 1860 Deed it has to be recorded that there are not as many copies of it in existence as there should be. As a legal document it has been quite elusive. For one thing there should be a copy in the Public Record Office. There is not. There should also be a copy in the Parish but there is not. Thereby hangs a tale. In 1940 the Diocese were trying to find a copy of it. The vicar of Bream at that time, Arthur Parr, did not have a copy but thought it was in the diocesan registry. It was not. The vice-chair of the Diocesan Council of Education, Henry Herrick, then wrote to Lambeth Palace to see if they had a copy. At Lambeth their record keeping was (and still is) immaculate and they replied to Herrick that the vicar of Bream, Francis Eales, had sent the parish copy of the deed to them in 1900 when he was seeking a grant for the enlargement of the school. They had returned the deed to him on 12 January 1900 and he had acknowledged receipt of same by letter dated 15 January 1900. Thereafter, the parish copy appears to have disappeared.

The finger of blame does seem to point towards Francis Eales who in respect of his grant application in 1900 did write to Lambeth and confess 'I seem to have mislaid the claim form . . .' Had he also possibly lost the Deed? So if anyone comes across an 1860 Deed and a 1900 Grant Application form . . . please return them to Bream vicarage.

Planning, Funding and Building

It is possible that Francis Eales was having a forgetful moment in 1900, for he was preoccupied with a major building work to the school. Maybe the same had been true of Cornelius Witherby at the time of the building of his school in 1861. The grant had been signed on 14 December 1860. On 4 February 1861 Witherby wrote to the Office of Woods and Forests in Whitehall to acknowledge it. Unfortunately he dated his letter in error, 1860. It is not just people of today who forget to change the dates of letters and cheques at the start of the new year. The recipient in Whitehall played at teacher and changed the date of Witherby's letter to 1861 and did so emphatically and in red. Tut-tut! Clearly vicars are human after all.

Once Cornelius Witherby had his site he was keen to get the school built and operational as quickly as he could. He certainly succeeded. From the date of the deed being signed in December 1860 it was less than eighteen months to the completion of the building work and it being fully operational as a school. Almost certainly the process was far less regulated than it would be now. In one respect however, I think Witherby encountered a problem that many building projects encounter today – escalating costs. His final cost figure was considerably more than the estimate done only twelve months before. Witherby did not have the safety net of a contingency fund and was, I think, very fortunate that somebody with the means to be generous, came to his rescue.

Most Bream people are familiar with the Community Centre but to understand the original 1861–2 building it is advisable to study the plan as drawn up by William White, architect of Wimpole Street, London. White was a distinguished contemporary architect and it is interesting to speculate how he came to design Bream National School. It could be significant that Bream's young vicar had come from London. Possibly he knew White personally or knew of his reputation before becoming vicar of Bream in 1858. It is of further interest to note that William White carried out at least two other major architectural jobs in the Dean – the rebuilding of Bream Church in 1861 and the restoration of Newland Church between 1861 and 1863. We shall probably never know the connection that brought White to work in Bream. Suffice it to say that his design for Bream schools produced a magnificent building that is much revered in this community to this day.

When researching this book I fortunately came across a copy of White's 1860-61 drawing. However, for all his reputation and expertise it does contain one very basic 'schoolboy' howler. I am not going to point it out – look at the drawing and work it out for yourself. I would be disappointed if any year six pupil currently at Bream School could not discover it. On the plan, White's label 'Plan of Schools' is the High Street. The boys' porch, listed as 5 feet wide, is now the fire exit to the building but until recently was the main entrance/exit. The small classroom to the right of the boys' porch is the smaller room in the library and the connecting door on the plan is now a fire exit for the library. The room marked 'Girls and Infants Room, future Infants Room' is now the main library room. The room to the left of the boys' porch and marked 'Boys Room and future Girls Room' was the schoolroom, the main room in the school. Known now as room 1 or the carpeted room many of its original features have survived. It is still 16 feet 6 inches wide, the window facing the High Street is original as are the three windows that face the present day car park. The location of the original fireplace is still self-evident, as is the door leading to the boys' yard although it is now bricked up. It was not until I saw the plan that I became aware of the boys' yard and felt in a time warp when I went in there. In the corner of the yard marked as the WC the faded whitewash on the stone wall is still visible. In 1861 outdoor toilets were the order of the day. Recently Ron Watkins told me a story about attempting a challenge that only boys could attempt in that boys' urinal. He succeeded in 'watering' Mr Watson's garden on the other side of the wall. He was caned for his success. I am sure many boys the length and breadth of this country will recollect that challenge – it was not particular to Bream. Another time, another place, but I remember one of my contemporaries being caned for a similar offence.

The layout of the school reflects educational thinking at that time. The boys had their own designated yard presumably where boys games were permitted. The infants were coupled with the girls, presumably for safety reasons. Their yard, now the garden of the school house, could only be accessed via the infants and girls' porch. The thin lines drawn across the rooms show the architect's vision of where the desks should be and in the two big classrooms (now room 1 and the main library) the teacher would operate with his or her back to the one fire or stove that would heat the entire room (probably very inadequately). These two big rooms measuring 40 feet by 16 feet 6 inches (boys) and 30 feet by 18 feet 6 inches (girls and infants) were designed to accommodate eighty boys and eighty girls.

The school house was a luxurious property at that time with parlour, kitchen and scullery downstairs, three bedrooms upstairs, two fireplaces downstairs, two upstairs and, just discernible on the plan, a boiler in the scullery for doing the washing. No doubt the house was a strong selling point for a husband and wife team contemplating teaching at Bream schools.

The plan submitted to the Committee of Council for Education states that the external walls are twenty inches thick, that construction is of local stone and that internally it was plastered but the lower portion of the wall – no doubt to preserve it – was lined with brick. The floors were boarded on joists and five inches above the ground. The roof was slate and the rooms were ventilated and warmed by means of traps in the ceiling and gables (still to be seen) with open grates to admit fresh warmed air. The gutters and downspouts were iron. It is interesting to note the following regulation for school buildings on the form that Witherby completed. Written in italics for emphasis is the phrase *'All the materials used must be of the most durable kind and the best of their kind.'* This really is an example of the 'good old days' and William White's design in fact conformed to only a minimum standard; the external wall had to be at least twenty inches thick, the teacher's residence, if there was one, had to have at least three bedrooms and a parlour, kitchen and scullery.

I stated that the planning and building process was less regulated 150 years ago than it is now. Nevertheless, it was thorough enough to make sure the project had been properly analysed and costed to minimise risk, and ensure that what was being built would be maintained and would last.

An early stage in the process that Witherby had to undergo was to form a group of 'promoters' who would commit themselves to a document called a 'memorial' outlining how the school would be maintained in the future and pledging themselves to subscribe to the building of it. The promoters had to attest that seven tenths of families the school was intended for were Church of England (a likely pre-requisite for a National School) and that, while the school was open to children of all religious denominations, each child was required to learn the catechism and attend Anglican services unless a parent raised objection on grounds of conscience.

Ten Bream men signed the memorial:

Cornelius Witherby,	Bream Parsonage
Thomas Batten, Shoemaker	Bream
Richard Morgan, Miner	Bream

Daniel Simms, Shopkeeper	Bream	
Isaac Jones	Bream	
William Kear, Innkeeper	Bream	
Richard Howells	Bream	
Samuel Morgan, Gaffer of Coal Pit	Bream	
John Priest, Collier	Bream	
Thomas Ames, Grocer	Bream	

The promoters believed they could raise £111. 10s. per annum to maintain the school, made up as follows:

	£	s.
From annual subscriptions and donations	40	0
Annual collections	7	0
School pence (from parents)	52	0
Endowment (Mary Gough's Charity)	2	10
Other sources of income	10	0
	£111	10

The school was intended for the 'instruction of the children of the labouring poor' and one of the questions in the Memorial asked who was there ' besides the labouring population' that could give financial support to the school and resided in the area? This was very much a question to ascertain if 'middle and upper class' money could be available, if required, to support the school. Indeed the phrase 'middle and upper class' appears in the notes explaining the question. Witherby stated there were none in this parish but there were in parishes adjacent. He named the Dowager Countess of Dunraven (Clearwell), Sir James Campbell (Whitemead), six landed proprietors and two owners of Foundry Works. The population of Bream, Witherby stated as being 2,000, chiefly employed as 'miners and colliers.' The special reason, therefore, for applying for grant aid to build a new school was that the district was 'neglected and generally speaking ignorant.'

The architect's estimate for the cost of the building, which was sent to the Lords of the Committee of the Privy Council on Education, amounted to £655. This was made up as follows and dated 13 June 1861:

	£	s.	d.
School House	380	0	0
Teachers Residence	165	0	0

		£	s.	d.
Boundary walls and outbuildings		35	0	0
Desks, benches and fittings		15	0	0
Fittings of residence		5	0	0
Architects commission and expenses		35	0	0
Any other expenses		10	0	0
Sundries		5	0	0
Gratuitous cartage		5	0	0
	Total	£655	0	0

The details of how this sum was to be paid for was explained by Witherby and White as follows:

		£	s.	d.
Voluntary local subscriptions		79	11	7
Collections in church or chapel		7	13	2
Sale of old materials		202	0	0
Gratuitous cartage		5	0	0
Non-local collections		75	0	0
Diocesan grant		75	0	0
National Society (anticipated)		5	0	0
	Total	£449	4	9

Presumably 'sale of old materials' was the net proceeds from the sale of the Tufts school. The gratuitous cartage probably refers to moving furniture from the Tufts to the Eaves school which was presumably done with voluntary labour but was included here as part of a 'true cost' balance sheet. The grant from the National Society was applied for in April 1861 and realised £25 not £5 as per this budget. I have omitted the cost of the acre of land from this balance sheet because it was a free gift from the Office of Woods. If it were included in the cost of building the school, the price would have gone up by £160.

Thus we have a shortfall in the figures of June 1861 with an anticipated expenditure of £655 and an anticipated revenue of £449. 4s. 9d. The shortfall, or to use the Council of Education's technical phrase – 'deficiency to balance', was £205. 15s. 3d. This was the exact figure that the Lords of the Committee of Council agreed should be the Government grant to help build Bream schools. All could now proceed – unless of course there was to be an unforeseen escalation of costs.

The grant application process had been rigorous. One of the key elements in it was what we probably would call today 'local ownership of the project.' There was a strong expectation in Whitehall that local people would promote the plan for the school, contribute to its building and maintenance costs and have a vested interest in it having a viable future as a school. For this reason, Whitehall insisted on knowing how much of the proposed expenditure on the school had been raised by church collections and by voluntary local subscriptions. Indeed they went even further than this by insisting on a full breakdown of who had contributed what in Cornelius Witherby's 'local subscriptions' total of £79. 11s. 7d. Thus there is a document in the PRO, completed by the vicar, which is entitled 'Schedule of Contributions by Proprietors, Residents or Employers of Labour.' Residents in this case would probably mean owner occupiers who had resided in the community for some time. The labouring class would not be expected to be included in the schedule because they probably could not afford a contribution and were likely to be migrant poor who moved around as job opportunities came and went. Primarily the schedule was aimed at property and substance and would target tradespeople and shopkeepers and the more well-to-do. I have no doubt it is a document of considerable local interest and I have therefore included full details.

Name	Address	Contribution		
		£	s.	d.
William Savage Poole	Pastors Hill	10	0	0
Reverend C Witherby	Parsonage Bream	5	0	0
Daniel Simms	Bream's Eaves	10	0	0
Isaac Jones	Bream's Eaves	1	0	0
John Preest	Bream's Eaves	5	0	0
Samuel Morgan	Bream's Eaves	10	0	0
Richard Morgan	Bream's Eaves	5	0	0
William Kear	Rising Sun Inn	10	0	0
Henry Kear	Bream	5	0	0
Richard Morse	Bream	5	0	0
Thomas Batten	Bream	5	0	0
A Friend	Bream	4	0	0
William Addison Esq.	Warren House, Lydney	1	0	0
Emmanuel Lucas	Priors Farm, Bream	5	0	0
Thomas Ames	Bream	10	0	0
Geo. Smith	Bream's Eaves	10	0	0

Walter Price	Bream's Eaves	10	0	0
Hugh Preest	Bream's Eaves	10	0	0
Mr Evans	Bream's Eaves	10	0	0
Richard Howells	Bream's Eaves	5	0	0
Mr Walwyn	Parkend	5	0	0
Geo. B Keeling Esq.	Lydney	1	0	0
Mrs Raikes	Bream	5	0	0
Mrs Isaac Preest	Bream Woodside	10	0	0
Mr Sam Moorhouse	Bream	1	0	0
Mr Thomas Kear	Bream's Eaves	10	0	0
Henrietta Robins	Bream's Eaves	1	0	0
Mr John Morse	Bream's Eaves	5	0	0
Countess Dunraven	Clearwell Court	5	0	0
Charles Bathurst	Lydney Park	30	0	0
Miss Constant	Noxon Park Farm	5	0	0
Collections by Committee		9	6	7
Sir James Campbell	Parkend	5	0	0
Miss E H Ridout	Bream Parsonage	3	0	0
	Total	£79	11	7

Crisis?

One prominent name appears to be missing from the above list of contributors – that of Miss Alice Davies, sister of Mr Edward Machen (Deputy Surveyor of the Forest, 1805–54). Nicholls in his *'Personalities of the Forest of Dean'*, published in 1863, refers to the 'considerable gifts' of Miss Alice Davies to the building of the school and school house. Why then does her name not appear in the list of contributors?

The probable answer lies in the fact that Alice Davies had just made a massive contribution to Bream church. In 1855 she had donated the land on which the vicarage was subsequently built and had largely funded the major rebuilding of St James church (by William White), out of her own pocket. She had more than done her bit for the village. Anyway, Cornelius Witherby had no reason to request money from her – his estimated costs for building the school were matched by his actual and anticipated revenue of £655. All would be well – or would it?

Funding a major building project can be a hazardous process and costs can spiral to the point where they are out of control. A twenty-first century example is the new Wembley Stadium, now completed long after it was due and costing far more than was originally anticipated. In fact it is customary now to budget in to building costs a contingency fund of 20–25 per cent to cater for all eventualities.

Cornelius Witherby's 1861 balance sheet contained no such rainy day contingency fund. If costs were to escalate there could be a crisis. They did and there was. Building work went on during the autumn, winter and spring of 1861–2 and by May, Cornelius Witherby was in a position to send off the completion balance sheet to Whitehall. This showed an increase in costs of over 30 per cent. The estimated cost of £655 in 1861, had risen to a final actual cost of £860 10s. 5d., an overspend of over £205. How had the vicar raised this sum? His balance sheet shows an increase in donations from non-local contributions from £75 to £88. 7s. but by far and away the biggest element was the huge increase in local subscriptions from £79. 11s. 7d. to £256. 15s. 0d. This was a truly remark-able increase which can only be adequately explained by Alice Davies' generosity. It may even be that Alice Davies was always intended to be the contingency fund. Perhaps this was why her name does not appear on the list of contributors; she was in reserve and until 1862 it was not known what her contribution would have to be. Whatever the truth of the matter, there is no doubt she contributed some £190 to the building of the school, over 20 per cent of the final cost. In the light of her contributions to Bream vicarage and church this was a stunning act of largesse. Bream owes Alice Davies hugely.

The final balance sheet is in the Public Record Office (ED103/42) and is as follows:

Debtor	£	s.	d.	Creditor	£	s.	d.
Local							
Collections in Church or Chapel	7	13	2				
By value of site (if given)	160	0	0	By value of site (if given)	160	0	0
Sale of old materials	202	0	0	Buildings	659	17	7
By other means	256	15	0	Sundries	7	0	0
Not Local							
Contributions	88	7	0				
Grant – National Society	25	0	0				
Grant – Diocesan Aid Board	75	0	0				
Total already received	£814	15	2	Total already paid	£ 826	17	7

Grant to be received from Committee of Council on Education				Payments to be made: Architect	40	2	0
	205	15	3	Builders and Joiners	153	10	10
Total	£1,020	10	5	Total	£1,020	10	5

NB: The total in both columns includes the notional sum of £160, the value of the site itself, which had in fact been given free.

This final balance sheet was part of the Certificate of Completion signed by the architect William White and dated 28 May 1862. The certificate was also signed by Cornelius Witherby and his curate Henry Thomas Hewitt, the school managers, William Savage Poole and Robert B Poole and the named members of the building committee; Thomas Batten, Thomas Ames, Samuel Morgan, Richard Morgan, William Kear and Richard Howells. The signatories attested that the building had been completed to specification, that the deed was safely lodged in the parish strong box along with the registers and that the deed had been enrolled in Chancery. This latter statement is doubtful since there is currently no copy of the deed in the PRO; if it had been enrolled there would be.

A Potential Rival?

Nonconformity was growing significantly in Bream in the middle of the nineteenth century. In 1851 the Bible Christians had built a chapel in Parkend Road and in 1859 rebuilt it and added a schoolroom alongside. In 1859 the Primitive Methodists had built a chapel at Bream Eaves (now the Eaves Centre). In 1860 the Wesleyans built a new chapel at Woodside (now the Pentecostal chapel). All three chapels built schoolrooms in 1859, 1903 and 1913 respectively which were principally used for Sunday school. One of the chapels however, the Bible Christians in Parkend Road, did set up one as a day school at the identical time that Bream National School was about to be built. Whether there was a degree of rivalry in this or not is impossible to say at this distance in time but it is certainly true that some developments were remarkably coincidental. We know that the National School at Bream Eaves was bursting at the seams by 1859, the very year that the Bible Christians were building their schoolroom. Further, the deed for Bream National School acquiring land at the cross roads was signed in December 1860 and the following month the Bible Christians opened their day school at Parkend Road chapel.

From one perspective this could be seen as an attempt to establish a chapel rival to the Anglican National School. Another perspective could argue that Parkend Road day school provided much needed support in a situation of desperate overcrowding.

Reference has already been made to the Reverend John Moxley describing Bream people as being 'little better than a horde of freebooting banditti.' The school in Parkend Road was run by his son and opened on Monday 14 January 1861 when twenty children were enrolled. This number grew rapidly, rising to thirty-eight in week two, forty-five in week three and fifty-five in week four. By this stage the Bible Christian day school itself may have been approaching overcrowding and was teaching nearly as many children as the National School at the Tufts. We do not know how long this school existed for. I suspect it was short-lived because a statement made by Cornelius Witherby in April 1861, only three months after it opened, when he applied for a National Society grant for his building stated the following. In answer to a question about non-Anglican educational provision he wrote that there was 'a dissenting school' which 'charges 2d. for reading with writing' but 'is thinly attended except by young children, about 20.' Clearly the new Bible Christian day school was in decline a few months after its inception and it almost certainly would not survive the opening of a purpose-built new school set in one acre of ground in the centre of the village. That said, Parkend Road Bible Christian schoolroom continued as a Sunday school for many years.

At the beginning of this chapter, reference was made to Cornelius Witherby telling the Commissioners of Woods and Forests in 1860 that the school site at the Eaves had been sold by public auction, though possession was not to be given till spring 1861. Clearly this could present a problem with transferring from one site to another if the new site at the Eaves was still being built in 1862, which it was. However, this difficulty appears to have been successfully managed. The minutes of Gough's and Paulett's Trust confirm that the trustees held their annual meeting in the schoolroom in January 1861 and again in January 1862. Obviously the Tufts school operated until the Eaves schools were finished.

By the spring of 1862 the new schools were built. With pride Cornelius Witherby wrote in May to the National Society 'I am happy to say that these schools are now completed and in use.' He also wrote to the Office of Woods on 6 June in a similar vein; with justifiable pride he told them that the schools were now in operation with 130 children and a certificated master and his wife. With an eye to the main chance he also thanked them for their liberality (in granting the land free of charge) and their annual grant of £15 and asked whether, because the schools had now doubled in size, they could possibly increase the grant. They duly did – to £20. When Cornelius Witherby was in persuasive mood nobody said no to him.

Cornelius Witherby had every reason to feel proud. He had created a magnificent building in the centre of the village and had surmounted every difficulty he had encountered. His project had begun with his letter of 6 December 1858 to the Lords Commissioners for Woods and Forests to ask for land for a new school. The project finally came to fruition on Monday 24 March 1862 when the new schools opened their doors to pupils for the first time. A remarkable achievement.

When it all began in 1858, Cornelius Witherby had been just twenty-four years old.

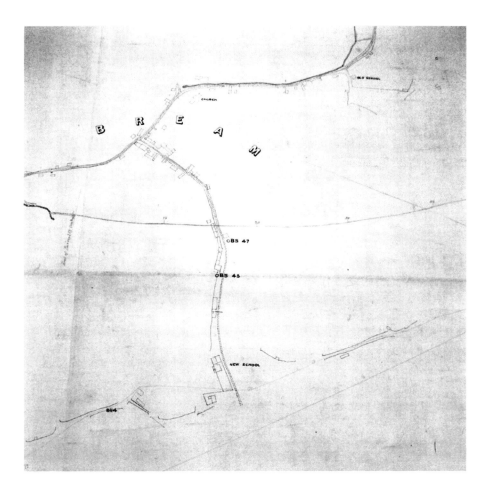

Map of Bream village c.1862-3 believed to be drawn by Thomas Sopwith. The map shows the location of the Tufts (old) school and the Eaves (new) school. *Courtesy of Gloucestershire Archives, D232*

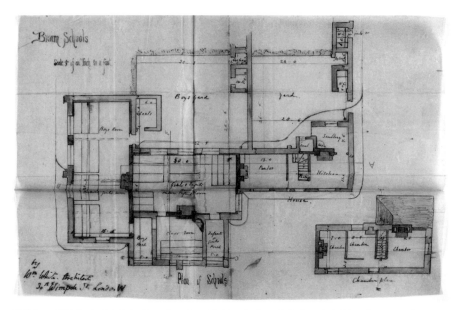

William White's initial plan for the 1862 National School. This plan was later modified.
Courtesy of Lambeth Palace

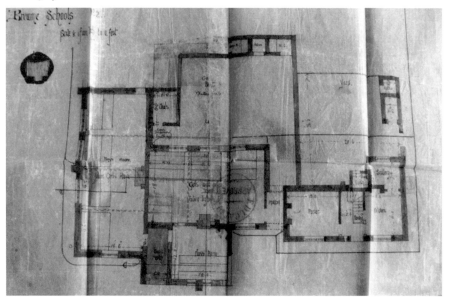

William White's modified plan for the 1862 school. In this new plan the school house has been brought forward and the infant/girls' porch has gone into today's library.
Courtesy of Gloucestershire Archives D2186/94

The 1862 doorway connecting the boys' schoolroom to the yard.

The view across the boys yard into the corner designated in 1862 for ash/WC

CHAPTER FOUR

1862–1907: The Big Picture

Headteachers 1862–1907

Boys/Mixed School Heads	Girls School Heads	Infants School Heads
Joseph A.L. Littlewood 1857 – ?	Janet Smith 1862? – ?	
Ambrose Henry Smith 1861?–1867	Mary Anne Leete 1865–7	
Albert Carey 1867–74	Marianne Carey 1867–74	
Augustus Dickson 1875–76	Mary Dickson 1875–76	Selina Durnell 1875–96
Edward Wall 1876–7	Emma Wall 1876–77	Clara Jane Brain 1896–1902
Thomas John White 1877–78	Sarah Ann Mann 1878–82	Annie M Williams 1902–1913
Henry L. Poole 1879–85	Mary Grace Newman 1882–88	
William F Mullan 1885 – 1918		
(w.e.f. 1888 head of mixed school)		

Premises – Fit for Purpose?

1. Expectations

It might be expected that once Bream National Schools had moved into their fine new premises at Bream Eaves in 1862, matters would stay much as they were for at least the foreseeable future. Wishful thinking! Within the next forty years – largely due to continued population growth in the area – the 1862 building was to undergo two major extensions that significantly increased the size of the original building. The first of these, in 1872, virtually doubled the size of the 1862 schoolroom. The second extension, in 1900, was even bigger than that of 1872. That said, both extensions were very much in harmony with the original building and in no way detracted from its architectural appeal. The joins were virtually seamless.

There were in fact other – and lesser – developments to the site even before the 1872 extension. The first of these was the erection of a gallery in the infant classroom over a two-day period, Friday and Saturday the 12 and 13 February 1863. At this point the school had been in operation for less than a year and it may be that the gallery had been intended as part of the original building plan. Presumably as a result of the gallery (a fairly common feature of Victorian schools), the teacher would be able to see clearly every one of the infants in the room. However, some forty years later, an infant school inspector was to write 'the cumbersome gallery must be removed without further delay.' It duly was – in 1904. Educational fashion, like its counterpart in the high street, has a habit of coming full circle.

The second development was a conveyance of land measuring some 44 feet by 27 feet which presumably was an addition to the land the school site occupied. The trust deed for this conveyance is dated 1867 and is, unlike the 1860 trust deed, correctly lodged in the Public Record Office (PRO). As the law stood between 1836 and 1903, any conveyance of land for charitable uses, expressly including school buildings and schoolmasters' houses, had to be enrolled on the Close Rolls of Chancery which are now stored in the PRO. The 1860 Deed, as previously stated, should have been enrolled in Chancery but for some reason was not. The far less important 1867 Deed was.

The 1867 Deed was arranged correctly by a local solicitor, William Roberts of Coleford. Interestingly, the deed is a gift from the vicar of Bream, Cornelius Witherby, to Bream School whose site ownership is in his name as vicar of the parish. Consequently Cornelius Witherby, acting in his private capacity as an individual, conveyed the land to the incumbent of Bream (in other words to himself in his public capacity as vicar). Thus the man conveyed the land to the office. The deed also contained the key legal phrases that Witherby made the gift 'freely and voluntarily and *without valuable consideration.*' I do not know whether the land concerned was a gift to Cornelius Witherby or bought by him out of his own pocket.

2. The 1872 Extension. Whitecroft Deprived

There are some facts that are so blindingly obvious that many of us are totally unaware of them until they are pointed out. The fact that Whitecroft does not have a school and never has had one is a case in point. Why should Whitecroft as a Forest community not have a school when all of its neighbours, Pillowell, Yorkley, Parkend, Bream and Ellwood have? The answer is as follows.

In 1868 Cornelius Witherby left Bream to continue his ministry in Bristol. He was replaced as vicar of Bream by the Reverend John Frederick Gosling. Within a few years of his coming to Bream John Gosling was to face a problem with Bream National Schools of a very similar nature to that faced by Cornelius Whitherby in 1860 – the schools' incapacity to cope with the number of children who needed education. His initial answer in 1871 was a creative one – to build a new school at Whitecroft for 200 children and hope that in the future this would lead to a new church at Whitecroft. This new church in his plan was to be dedicated to St John.

The records of this episode are in Lambeth Palace under the intriguing heading of Bream St John/Whitecroft. John Gosling, in conjunction with his church wardens and the vicar and church wardens of St Paul's Parkend, had established a trustee board for the planned new school in 1871 and submitted a bid for grant aid from the National Society in April of that year. The plan would certainly have relieved the pressure on Bream schools by building a new school for 100 boys and 100 girls. The infants in this catchment area, as per plan, would be taught at the already existing Yorkley Wood school (more on this particular establishment later). The new school was to consist of one big room with a partition which, when closed, would provide two rooms measuring 45 feet by 18 feet for 100 boys and 100 girls respectively. John Gosling's estimated cost for this building, on freely given Crown land, was £700 if built of stone and £500 if built of concrete. Stone was the preferred option. In the long term Gosling hoped that the new school would be used for Sunday services (like Yorkley Wood) and form a basis 'for the erection of a Church and the formation of a regular district,' hence his application in the name of St John's, Bream St James' and Bream St John's (Whitecroft) had a certain ring about it.

Gosling's plans in 1871 for a new school were not however as meticulous as Witherby's had been in 1860. No local funds had been collected or anticipated and all that he had to offset the estimated building cost of £700 was a £100 grant from the diocesan board and a hoped for subsidy from the Committee of the Privy Council on Education of c.£200 – a comparable figure to that given to Witherby in 1860. The National Society agreed to a grant of £50 but even so there was still a shortfall of £350. The embryonic trustee board of Whitecroft school had no means of raising that sum of money and consequently abandoned the plan. On 10 June 1872 John Gosling wrote to the National Society to confirm that the trustees had been obliged to give up the scheme 'from want of money.' Thus Whitecroft never did have a school, never became an ecclesiastical district and never had a church dedicated to St John. Gosling's creative solution had failed.

This failure well and truly brought the focus back onto Bream's overcrowded National Schools where the situation was now critical. Indeed Gosling's lack of funding for his Whitecroft school led directly to his 1872–3 extension of Bream school. Here again though his funding plans were somewhat tenuous and were to encounter problems.

3. The Gosling Extension at Bream, 1872–3

In September 1872, John Gosling wrote to the Commissioners of Woods and Forests to inform them that the Education Department had decided that Bream National Schools were not big enough. Gosling and his fellow managers had therefore decided to enlarge the school by the addition of a room capable of holding 100 extra children at an estimated cost of £340. He asked the Commissioners if they could see their way to making a capital grant to help towards the cost. The Commissioners then wrote to Sir James Campbell at Whitemead Park seeking his recommendation. He advised a sum of £50 would be appropriate.

At this point the commissioners voiced concern as to what other sources of funding were available and what practical steps the managers had made to date to raise the considerable sum of £340? James Campbell's reply to this question in November 1872 was staggering. He stated 'because of the need for additional accommodation and the late period of the year, work has already begun and the vicar has made himself responsible for the whole amount required.' The extension really is the Gosling extension. He paid for it.

Sir James Campbell's suggested £50 from the Commissioners of Woods never in fact materialised but there were other sources of income as evidenced in the final balance sheet that Gosling sent to the National Society.

His receipts were:

	£	s.	d.
Local subscriptions	38	2	0
Diocesan Grant	50	0	0
National Society Grant	26	0	0
Total	£114	2	0

His outgoings were:

	£	s.	d.
Cost of new schoolroom	341	0	0
Fittings	84	1	9
Total	£425	1	9

This left a shortfall of £310. 19s. 9d. and Gosling paid the entire sum of out of his own pocket. Clearly he was a vicar with very considerable private means!

Why was Gosling in such a hurry to extend the school that he was prepared to use his own money to do so? Initially Gosling had been optimistic that the overcrowding issue would be resolved by building a Whitecroft school in 1871–2. That plan fell by the wayside in the summer of 1872 by which time something else, quite apart from the overcrowding issue, was galvanising Gosling into urgent action. In 1870 the Government had passed the so-called Forster Education Act (Forster was the vice-president of the Council for Education). This act stated that, in areas where the schooling system was inadequate, a school board should be established with the power to build board schools funded by the local rates. This seriously alarmed Gosling as evidenced by his letter to the National Society when asking for a grant for his extension. If Bream National Schools were not extended and quickly, they would be overtaken by events. Gosling foresaw the establishment of a school board in the Forest (this did happen but not until 1875) and then, if the National School was not providing adequate education for all the children in the area, a board school would be 'erected close at hand' or as happened at Woolaston the new school board would take over control of the National School. If that were so the Anglican monopoly of education in the village would be broken and, as he himself expressed it to the National Society, 'I am desirous to keep the school in connection with the Church of England.' The extension became something of a race against time while the school board was still only a distant threat. Even so it was doubtful if the proposed extension would provide a long term solution to the overcrowding problem since it would only provide 103 extra places and the Education Department at Whitehall believed 155 were needed.

In his application to the National Society Gosling stated that the current average attendance for the schools was 153.7. Essentially this was divided as follows: boys taught in the current room 1, girls in the current library and infants in the current junior library. The extension changed this and moved the boys into the new part of the school. In effect the extension led to an approximate mirror image of room 1, the same width but slightly longer and on the Brockhollands/Lydney side of the school, in other words across the present room 2 and into the café. There is a porch to the rear of the café and this would after 1873 have become the boys' porch. They would still have used the same playground as they had previously. The way was now clear for the girls to move into room 1 previously occupied by the boys, and for the infants to spread into the library.

The new extension was opened – appropriately by the vicar who had after all paid for it to be built – on Monday 5 May 1873.

Subsequently Gosling went public in his hostility to board schools. In 1881 he wrote to *The Dean Forest Guardian* to voice his 'unqualified disapproval' of the school boardsystem.

4. The Eales' Extension: Off to the Pub

The 1872–3 extension, welcome and necessary as it undoubtedly was, would not provide other than a temporary respite to the accommodation problems at the schools. Indeed it seems to be true of Bream schools building generally throughout the nineteenth century that the process was a reactive rather than a proactive one. What was built did little more than paper over the cracks and did not provide a long term solution. Money was the crucial factor in the process and caused problems with both the 1872–3 and 1900 extensions. Thus, what was done was what they could afford to do and not necessarily what they should do or even wanted to do. Perhaps it has always been so in education.

The school inspectors were making adverse reports on accommodation as early as 1891 and thereafter on an almost annual basis. In 1893 the inspectors threatened to withhold the grant for the infant school if there were not improvements specifically to the infant accommodation. The managers had to act on this directive but within three years the inspectors were again complaining of inadequate accommodation for the infants. The managers coped with this in part in 1899 by refusing to admit into the school children under the age of four. This however was only a sticking plaster answer and the issue was not going to be finally resolved until the county council took on the responsibility of building a new infant school.

The mixed school of boys and girls was separately inspected but similar criticism was made. In 1891 the inspector's report stated that the toilets, referred to at the time as 'the offices', were inadequate. The 1898 report was so critical of the overcrowding that the grant to the mixed school was only made on the condition of the proposed enlargement of the school taking place. The school was significantly enlarged in 1900. Even so it was still overcrowded. The inspector's report in 1901 stated that the alterations had much improved the schools but the premises were still insufficient for the average attendance. Salvation was only to come with the building of the new infant school and the subsequent release of the infant accommodation for use by the mixed school.

In the light of the inspectors' adverse reports modest improvements had taken place in the 1890s to keep the schools operational. In 1893 the infant classroom (junior library) had been enlarged and its window space had been increased. New toilets or 'offices' were provided for boys, girls and infants in the same year. The details of the 'office' system are apparent from a file in the PRO and a county council surveyor's report in 1903. The urinals were a wooden trough. The closets or offices proper cannot be described as toilets because they had no running water flush. Technically the 'offices' consisted of 'hopper pans' which were flushed, according to the 1903 surveyor, 'by hand' using a pail of water which carried the waste down a long unventilated drain to the cesspool, which must be 'foul and dangerous to health'. This cesspool was on site A of the proposed infant school site offered to the county council by the Office of Woods in 1905.

These improvements were carried out by the Reverend Edward Dandy in 1893. In 1896 he was succeeded as vicar of Bream by the Reverend Ernest F Eales. It was Ernest Eales who carried out the third major development of the 1862 school site. This resulted in the erection of a new main room for the schools (the current rooms 2 and 3) coming out at ninety degrees from the line of the 1862 and 1873 building.

As previously there were funding problems with the 1900 extension. In a letter to Whitehall in January 1899 Eales explained that the managers were submitting plans for a new main room and boys cloakroom but were not at present going to do anything about girls' and infants' offices or the infants' cloakroom. Presumably this was for financial reasons. At this point Whitehall sent an inspecting architect who found that the office accommodation (toilets) was inadequate. Eventually the managers were given permission in June 1899 to proceed with their plans to create a new main room and a boys' cloakroom which Eales refers to as a 'cap room.' Caps were standard wear for schoolboys.

Work began in the summer of 1899 and lasted the best part of a year before it was completed. Inevitably there was a lot of noise and dirt while the work was ongoing and the functioning of the schools was seriously disrupted. The August holiday was extended to 31 August, but even by then there was still much to do. How could the schools cope with this difficulty?

On 14 August 1899 Eales submitted to Whitehall the managers' emergency plan to continue operating the schools. The plan was to send the infants to the pub. A creative solution!

In actual fact it was a very practical and meritorious solution. What the managers were proposing to do was to hire the assembly room (otherwise known as the Skittle Alley) at the Rising Sun. This would then free up the use of the infant schoolroom (today's library) and its classroom (today's junior library) for the mixed school.

Eales' letter to their Lordships in Whitehall stressed the advantages of the proposed arrangement and was most reassuring in respect of infants being near licensed premises. The Rising Sun, kept by Mrs Elsmore, was a 'very respectable inn' and the children would 'not be obliged to pass within 24 yards of the inn door' – one can imagine the vicar pacing this out. The assembly room itself was commodious, being nearly 60 feet long and 20 feet wide, had four good windows in front (the north-west side), two smaller ones in the rear and had two fireplaces and two doors. At the time the room was used as a girls' Sunday school and religious services were sometimes held there. There were no 'offices' but Eales was optimistic that it would be easy 'to erect a sufficient number in the garden behind the room.' Their Lordships were convinced and gave their consent. Thus Bream Infant School, when it reopened after the holidays on Monday 4 September, was held at The Rising Sun. It was to continue there for over seven months.

The cost of the extension, as per the balance sheet that Eales sent to the National Society, was £486. 19s. 0d. (some £35,110 in 2005 terms). Receipts towards this were as follows:

	£	s.	d.
Crown grant: Office of Woods	40	0	0
Local subs	312	3	6
Bazaar (1902)	44	15	6
Bishops fund	50	0	0
National Society Grant	40	0	0
Total	£486	19	0

As in 1861–2 the local effort had been inspirational. The 1902 Bazaar had been specifically to raise money to clear the debt still owing on the job but it had in turn been preceded by similar bazaars in 1899 and 1900. Funding the work had been a very long process. For example, the National Society had agreed their £40 grant in January 1900 but did not make payment until October 1902.

The extension had been a magnificent local effort by the community and specifically by the church. However it was a case of too little too late. Even in 1901, HM Inspectorate of Education (HMI) were damning with faint praise by reporting that 'the alterations have much improved the accommodation' but 'the mixed school accommodation is insufficient for the average attendance. The attendance should be reduced or the accommodation increased.' But community and church were probably financially exhausted by the 1900 extension. They could do no more. I am sure this problem was country-wide – the funding requirements of an education for all policy was becoming impossible for the voluntary societies.

Fortunately, help was to hand as a result of the 1902 Education Act. Not only would the mixed school gain financial support from the County but any new school could be totally funded by the county council. The Church would lose some degree of control of education but, in realistic terms, there was no other way forward.

Horace Household, the new secretary to the County Education Committee, was coming to the rescue as early as 1903. In that year the HMI report on the mixed school pointed out in very blunt terms the extent of the overcrowding problem. The mixed school had 255 boys and girls on their books, sixty children were due to come up from the infants and yet they only had room to accommodate an average attendance of 240. Household himself wrote to inform the Board of Education in London that the managers were not in a position to carry out the required enlargement 'through lack of funds.' He advised that the County Education Committee were holding a local enquiry at Bream on 27 January 1904 'to ascertain the opinion of the inhabitants of the District on the matter.' At the meeting Mr Household made public the overcrowding in both infant and mixed schools.

The infant school allowing 10 square feet per child (it is now 6.3 square metres per infant, a much larger area) could accommodate ninety-one children; in fact there were 155 on the books and the average attendance was 129. In the mixed school the accommodation could house 219 but there were 283 on role and 253 in average attendance. The meeting agreed the only realistic option was for the council to build a new infant school nearby and the mixed school to then take over the vacated infant premises. Over to Mr Household and the 1907 building project.

5. The 1903 Premises Survey

As a result of the 1902 Education Act, the county surveyor carried out a detailed survey of the school premises at Bream. We are fortunate that this survey has survived and gives a fascinating insight into the mixed and infant schools site.

In summary the key features of the schools are as follows:

Water supply: There was no mains water. A well in the yard was fitted with a pump which supplied three water tanks.

Playgrounds: The boys' playground was the present day car park but in a rough state. The girls used the field in front of the schools (the present sports club car park area).

'Offices': As previously mentioned these were hopper devices flushed by a bucket of water. The boys also had a urinal but in 1903 at the time of inspection the outlet was choked and the urinal was overflowing 'down the face of the wall.' The 'offices' drained into a cesspit in the teacher's garden.

The wash basins in the schools deserve special mention. They were made of china but there were only three of them in schools accommodating over 400 pupils and, as the report noted, they were 'rarely used.' Should our reaction to this wash basin situation be based on 2007 or 1902 standards of hygiene?

In respect of rainwater drainage, some water was fed into the cold water tanks, the rest was conveyed by a drain across the boys' playground (as now) and into a ditch in Parkend Road.

Heating: Was by portable stove in each large room. There was no central heating.

Lighting: Was by oil lamp.

Furniture: The surveyor compiled inventories of the complete contents of both infant and mixed schools. Imaginative use of these lists can give us a real insight into how Edwardian schools actually were. The lists are here produced in full (see page 106) and no further comment is necessary other than the reminder that the infant school could house about 150 children and the mixed school about 250.

Staff – Fit for Purpose?

1. The situation in which staff were working

The opening of the new National Schools at Bream Eaves in 1862 coincided with momentous developments in elementary education. This was the introduction of the Revised Code for Education.

Previously the Prince Consort, Albert, had chaired an elementary education conference in 1857 that established that there were only some two million children in elementary education and that of those that did attend nearly half did so for less than a year. This led the Government to set up a royal commission in 1858 under the chairmanship of the Duke of Newcastle to investigate elementary education and recommend a way forward.

The Newcastle Commission discovered that over 80 per cent of children had left elementary education before the age of twelve and that more than half attended school for less than 100 days per year. Most left without attaining what the commission regarded as a basic standard of learning. This consisted of being able to spell ordinary words correctly, to write a letter that was legible and intelligible, to make out or check a common bill, to have sufficient geographical knowledge to know the position of the countries of the world; above all, to be sufficiently acquainted with the Scriptures to be able to follow 'a plain Saxon sermon.' Many did not achieve this standard in 1858 and, of those that did, some lapsed within a few years of leaving school.

Faced with this problem and driven by a government that wanted economy and efficiency the Commission recommended a 'payments by results' system which was adopted as the Revised Code of Education in 1862. Nowadays in education we use the phrase 'best value' as though it is a new concept. But is it? I suspect it may very well be yet another wheel that has been reinvented. Certainly Robert Lowe who introduced the revised code to Parliament was determined that the Government was going to get value for money out of its elementary education system.

Under the revised code the grant to the school was dependent upon the attendance of pupils and their individual success in passing an examination in the three Rs (reading, writing and arithmetic) and needlework for the girls. This examination was administered by an inspector who reported on the school every year. Failure to reach the required standards in the code led to a deduction of grant. I know teachers nowadays feel pressure. I wonder how they would have felt working during the thirty-year existence of the, where they would have been subject to annual inspection and their salary would have been determined by pupils' attendance and exam performance. The revised code was truly bad news for Bream schools and their staff.

In practice, the code penalised the bright child. Teachers prioritised, bringing slower pupils up to grant-earning standard in the three Rs. Teachers became 'crammers.' They became demoralised and their lives became dominated by percentage passes. Sharp practices developed such as sending round exam questions from school to school, shipping backward children to some other school on examination days to avoid bringing down their percentage of passes and, as certainly happened at Bream, marking up absent scholars in order to improve attendance figures.

The code was generally unpopular with teachers, managers and inspectors. But few probably dared to be openly critical. The instigator of the code, Robert Lowe, fended off would-be opposition when he said 'teachers desiring to criticise the code were as impertinent as chickens wishing to decide the sauce in which they would be served.' It truly was a crude and blunt instrument and a dead weight on any creative teaching. On one specific matter it is an interesting point of debate in our politically-correct society as to whether an all-male inspectorate was qualified to judge girls' needlework.

Teaching under the code was still dependent on the monitorial system. Pupil-teachers were apprenticed to the head for five years from the age of thirteen to eighteen – though this rule was also broken, in Bream. They were paid for those five years, at the end of which they could sit for an exam and, if successful, go on to a three year course at training college. After college they qualified as certificated teachers. Pupil-teachers who did not go on to do three years' training became uncertificated or assistant teachers. Obviously it was usual for a pupil-teacher to have been a pupil at that school. In Bream pupil-teachers did stay on as uncertificated teachers and even returned as certificated ones. Below the pupil-teacher in rank and age was the paid monitor. In the infant school the monitor could be as young as eight.

2. School or Schools?

The perennial problems with Bream, whether it was one single school or separate schools, was an issue in the late nineteenth century. Essentially there was one National School on one site in 1862 but it was probably called the schools because it had a boys' department under a master and a girls' department under a governess. The master seemed to have some jurisdiction over matters concerning the girls' department.

In 1865 the situation changed and there was a separation into the boys' school and the girls' and infants' school. This changed again in 1875 when the little ones were separated out from the girls' school to form the infant school with their own separate headmistress. In 1892 the boys' school and girls' school amalgamated into a mixed school again, the infants staying independent.

In Summary
1862 One mixed school of boys, girls and infants.
1865 Two schools; boys school, and girls and infants school.
1875 Three schools; boys, girls and infants.
1888 Two schools; mixed school of boys and girls, and infant school.

It is much simpler to refer to the site, as historically has always happened, as 'the schools.'

3. 1862–82 – The Teachers' graveyard

I stated previously that the Revised Code of 1862 was bad news for Bream schools and their staff. And so it was. It is still true now, but in the more divided society of nineteenth century Britain, it was even more true that children who were going through education were not starting from the same base point. In the nineteenth century the children of parents who were themselves educated and with homes that contained books would have had a head start. At the time and bearing in mind Payler Proctor, John Moxley and Elija Waring's comments about the level of education in the Forest – and Bream in particular – teaching in the village must have been an uphill struggle. No doubt rewarding but still uphill. Bream was almost exclusively a working class mining and colliery area. The parents would themselves have been – and not in any pejorative sense – illiterate. There would have been no books at home and the parents themselves could not impose educational standards if they had no personal experience of the education process.

To judge Bream schools in 1862 against a national standard would inevitably find the schools a failure because there was so much leeway to make up. For at least twenty years after the code was introduced the schools *were* a failure. Bream was a graveyard for aspiring heads; they came, they failed and they went – no matter how good they were. It took some twenty years to make up the leeway and by then six masters and six mistresses had fallen by the wayside. It was a no-win situation, well illustrated by one discerning diocesan inspector in 1866 who wrote 'the progress [is] as much as could reasonably be expected considering the material out of which the school is formed. The children coming from a district where education has not been much valued or attended to . . .'

If we were to explore our perceptions of the teaching profession in the nineteenth century, I suspect most people would assume that most teachers would work in the district where they had been born and bred, that for most of them the school where they worked would be a job for life and if they were to move they would do so locally. The evidence at Bream would indicate that none of the above statements is true, certainly for teachers in the upper reaches of the profession, those with certificated qualification. In fact it is possible to argue that there may well have been more mobility in the nineteenth century teaching profession in Gloucestershire than there is today. It would be a huge exercise to test that hypothesis but there is certainly a case to be made for it to be true of Bream. Another hypothesis from Bream that would probably stand scrutiny in a national context is that National Schools were staffed by husband and wife teams. It was almost a travelling circus at Bream where a husband and wife came to live in the schoolhouse, the master taught the boys, the mistress taught the girls and after a few years they moved on to another National School in another area. At Bream they had an added inducement to move on – a critical inspector's report and consequently a reduced salary.

As previously mentioned Joseph Augustus Lewis Littlewood and his wife Margaret took over Bream Tufts school in 1857. When appointed to Bream he was teaching in Edinburgh. The census gives his birthplace as the Isle of Wight and Margaret's as being Northumberland. They did not stay long in Bream; in 1861 they were master and mistress of a school in Walton on Thames, Surrey.

Probably taking over from Joseph Littlewood was Ambrose H Smith. The 1861 Census states that he was aged twenty-five, a bachelor and he was lodging with the Sims family on Mill Hill. Almost certainly he was the first schoolmaster to live in the new schoolhouse at the Eaves. Possibly he married soon after since the 1863 *Post Office Directory* names the schoolmistress as Mrs Janet Smith. The parish magazine for 1867 tells us that Ambrose Smith was also choirmaster at St James and that when he left the school in 1867 he was presented with an inscribed teapot and a purse containing £6. 11s. 6d. Thereafter the Smiths may well have left the county since they do not appear on the 1871 Census. Mrs Smith may well have already ceased employment at the schools because in 1865 when the girls' and boys' schools were separated Miss Mary Anne Leete from London was appointed schoolmistress.

Mary Leete's first inspector's report in 1866 was encouraging. The test results were poor but, as Miss Leete pointed out to the inspector, there was much leeway to make up (a very human trait to damn what has gone before!). The inspector quite understood, praised her skill and was confident of an improvement during the year. It did not happen. In the meantime Miss Leete had fallen for the church organist, Simeon Dobbs, and the girls' exam results were again poor. As the inspector said 'it is abundantly clear that the mistress' heart has not been in her work.' It was elsewhere. She had fallen in love. There was a deduction in the grant and Miss Leete left the school shortly afterwards. Her marriage was good news for the girls – they were given a half day holiday from school on 1 January 1868 in honour of their former mistress' marriage. The Dobbs left Bream in 1867, Simeon having got a job as an organist in Berkshire. In 1871 they were in Worcestershire and in 1881 in London.

The inspector's reports on Ambrose Smith's work in the boys department followed a similar pattern. In 1865 the inspector wrote that the expected improvements from previous years had not taken place. A deduction in the grant was made and the school was also seriously criticised for employing a teacher who was under thirteen years of age. This was pupil-teacher William Morgan. Again in 1866 there was a deduction in the grant. The inspector commented 'the failures in the two lowest standards have been so numerous as to indicate something wrong somewhere.' In 1867 the boys' inspection took place at the end of April. Some improvement was reported but 'it is still far from what might and should be.' Ambrose Smith left the school on 10 May, just four days before the inspector's written report arrived. There may have been a previous oral report to the vicar and there is the distinct possibility that Ambrose Smith was dismissed since, when he left suddenly on 10 May, the school was without a master till a new one was appointed at the end of June. The school had to be taken by the clergy in the intervening period.

Next up were the Careys, Albert Carey and Mrs Marianne Carey from Stourport. He began as master on 27 June 1867, she as mistress four days later on 1 July. Like the previous master, Ambrose Smith, Albert Carey was also choirmaster at church. The Careys stayed at Bream schools for seven years and during that time, there seems to have been a gradual improvement in standards. Inspectors were still critical of performance in arithmetic – that Bream perennial – but in other respects the schools were approaching a satisfactory standard.

In 1873, with the Gosling extension in place, matters started to go wrong for the Careys. For one thing their income went down. In February

1873 an inspector visited the girls' school and reported finding 'nine scholars marked as present in the registers who were absent.' This breach of the 1862 Code was punished by a deduction of 10 per cent in the grant and consequently a lower salary for Mrs Carey. A further deduction in salary was to happen in September 1874 when, facilitated by the new extra accommodation and faced with continuing criticism of how badly the infants were taught, the managers decided to separate the infants from the girls' school and appoint a specialist infant teacher. This could well have halved Marianne Carey's salary. On top of this Albert Carey received an HMI report that was very critical of the spelling in the boys' school – 'decidedly poor' – and stated that 20 per cent of the boys qualified for examination had been 'purposely kept back.' Albert Carey, stung by this criticism, replied in the log book that this had been an infant school decision – a classic case of 'not me gov'.' He was in effect blaming his wife who at that stage still had responsibility for infants.

It is impossible at this distance to know the relationship between the master and his wife but the girls' school log book contains a rather odd entry for 14 August 1874, the day that Marianne Carey left the girls' school. There were pupil-teachers in the boys' and girls' schools who were in effect apprenticed from thirteen to eighteen and mainly taught the younger children, and received ongoing instruction on how to do so. Marianne Carey's log for 14 August states that the pupil-teachers had their instruction from 6.30–7.30 p.m. from the master but *always in my presence.'* The latter phrase seems odd. No other mistress made such a log entry.

The Careys seem to have departed under something of a cloud. Once again the clergy had to step into the breach. Between August 1874 and March 1875 the schools were without a master and mistress. Meantime the Careys continued teaching and the 1881 Census saw them both plying their profession in Devon.

While they were in Bream the Careys had several children. In this respect the boys' log book for January 1868 gives us an interesting insight into family life at that time. Nowadays ordinary maternity leave is defined by statute as being twenty-six weeks. On Monday 13 January 1868, Marianne Carey was confined and gave birth to a son, John William Moore Carey. She was back in charge of the girls and infants on Monday 3 February, just three weeks later. In the meantime the master, as the only adult teacher, took responsibility for all 126 children in the schools.

A further interesting development occurred under the Careys, a 'first' as far as I know. On Thursday 25 June 1874 groups of boys and girls were photographed. I wonder if any of these pictures have survived? Sadly, as a consequence of the photographs, playtime was cancelled. One cannot have too much excitement in one day.

The next couple to work at Bream schools were Augustus and Mary Dickson. Their tenure of the schools was fleeting, taking up post in March 1875 and resigning in August 1876. They seem not to have enjoyed their time in Bream very much; in the summer of 1875 Mary Dickson was taken home to Nottinghamshire by her father because of illness. Augustus Dickson, from his log book, had little enthusiasm for the school. His one dramatic gesture occurred in July 1876 when he wrote that he had dismissed the grandly named Admiral Jones for 'outrageous conduct.' He went on to say 'He has proved himself to be the worst boy in all the school.' Unfortunately we are left in the dark as to what the boy did. The grandly named Admiral Jones must have eventually returned to school sometime since in the 1881 Census he is described as a seventeen-year-old pupil-teacher. He became a well known character in Bream with a road named after him – Admiral's Lane – now known as Blue Rock Crescent. The 1881 Census recorded the Dicksons as schoolmaster and mistress back in Nottinghamshire.

The next married teachers at Bream were there for an even shorter period than the Dicksons and their time at the schools was truly tragic. Edward and Emma Wall came from Whiston school in Prescot, Lancashire. They took charge at Bream in October 1876 and left at the beginning of August 1877. Both received dreadful inspectors' reports. The girls' school report stated 'the percentage of passes here is very poor, but still this school is not in quite so low a state of instruction as the boys' school.' The boys' school report stated 'the state of attainment is anything but creditable to Mr Wall's seven months here, even after due allowance is made.' The 'due allowance' being made was a reference to a family tragedy. The boys' log book entry for 31 May 1877 reads 'At noon on Thursday an infant daughter of the master and mistress was accidentally suffocated by falling on top of a small tub of water. An inquest was necessary.' The girls' log is even more poignant. 'Thursday. I was called out of school. My little girl died suddenly.' The infant was named Edith. She was aged one. The subsequent coroner's inquest reported that Edith was in the care of her twelve-year-old sister Anne who was busy with housework in another room. The Walls left in the summer and he became schoolmaster of Kingsland National School in Herefordshire.

At this point, September 1877, the married-couple mould was finally broken. Thomas John White was appointed master and in January 1878 Sarah Ann Mann took charge of the girls' school. There was, however, no change in standards in the schools. They continued to be abysmal.

Thomas John White only had one inspector's report at Bream. The report stated 'attainments still very low and the discipline is weak also.' White left a few months later.

Under the leadership of Sarah Mann the girls' school showed some initial improvement but by 1880 the school was again being castigated for poor results in arithmetic and a deduction in the grant was threatened. The deduction was made in 1881 and another 10 per cent made in 1882. When the school broke up for Whitsun at the end of May 1882, Sarah Mann seemed to leave in haste from a school that was in trouble. The log book indicates there were parental complaints coming in and at least one of the managers seemed to be in school every day – a bad sign. Whitsun was an unusual time to leave a teaching post but, as she herself wrote in the log book, 'I do not come into school again, having resigned the Mistress-ship.'

Henry Poole, who took over from Thomas John White, was at least the sixth master in the seventeen years the school had been open at the Eaves. This was not good for the stability of the school and standards had consistently been unsatisfactory. Under Henry Poole, who stayed as master for six years, the school at last did gain some better reports. Was there light beginning to come through at the end of the tunnel? His worst report was his final one in the summer of 1885. The inspector was critical of arithmetic (again) and very hesitant to award a grant for English. He was also critical of the school cesspool; that was too close to the buildings and should never be allowed to become too full. School inspectors really do have a view on everything. Henry Poole subsequently resigned from Bream in November 1885 to take up a headship in Buckinghamshire. His successor was one of Bream's greatest schoolmasters – W F Mullan. Under his very capable leadership the school was to go from strength to strength.

4. Turning the Corner

As previously stated, the imposition of payment by results against a national standard in 1862 put Bream schoolteachers – irrespective of their quality – into a lose - lose situation. Until they could establish a culture of education in the village there would never be a level playing field by which Bream schools could be judged against other, more advantaged institutions. To make up the leeway was going to be a hard job.

Crucially in 1874, following the Gosling extension, the managers took a decision that really did have momentous consequences for the schools and built on the improvements already put in train by the Careys and Henry Poole. They appointed a specialist infant teacher in September

1874 who became the first head of Bream's infant school when it was separated from the girls' school on 30 April 1875. Her name was Selina Durnell and she served Bream Infants School with exemplary distinction for the next twenty-one years.

Until 1874 the infants had been, as evidenced in the inspectors' reports, badly taught by pupil-teachers who themselves were being instructed by a master who only taught older pupils. By the 1870s infant schools were growing in popularity in Gloucestershire and infant teaching was seen as a speciality. As soon as Selina Durnell was appointed standards began to improve in the infants and, as those children progressed into the boys' and girls' schools, standards there would also improve significantly. Thus from 1875 onwards Bream schools really turned the corner and made significant progress. This was down particularly to the superb heads – Selina Durnell, head of Bream Infants School 1875–96, and W F Mullan, head of the boys and subsequently mixed school 1885–1918.

5. Selina Durnell

Selina Perks Durnell was born in Shropshire in 1854 and started work at Bream as an 'attested infant mistress' in September 1874. She was twenty years old and lived on Mill Hill. Just prior to her arrival, the Careys had left their posts as master and mistress and the schools were under the supervision of the vicar. As a result of this, Selina Durnell, on arrival, was given the job of supervising sewing and knitting in the girls' school as well as teaching the infants. At Christmas 1874 she sat for her certificate exam and passed. As a result she was appointed the first headmistress of Bream Infants School in 1875. When she finally left in the summer of 1896 it was not for another teaching post. Like Mary Ann Leete before her she left to get married.

Selina's impact on the school was immediate and the consequent improvement was mirrored in the inspectors' reports. There were minor HMI criticisms in the early years of her headship – in 1875 some adverse comments on discipline and in the following year 1876 over the fact that six-year-olds were counting on their fingers in arithmetic, but the overall pattern was one of consistently high quality work. 1877 to 1896 reports on Bream Infants School were full of praise. In 1881 the inspector delivered the following report 'The infants are carefully and thoroughly well taught; discipline is good and the sewing is the best of any infants school in my district. Miss Durnell deserves praise for steady and successful work.' The 1887 inspector actually observed the children 'were interested in their work' (was this an unusual event?) and the report in 1890 made an observation which probably was a result of the fact that the children enjoyed school when he wrote that they were 'attending with unusual regularity.'

By 1895 the HMI reports had been so good for so long that the school was given an exemption from an annual inspection – the first for any of the schools in Bream and a fitting tribute to a great headmistress after twenty years' excellent work in the school.

The log book for the infants school, completed by Selina on a weekly basis, gives a detailed picture of the operation of the school and an insight into her qualities. She was efficient, flexible, educationally up-to-date and very caring of her charges. She could also, when the need arose, be tough with parents and the staff under her control. In 1875 an inspector criticised the school verbally for not having an object box containing object cards; an object box arrived in school on 16 July, the very same day the inspector's written report was received. She split the infants up, probably for the first time, to promote better learning; in 1877 she organised the school into three classes and in 1878 divided the six and seven-year-olds into two divisions (sets) so they 'may be taught to read better.' She could also be flexible in her working arrangements with other professionals.

In 1883 a new head of the girls' school, Miss Newman, arrived with her own particular strengths and interests. Soon afterwards the two schools exchanged teachers in certain subjects; Miss Durnell taking the girls' school for singing and Miss Newman taking the infants for drill. This became a weekly exchange.

Several specific instances reveal her concern for her children. In January 1888 the weather was so dull that in the arithmetic lesson she decided it was too dark for the children to see the figures on their slates so she read to them instead. A few months later, when hearing the children read, she quickly worked out the reason for one little girl's reading problem. She could not read because she couldn't see the words. In January 1895 the weather was so bad there were only thirty-one children in school. Her reaction to this was to amalgamate the classes that day, teach them herself and send the two other teachers home — a humane touch.

In 1876, twelve months after taking over as head of infants there were 145 children on the books with ninety-three in average attendance. It is as well to remember that to teach these children Selina Durnell had the assistance of just one teenage pupil-teacher and a monitor who could be as young as eight. At times she was very strict on both and her criticisms of their behaviour and teaching give an insight into her philosophy as a teacher.

In 1879 she castigated her pupil-teacher Annie Morse and her monitor, Clara Brain, on the highly commendable grounds that 'they don't make their lessons attractive to children.' The culprits at the time were aged approximately sixteen and seven respectively. From the perspective of their age Selina's comments may seem harsh to us today but we have to remember that it was standard practice at the time, under the revised code, for pupil-teachers and monitors of comparable ages to have responsibility for teaching classes of children. Clara Brain was eventually to progress from being a monitor to being a pupil-teacher at Bream and eventually taking over as infant headmistress when Selina Durnell left the school in 1896.

Clara also got a scolding when Selina observed her lesson on the subject of 'cotton.' The criticism was 'too many answers from the same children while others did nothing. Children are not made to work for themselves.' Selina Durnell's qualities as a teacher were timeless, she would have been successful with children irrespective of the era in which she taught.

One particular monitor who was frequently in trouble was Ellen Livinia Worgan who became a monitor in 1882 at the age of nine. Ellen was cautioned several times for slapping the little children. This had led to a number of parental complaints; in fact one parent, Jane White from Woodside, came up to school and gave the monitor herself a slap. I do not know if any legal action was taken against Jane White for this but a couple of months later, when Ellen was still hitting the little ones, Selina referred her to the vicar for a formal warning. The vicar, Henry Dandy, wrote in the school log 'I have spoken to Ellen Worgan and she has promised me not to use her hands, stick or pencil to punish the children but will send all such cases to Miss Durnell.' A couple of months later complaints were coming in again about Ellen's behaviour. Shortly after, she resigned – or was forced to do so.

Another monitor who had a bad press in Selina's log book was Sarah Nash. Anyone who has been in the teaching profession has a dread of freezing in front of a class. This happened to Sarah when she was an eight-year-old monitor at Bream. The headmistress wrote 'I told Sarah Nash to give a lesson this morning she was unable to say anything.' Oh dear! A few months later she was criticised again on an observed lesson – 'her manner is too listless.' Later when she was giving a lesson on 'The Goad' she attracted the following rebuke 'Attention of class not kept up. Spoke to her again about speaking distinctly and being bright in her manner.' Feedback on lessons was very forthcoming from Selina Durnell.

Sara Nash did come through in the end and completed her time as a pupil-teacher at Bream.

Selina's time as headmistress was punctuated by bouts of ill health. She was away ill from January to March 1880, when the school had to employ a 'supply' head. In September 1882, when considering her state of health, the managers instructed her to exercise 'general supervision only' of the school for that month. In March 1888, the vicar told her that she could leave school at any time on grounds of her health.

In the late nineteenth century the link between Anglican Church and school was always very close. In Selina's time that link became even closer. In 1867 Mary Anne Leete, the girls headmistress, had married the church organist. Selina went one better. She married the vicar. Whatever could be said of this arrangement it certainly was not a whirlwind romance. Selina Durnell had been head of infants for five years when Henry Dandy MA arrived as curate of Bream in 1880. Three years later Henry Dandy became vicar of Bream and in 1896, sixteen years after making Selina's acquaintance the couple were married.

The marriage took place on 5 August 1896 in Bath. By that time Selina had already left Bream Infants School and was living in King Street, Bath. Henry Dandy had also left Bream to become vicar of Kingswood in Bristol. Interestingly the log book of the school gives no reason as to why she was leaving and the *Dean Forest Guardian* dated 24 July, which reported Reverend Dandy's presentation evening, makes no mention of his forthcoming marriage less than two weeks away. It is fascinating to speculate whether their marriage plans had been kept secret. At the time of the marriage the bride was forty-four and the groom thirty-eight.

Selina Perks Dandy kept her links with Bream. At the time of the 1901 she was staying with her Phipps relatives on Mill Hill. She died 12 July at Kingswood vicarage and Henry Dandy, no doubt in accordance with her wishes, arranged for her to be buried outside the east window of Bream Church. She was aged fifty-five.

It is appropriate that she was buried in Bream. She had been Bream Infants School's first head and had led the school superbly for over twenty years.

6. William Frederick Mullan

W F Mullan's career as a head at Bream School overlapped Selina Durnell's leadership of the infants school by some eleven years. He built on her excellent work in the infants and created a National School that achieved a consistently high standard of education throughout the period of his very long headship – a headship that saw major changes in the structure of the school. On arrival in 1885 he was head of a comparatively small boys' National School and was assisted by one pupil-teacher and a monitor. His leadership of the boys' school however was so outstanding that by 1888 he was in charge of the girls as well and Bream became a mixed school. As the school grew under his leadership the premises became so overcrowded that the temporary school came into use in 1905 and the new infant school was built in 1907. Even so numbers in the mixed school continued to grow – by 1909 there were 364 on roll – and in 1912 it became necessary to teach standard II in the infants rather than the mixed school. Despite the problems of overcrowding, there was no diminution in standards while W F Mullan was head. He took early retirement aged fifty-eight on health grounds in 1918. The staff by then numbered seven full time teachers.

William Frederick Mullan was born in Manchester in 1859. He began teaching in the Everton suburb of Liverpool (missionary work no doubt). His teacher training was at St John's, Battersea, London and later at St Mary Radcliffe, Bristol where he met two people who were to have a profound effect on the rest of his life; Henry Dandy and Rosina Boon, his future employer and his future wife. When the headship of Bream boys' school became vacant in 1885 the newly appointed vicar, the Reverend Henry Dandy, invited William Mullan to take the post. Some six months after taking up residence at the Bream school house he then married Rosina Boon, a photographer's assistant he had met while training in Bristol. The wedding took place in Barton Regis. Both were to spend the rest of their lives in Bream. They were to have three children. Amy Boon Mullan became a pupil-teacher at Bream School, went on to Cheltenham Training College and taught in Bristol. Frederick William Mullan lost an eye serving as a stretcher bearer with the Royal Army Medical Corps in the First World War and subsequently practised as a dentist in Bream and Lydney. A third child, Lily, died in infancy in 1891 and is buried in Bream churchyard.

It is the way of the world for teachers to acquire nicknames and I was keen to discover if any nickname was given to Mr Mullan. In the village he was a highly respected figure and seemed to be known as Mr Mullan, William Mullan or William F Mullan. Logically his nickname should have been a derivative of, or pun on, his first name or surname but it was not. Angus Cooper, who was a choirboy when William Mullan was in the choir, assures me that the children called him 'Old Joe.' There is a peculiar kind of Forest or Bream logic in that. A similar logic was at work with his son Frederick Mullan who was known to everyone as Teddy. When I asked Angus why that was, he assured me that at that time in the Forest anyone with the Christian name of Frederick was known as Teddy. Correspondingly, I suppose anyone with the Christian name of Edward should be called Freddy. That is Forest logic – long may it flourish.

The records of Bream School during William Mullan's headship reveal a man with a human touch and a sense of humour. On 6 April 1903 a travelling circus came to Bream with the consequence that only 175 out of 280 children attended school on that day. Some heads would have reacted furiously to this but not William Mullan. His log book entry for that day realistically records 'The attractions of a travelling circus have proved too much for a large number of the children.' A similar event and low attendance in August 1893 was recorded with the dry entry 'several attractions in neighbourhood more potent than the school.' In recording a lateness misdemeanour by one of the girls, Fanny Wintle, in February 1900 the entry is as follows 'Fanny Wintle went home – told to do so by her mother if punished for being late. Her attendance was cancelled and a message was sent home regarding the effect on discipline such conduct was likely to cause. The girl only lives 100 yards from school!' William Mullan had the capacity to see the funny side of any situation.

The other side of this coin though was his firmness as a schoolmaster that won him universal respect inside and outside school. He started at Bream on Monday 16 November 1885 and lost no time in establishing his authority. Less than three weeks after he arrived one of the boys, George Masters, had been expelled 'for insubordination and persistent bad conduct after repeated warnings and appeals to parents.' This no nonsense approach was followed a few weeks later when Albert James was sent home for 'cursing and attempting to kick the master.' In common with every schoolmaster in the land at that time, William Mullan used the cane, but, if discipline was good, which it was, he would use it rarely. It could be and was used for misdemeanours outside school as well as inside. In April 1894 Fred Moore was punished for beating a donkey on his way to school. The following year Leonard Treherne was likewise caned for 'ill-using donkeys on the green.'

The quality of William Mullan's leadership of Bream School is amply evidenced in HMI reports. In 1887, less than two years after he arrived, HMI were reporting 'The Master deserves praise for the creditable improvement which has taken place . . . the school is now in a good state of efficiency.' In 1894, HMI stated 'The order and organisation are very good and the instruction is in all respects thorough.' The following year the school gained exception from the annual inspection. The 1897 HMI report gives a real insight into William Mullan's talent as a teacher when it records that the top class or first class which he taught consisted of five different standards of pupils – from standard III to standard VII – the highest standard in elementary education at the time. Couple that range of ability with the number of pupils in a class gives an impression of a truly daunting task for any teacher, even one as good as William Mullan. A staff list exists for 1907 which states the maximum number of pupils staff could have in a class. Because he was headmaster William Mullan was limited to fifty pupils. His 'certified assistants', Mrs S A Wrighton and Mr G White, could teach up to sixty. The uncertificated, Article 50 staff, Mr H L Cooke, Mr E B Barlow, Miss A Williams, Miss M A Phipps, Miss M W Smith and Miss E Hatch were limited to forty-five pupils. In practice these guidelines could be broken. In 1906 HMI observed an uncertificated teacher in charge of a class of eighty-three and during one week in March 1911, because of teacher sickness, two teachers were dealing with 180 girls in three rooms. Even in those days teachers were expected to work miracles.

Despite such a challenge of numbers William Mullan was very keen on high attendance since he firmly believed that progress was directly linked to good attendance. In May 1886 he sent a letter out to parents pointing out the necessity of regular attendance if progress was to be expected. In 1889 he introduced a ticket scheme for good attendance whereby children who attended for one year without absence were entitled to a prize. In 1892 if a child was absent without explanation a message was sent home to enquire why. Subsequently the attendance officer was sent round. By 1917 William Mullan even had an attendance committee of school managers whose sole function was interviewing parents of 'irregular children.'

Among the specific developments that occurred during William Mullan's tenure of Bream School was the setting up of a 'penny bank' in 1892 allowing children and parents to save. In 1896 a football was purchased for the use of the boys. The following year, 1897, the curate Reverend Walter Frederick Adams presented the school with a horizontal bar, used at the time for 'drill' – the forerunner of today's PE. This was exclusively for the use of the boys. In 1898 Reverend Adams presented a trapeze bar – also exclusively for the boys. Clearly exercises on the horizontal bar or the trapeze was not for the girls. Their drill lessons were apparently more sedate. I wonder if any of them challenged the adult view of what exercise the different sexes were allowed to undertake? In reverse the boys were not allowed to do needlework and their equivalent was technical drawing. The Reverend Adams was obviously keen on drill. He not only presented the school with items of equipment but also taught the older boys their use – 'muscular Christianity' at work.

In May 1900 there was to be an eclipse of the sun. William Mullan took advantage of this to give a lesson on the principle of the eclipse. Three days later playtime was extended and the children were issued with smoked glasses so that they could observe the progress of the eclipse. William Mullan also set up a school museum. In September 1900 a Sergeant Gregoire of the 3rd Grenadiers who had recently been on service in the Boer War in South Africa presented five mauser cartridges from Paaderburg to the school museum. To the victor the spoils – the Mauser rifle was standard use among the Boers in their war against the British, 1899-1902. Another novelty for the children occurred in April 1903 when the vicar, G W Leonard Cass, brought his wind-up gramophone into school for the children to listen to. This really was a treat because very few of them had ever heard one. Another development under William Mullan was the acquisition of a flagpole for the playground in 1909, presented by Dr Bowles of Priors Mesne – and in time for the celebration of Empire Day when the Union Jack was hoisted and saluted by all the children who then sang patriotic songs. Another acquisition was some land in 1912 given by Ralph Williams which was to be a garden, again solely for the use of the boys. The current educational thinking was that the boys learned to grow vegetables while their future wives were learning how to cook.

While these local developments were taking place in the school there could also be national events that had an impact on the village and the school – events such as the Boer War, the First World War and the death of Queen Victoria. In respect of the Boer War, apart from the visit of Sergeant Gregoire, the children were all given a half-holiday in March 1900 to celebrate the relief of Ladysmith. They were also sent home early on 2 June 1902 in celebration of the Declaration of Peace.

The First World War had an even bigger impact on the school and its headmaster. When the Soldiers Fund Committee was formed in the village in 1917 to raise money for presentations to soldiers home on leave, William Mullan was its secretary. Other events relating to the mixed school and the First World War will be dealt with in a later chapter.

The Death of Queen Victoria

The death of the Queen in 1901, after sixty-four years on the throne, was another national event which permeated the life of Bream School when William Mullan was head and in an indirect as well as a direct way. Directly, in that when news of the Queen's death was released on 22

January 1901 the vicar, Reverend Eales, came into school to lead the children in a special tribute accompanied by prayers for the Queen and members of the royal family. A few days later Union Jacks, draped in black crepe, were fixed to the walls of the school and on the day preceding the funeral, scheduled for 2 February, William Mullan held a special assembly for the school to tell them of the Queen's life and reign.

An indirect connection between Queen Victoria's death and Bream School occurred at her funeral when all the crowned heads of State in Europe followed behind a simple sailor boy who had recently left Bream School, Thomas Richard Wildin.

Thomas Wildin had been born in Bream on 5 January 1882. He attended Bream School until 1894 when, aged twelve, he left to become a live-in apprentice at a shop in Lydney. He lived at the shop, Monday to Saturday, returned home on Sunday and had a half day off on Thursday. One Thursday afternoon, kicking his heels in Lydney High Street, he was invited by a Lydney resident, Samuel Pocket, to join him on a boat trip across the Severn because Sam was going to see his bank manager 'over there.' Thomas gladly agreed and while Mr Pocket was in the bank, Thomas wandered into the nearby Naval Recruiting Office. The rest, as they say, is history. Thomas duly signed on, aged fifteen, as a boy sailor and embarked that day on a train to Portsmouth. Mr Pocket had the unenviable task of returning to Lydney minus one fifteen-year-old travelling companion and getting someone to break the news to Thomas' family.

On 2 February, 1902 Able Seaman Thomas Wildin, seven years out from Bream School, was on duty as part of the naval detachment at Windsor railway station. The detachment was detailed to provide part of the escort to take the Queen's coffin from the station to the state funeral at St George's Chapel.

The Queen had died at Osborne House on the Isle of Wight. The original plan for the State funeral was that when the coffin arrived at Windsor station it was to be placed on a gun carriage and pulled up the hill at Windsor by a troop of horses from the Royal Horse Artillery (RHA). Following the gun carriage would be the funeral cortège led by Edward VII and Kaiser Wilhelm II followed in turn by the greatest number of crowned heads of state ever seen together anywhere.

At this point the plan started to go wrong. The train carrying the coffin was late arriving by a couple of hours. It was a bitterly cold day. The RHA horses that were due to pull the gun carriage had, in honour of the occasion, been specially shaved and polished. At this point the explanation of what happened next is controversial. Thomas Wildin's account –

no doubt the naval view of the event – was that, because of the cold and the delay, the horses were too restless to pull the gun carriage and the naval detachment pulled it instead. The RHA version of events was different. The horses were harnessed to the gun carriage but just as they started to take the weight one of the traces broke. An improvised attachment could easily have been made but before that could happen the naval detachment had seized the drag ropes and started the cortège off up Windsor High Street. The Navy is not called the senior service for nothing and – more to the point – huge crowds had already been waiting for a couple of hours on a bitterly cold February day.

The accompanying photograph shows the funeral procession in Windsor High Street on its way to St George's Chapel. Directly behind the coffin is King Edward VII and on his right is Kaiser Wilhelm II. Following them are members of every European royal family. The sailor level with the front of the coffin and on the far side is Able Seaman Thomas Richard Wildin. And so it came to pass that at Queen Victoria's funeral all of the crowned heads of Europe followed a sailor boy from Bream.

It is pleasing to record that the RHA eventually had their pride restored when they took the coffin, after its lying-in-state for two days, to its final resting place alongside the coffin of Albert, Prince Consort, in the Mausoleum in Windsor Great Park.

I am grateful to Thomas Wildin's daughter, Peggy Baynham, for this story and the photograph from the *Windsor and Eton Gazette*. Thomas Wildin became a Chief Petty Officer and served over twenty years in the Royal Navy. His three sons, Len, Walter and Geoffrey also served in the Navy and Walter is recorded on Bream Cenotaph. He served eighteen years in the Navy and held the rank of gunnery officer when his ship, *HMS Charybdis*, was torpedoed and sunk off the Channel Islands on 23 October 1943. He is the only officer on Bream Cenotaph's list of Second World War fatalities.

I have no doubt that William Mullan would have known that one of his ex-pupils took part in the Queen's funeral and was proud of that fact.

William Mullan finally left Bream School on 31 July 1918. His last entry in his log book reads 'Today I conclude my services as headmaster after thirty-three years work. I wish to convey my appreciation of the unvarying kindness and courtesy I have received from the managers and also the loyal co-operation of the staff.' He was Bream's longest serving head and was aged fifty-eight. Technically he was not of retirement age but he had no option. He had lost his hearing. His deafness had been worsening for a while and he had previously had a week off School in

November 1915 for hospital treatment from an ear specialist. Angus Cooper remembers, when he (Angus) was a choirboy, being amused when Old Joe finished the hymn a line after everybody else.

On retirement William and Rosina Mullan had to leave the School house. They retired to a house called Ravenswood. Eventually Teddy Mullan the son used the house as a dental practice. Subsequently it became a public house, officially known as 'The Cross Keys' but known, unofficially for many years, as 'The Dentist's Arms.'

William and Rosina Mullan had a long retirement, Rosina dying in 1937 aged seventy-nine and William Mullan dying in 1944, aged eighty-five.

I do not think anybody would argue with the judgement that Old Joe Mullan was a truly great Schoolmaster.

7. Other Schools in Bream?

There were certainly four, possibly five, other schools in Bream Parish in the late nineteenth century. Mostly these were private or 'Dame' schools and consisted of a few children attending a private house. Such 'schools' were not inspected and any written record of them is minimal or non-existent. We know that William and Sophia Webb still described their occupations as schoolmaster and schoolmistress in the 1861 Census when they lived at Colliers Beach. By this time they had already been dismissed from Bream National School and it is quite likely that they then ran a small private school in their house and charged probably a comparable rate to the National School – 2d. per child per week.

There was another private school on Forest Road in the house now known as 'The Cherries.' An 1862 conveyance on the property states 'all that tenement or dwelling house with the building or schoolroom thereto adjoining and built by the said Isaac Cullis.' The 'adjoining schoolroom' is now part of the house but it clearly was built separately but with a connection through to the domestic quarters. Confirmation of this building being a small private school comes from a written account of the recollections of Miss Eva Jordan, kindly lent to me by John Hale. Eva, born November 1888, wrote of the building 'the little cottage where we lived was used previously as a school where, for a few pence, children could get some education, if only to learn to read and write.'

Another Dame school appears to have existed at the entrance to Bowson Square. Margaret Addis remembers her father, William Thomas Preest, telling her about this little school which he attended. Bill Preest had been born in 1876. There were only about eight children who attended the school and it cost 3d. per week. The curriculum – if such it

102

could be called – consisted of the three Rs (reading, writing and arithmetic). The 'Dame' set the children some work to do and then disappeared to do her household chores such as the washing. Bill left that school at aged eleven and went to work at New Fancy Colliery (he walked there and back) for 4/- a week, tipping slag onto the slag heap (now New Fancy View).

There was also a Dame school in Admiral's Lane, now Blue Rock Crescent. Fortunately a photo exists of this school which has kindly been provided by Joyce James. Joyce's granny, Mary Laura Heath, who was born c.1875, attended this school and is on the photograph. The location of the school was Jasmine House (now called Holly Cottage). The photo dates from c.1882 (see page 109). The Dame is on camera left (and looking rather formidable) with her two monitors or pupil-teachers alongside her and her assistant at the other end of the front row. Two teachers, with two monitors, to teach seventeen pupils would make this an expensive school, a theory born out by the boots and clothes the children are wearing. Indeed a number of the girls are wearing necklaces and the two oldest pupils, a boy and a girl, appear to be wearing buttonholes. Despite the formidable appearance of the Dame she has a very supportive stance in respect of the little girl next to her – one hand round her shoulder and the other holding the little girl's hand. Her assistant also has a comforting hand on her nearest charge. This really is an evocative photograph.

There was also a sewing school for girls based at the Hollies in Lydney Road. Beyond its existence, nothing is known of it.

One other school merits mention and that is in the far corner of the parish at Yorkley Wood. Bream clergy held services in Yorkley Wood chapel from 1867 onwards. The chapel during the week was then used as a Church school and is referred to in John Gosling's 1871 Whitecroft school plan as mainly teaching infants. The Yorkley Wood school probably only had a short life with the building of Pillowell board school in 1877 and later Yorkley council school in 1909.

It is perhaps as well that these other schools existed in the parish in the late nineteenth century. Without them the pressure of numbers on the National Schools at the Eaves would have been truly impossible.

The recent demolition of the 1950 toilet block revealed the 1872-3 Gosling extension (now the kitchen).

Reverend Gosling who used his own money to build the 1872-3 extension to Bream schools.
Photo courtesy of Roy Haviland

Revd Henry Dandy, responsible for further improvements to the schools in 1893.
Photo courtesy of Roy Haviland

Painting of the National School, believed to have been a Christmas gift in 1893. The artist would have been near the pond. The Witherby – Gosling school can clearly be seen. The Eales extension is yet to be added. The painting is reputed to have belonged to Sam Thomas.
Courtesy of Gloucestershire Library Service

The 1903 furniture lists for the mixed school written by Leonard Cass, vicar of Bream.
Courtesy of Gloucestershire Archives AE/R4/347

The 1903 furniture lists for the infants school written by Leonard Cass, vicar of Bream.
Courtesy of Gloucestershire Archives AE/R4/347

The funeral of Queen Victoria passing up Windsor High Street on 2 February 1902. On the far side of the carriage and level with the front of the coffin is Able Seaman Thomas Wildin from Bream. He is being followed by all the crowned heads of Europe.

Photo courtesy of Peggy Baynham

William Frederick Mullan. Headmaster at Bream 1885-1918.
Photo courtesy of Briget Thomas

W F Mullan in old age in the parlour of his house at Ravenswood now 'The Keys'.
Photo courtesy of Briget Thomas

The Dame School at Jasmine House – now Holly Cottage – circa 1882. *Photo courtesy of Joyce James*

CHAPTER FIVE

1862–1907: At the Chalk Face

The previous chapter attempted to paint the larger picture of Bream schools in the latter half of the nineteenth and the early years of the twentieth centuries. This chapter attempts to explore the finer details of what education was like in the village at that time. The fact that such a detailed examination is possible is down to the emergence of a particular set of educational records – school log books.

School log books began to make an appearance in some schools in the 1840s. At Bream the first log book appeared in 1862 soon after the new school opened at the Eaves. Like the ship's log kept by a sea captain it was a record kept by the headmaster/headmistress of major events in the life of that particular school. Consequently, at Bream there were different log books to reflect the degree of independence of the school or department concerned. For example, the infants' log book did not begin until 1875 when Selina Durnell was appointed head of the infants school. Prior to that date any serious issue concerning infants had been recorded in the girls' school log. Similarly a separate boys' and girls' log was combined into a mixed school log book when W F Mullan took over responsibility for both schools.

Usually the head kept the record on a weekly basis and, over a period of time, he or she would develop their own particular diary style that reflected their own personality. Thus, in one sense a log book was a formal document that fulfilled a regulatory requirement and in another sense, as recorded by an individual head, it could be, in turn, self-justifying, humorous, cynical, idiosyncratic and rich in experience of the world of parents, children, teachers and schools. On a superficial level the log book could also constitute a detailed record of the weather in the village since there was a formal requirement to log circumstances that affected children's school attendance. Thus, under some heads there are frequent references to weather events such as heavy rain, snow and even heatwaves that impacted on the schools. Given the individual nature of the entries recorded, I must state a historian's grateful thanks to all those heads from Ambrose Henry Smith in 1862 to Paul Woodward in 1997 who so faithfully found the time to maintain the weekly log of the school amidst so many other pressures on their precious time.

Before looking in detail at the record it is well worth considering our own individual or collective perception of those times. We all, for better or worse, have views on the past. Such perceptions generate thoughts such as:

- 'In Victorian times there was more discipline. Children were seen and not heard.'
- 'Teachers were always treated with respect.'
- 'If a child got into trouble at school they would keep quiet about it or they would get into trouble at home as well.'

All such thoughts are part-and-parcel of 'the good old days' – a utopian myth of past society.

Without becoming too philosophical, a constant theme of history is that of change and continuity. Life is always changing and yet it also has its constants, its universals or fixed points that remain the same irrespective of time. To evidence this, if we were to compare a child in a Victorian classroom to a child in a classroom today, much would be different – the premises, the subject matter, the size of class, the clothing, the technological aids used and so on, and yet there would still be a constant – a dynamic relationship between teacher and taught that, in a good lesson, would create a purposeful and rewarding learning situation that essentially would be the same in 1867 as in 2007. Selina Durnell reproached her teaching staff for not engaging all children in the class in much the same way – though probably more directly – as a present day inspector or head might.

That said, what views do we have of what education was like in the village between 1862 and 1907?

- How healthy were the children?
- What was their standard of living like?
- How do teachers salaries compare with those of today?
- Was there a price on schooling or was it free?
- How many holidays from school were there?
- Was school attendance/truancy an issue?

- What was children's behaviour like at school?
- How were they punished?
- How well did parents relate to the school?
- How well did the school link with the community?
- How well did the school relate to the church?
- What did children actually learn in the classroom?

Standards of Health

In 1851, life expectancy at birth in England and Wales was forty years for males and forty-four years for females. The present day equivalent for both sexes is over seventy-eight years. One of the principle reasons for the Victorian figure was a very high infant mortality rate which peaked in 1899 with a figure of 163 infant deaths per 1,000 births. Between 1850 and 1901 the chance of surviving the first year of life was 83 per cent (males) and 86 per cent (females). The current survival figure is well in excess of 99 per cent.

In Victorian times infants and children were particularly vulnerable. Not only was childbirth provision rudimentary but also, as children grew up, they were likely to suffer from a number of infectious diseases any one of which could prove fatal. It was true of our Victorian forebears that in the midst of life they were in death. This was particularly true of their children.

Standards of health and hygiene in a rural parish such as Bream would be better than in a late nineteenth century city. Even so – to a modern eye – the fatality statistics are truly appalling. An analysis of the burial records at Bream church for the period 1862 to 1907 indicates that in those forty-five years, seventy-eight children of school age were buried in the grave-yard. Two or three burials in any one year of five to fourteen-year-olds were common and some of them, residing as they were in an 'infected' house could be siblings. George Osborn Carpenter aged seven of Bream Eaves was buried on 18 December 1902. His ten-year-old brother, Albert Alfred Carpenter, was buried less than two weeks later on New Year's day. Both were victims of the 1901–2 scarlet fever epidemic that closed the school from 11 November 1901 to 3 February 1902.

The principle infectious diseases that plagued Bream schools were measles, scarlet fever, diphtheria, smallpox, whooping cough and influenza. There was also an outbreak of typhoid in 1874 that led to a fatality and an instruction that the children were not to drink from the school water supply. If a child caught one of the dreaded infectious diseases it

112

was common for all the children in that house to be excluded from school and quarantined at home. In the later Victorian period, when there was more awareness of public health issues, and a local Medical Officer of Health with power to order a complete school closure, this course of action became common. Between 1884 and 1907, a span of twenty-three years, there were no fewer than thirteen complete closures of Bream schools on the order of the local Medical Officer of Health.

It was not only infectious diseases that created risks for Bream school-children at that time. There could also be the occasional accident. On 17 December 1873 John Ruck, a ten-year-old boy in standard III, fell into a tank of hot water at the Bowson Pit. He was scalded to death. In May 1884, eleven-year-old Tom James died from tetanus at Aylburton Cottage Hospital. (This was the forerunner of Lydney Hospital. It opened in 1882 and transferred to Lydney in 1907). The log book entry for 5 May records that he was unable to attend school that day having cut his knee cap very badly with a hatchet.

Accidents such as these could occur at any time but, considering the ever present risk of disease, there is one inescapable conclusion. In terms of health, Victorian schoolchildren in Bream were very vulnerable indeed.

Standard of Living

Being well-to-do and being poor are relative. Most of us complain about never having enough money and yet outsiders looking in on our lives may well judge us comfortably off. It is all a matter of perspective. What is certainly true is that modern society has a safety net collectively called 'The Welfare State' with the consequence that very few people in this country today live on or below the bread line or experience hardship comparable to that of the Victorian working class.

School records in Bream do provide some evidence of real poverty and hardship. The clergy in their applications for funding for school building projects, regularly refer to poverty as being part-and-parcel of village life. Henry Poole in 1819 wrote of 'the poverty of the district' and reiterated that point in 1828 when he wrote to the National Society that 'the population is extremely poor' and could therefore not afford to contribute to the costs of schooling. In his application for money in 1860, Witherby also stressed how little the community could contribute towards a school, as essentially the inhabitants were working class miners and colliers.

Did the hard conditions at home impact on children's lives in school? Yes, it did. There are a significant number of references in the log books stating that the reason some children did not attend school was because they had no boots to wear or that the boots they had were so worn that they could not go out in wet weather. One entry as late as 1896 details the fact that there were a number of infants absent that week, 'nine with whooping cough, three with bad feet and two with no boots.' Sometimes it was not just lack of boots but, when the weather was cold, children could not attend school because of 'insufficient clothing' to wear. This could be such a problem that some children did not attend school in winter at all because they did not have the outdoor clothing to cope with the walk to and from school. However, even in those days, Bream was a caring and compassionate school and did what it could to alleviate the hardship – in the 1860s a clothing club was set up in school where parents could save small amounts of money and could buy clothes that were second or third hand. In effect this was an early form of jumble sale.

The photographic evidence from the private 'Dame' school in Jasmine House, discussed in the last chapter, certainly contrasts strongly with evidence from the National School where some of the children had personal experience of genuine hardship.

Staff Salaries

Discussions of hardship and poverty inevitably lead into teachers' salaries. We are fortunate that the salary record has survived for both the mixed school and the infant school for the beginning of the twentieth century, when W F Mullan and Miss Annie M Williams were the respective heads. Senior staff in both schools seem to have had an annual increase, payable with effect from 1 April usually amounting to £5 (worth £1,900 in 2005). In 1904-5 W F Mullan, a trained and certificated teacher and head, earned £164. 10s. per annum (£62,874) and was in charge of a mixed school of nearly 300 pupils. On 1 April 1908 his annual £5 increments ceased. He was then earning £180 per annum (£65,522). His deputy's salary went up by a similar £5 increment to a maximum of £120 per annum (£43,681). Salaries for uncertificated assistants and supplementary staff were not fixed by national pay scales but could vary slightly at the discretion of managers. The usual maximum salary at the time appeared to be £60 (£21,840), one third that of the head and one half that of the deputy. A pupil-teacher, just setting out on their profession, earned £16 (£6,081). Invariably the pupil-teacher would be living at home and working locally.

Annie Williams, in charge of an infant school that was only half the size of the mixed school, was paid an increment of £5 per annum rising to a maximum salary of £100 per annum (£36,401) in 1909. Uncertificated supplementary teachers in the infants were paid a mere £35 per annum (£13,302) with no increments.

The conversion figures above were calculated using an average earnings index. On whether teachers are better off or worse off now, or whether they are paid the rate for the job, I could not possibly comment.

The Cost of Schooling

State education today is 'free' but every parent is aware that there are some costs involved in sending a child to school. Usually there are costs in buying school uniform, costs for children to go on trips, costs in bringing children to and from school if we opt for a four-wheel method of transport and the unwritten expectation that parents will support such activities as the school fête and car boot sales, to bolster school funds. Did parents make similar contributions to school in the Victorian era or was education then truly 'free'?

Payment by parents in the nineteenth century was more formalised. Bream was a National School and operating on a shoestring budget. Reference has already been made to 'school pence' being part of the income coming to the Tufts school before 1862. Henry Poole (reluctantly) charged parents 1*d.* per week per child and John Beverstock increased that contribution to 2*d.* per child per week. School pence continued to be a necessary income source for the schools after the move to the Eaves in 1862 and the log books at Bream contain information on how the system worked.

The 2*d.* was collected from each child on a Monday morning, payment in advance for that week's schooling. Sometimes the money was collected by the head; at other times by the vicar. Frequently arrears built up because the money had been forgotten or the parents simply could not afford to pay that week. When arrears did build up, a bill was sometimes sent home or, a more drastic step, the child was sent back home for the money and schooling was refused until the arrears had been paid. Occasionally this caused friction between parents and the school – in 1869 Charles Preest was sent home by the vicar for his and his brother's money. Mr Preest came up to school, paid the money owing and in a fit of pique took both boys away from the school. Perhaps the best inducement to settle arrears was found in 1867 when Albert Carey announced that the annual school feast would be held on the last day of term (8 August) and that all school pence arrears had to be settled if children were to be eligible to attend. He nearly got trampled underfoot in the rush. The following month, September 1867 Reverend Witherby put out a gentle reminder to parents of the unfairness of sending children to school without paying the teacher. He advised the same to read Jeremiah 22: 13 and act upon it – *'woe unto him . . . that useth his neighbours service without wages, and giveth him not for his work.'* As well as paying the pence, parents were also expected to buy all consumables – copy books, exercise books and pencils.

The pence was not a universal levy whereby every child was charged the same. 2*d*. was the standard rate, though by the 1880s those who could afford it were expected to pay 3*d*. Fatherless children paid 1½*d*. per week. Under Reverend Gosling in 1869, a ceiling was fixed of 6*d*. per family per week so if a family had four children in the school they only paid for three. In cases of real hardship the pence were paid by the Board of Guardians who administered the poor law relief system. This however could have disadvantages because if the 'free children', as they were called, did not maintain a high rate of attendance the subsidy was withdrawn and the parent(s) had to pay.

Did the payment of school pence cause difficulty for parents? 2*d*. in 1862 converts, using the retail price index, to just over 50p in 2005. For some families, judging by the number of cases of arrears that built up, it could be a hardship to meet the payment at certain times. Perhaps the final word on this should rest with the Baker family. In 1868 the elder brother James Baker left school to go to work. His younger brother John then came to school in his place. The plain fact was that the Baker family at that time could only afford to pay for one child at school.

Holidays

Today there are far more holidays both for adults and schoolchildren than there were in the mid nineteenth century. The standard working week for an adult today is five days with a statutory guarantee of at least twenty leave days per year and the probability that bank holidays will also be holidays from work. It was very different in the mid nineteenth century.

For adults at that time, their holidays centred around the Holy days of the Christian calendar. Their working week consisted of six days labour with the seventh day, Sunday, being a day of rest on which attendance at church or chapel was expected. As the nineteenth century wore on this pattern gradually changed. Thursday afternoon increasingly became a half-holiday, as did Saturday afternoon when formalised sport started to be played. The coming of the railways in the mid century further changed working life, in that they created cheap transport that for the first time made the seaside resort accessible to the vast majority of the population. The day, or even the week, at the seaside became a regular family event. Finally, in 1871, bank holidays began for bank clerks and then spread rapidly into other jobs and professions.

Similar developments have taken place with school children's holidays. Now, children attend school for thirty-nine weeks of the fifty-two and have thirteen weeks as holiday. Bream schoolchildren in the late nineteenth century had less than half of that designated holiday time. Their school year began on 1 May and, administratively, it was divided into four quarters. The first quarter was May, June and July, the second was August, September and October and so on. The children were lucky if they had six weeks out of the fifty-two designated officially as holidays. Furthermore, there was usually a six day week as well. They attended school for five days and then most of them attended church or chapel Sunday school, where they were probably taught by the same teachers as during the week and performed similar reading and writing exercises in exercise books and copy books, though with the emphasis on religious education.

Of the holidays that Bream schoolchildren were given they always had time off for Christmas but were sometimes back at school before New Year. Easter holidays did not exist initially, the first at Bream being in 1869, though children were expected to attend church on Good Friday. The summer holiday could be as short as only three weeks and, reflecting the economic life of the village, began early to mid-August and was always referred to as 'harvest holiday.' As the turn of the century approached, the holidays for schoolchildren, as for their parents, gradually increased and the modern school pattern of two weeks at Christmas and Easter, half-term breaks and a longer summer holiday gradually emerged.

Holidays could of course also be enforced by adverse weather conditions. Anyone who doubts global warming should study the snow closure records of nineteenth century schools. At Bream a snow closure statistically occurred on average every other winter in the last fifteen years of the century. It was not only snow that could empty the schools. In those days all children walked to school and if there was torrential rain they would be soaked through on arrival at school. With one stove per room the school did not have the capacity to dry out all the children and may well then have sent them back home to dry off.

A further feature of Bream school holidays in the late nineteenth century was the existence of occasional days or half-days when the children were given a holiday for a particular event. These could be annual regular local events or occasional one-off happenings. Among the former category should be included Bream Flower Show, Bream Fair, the annual School Tea, the anniversary of the reopening of Bream church, the Harvest Festival, Ascension Day and the meeting of Gough's Charity trustees every January. All were designated as holidays for the children.

National events could also create designated holidays; events such as royal weddings in 1863 and 1893, the Queen's Diamond Jubilee in 1897 and her visit to Bristol in 1899. After 1906 Empire Day was also celebrated by a holiday at the suggestion of Gloucestershire County Council.

The school was also one of the few places in the village which could host a large gathering of people. Invariably the school would close for a half-holiday when the premises were required for specific events such as the Oddfellows Feast, the Co-op Society Tea, St James' Sick and Burial Society anniversary, the Parish Tea, the Poor Man's Friends' Club and the Cricket Club Supper and so on – all very much a case of the community 'meeting at the schools.'

Music recitals were a strong tradition in the Forest at the time and the choir and sometimes the whole school were often involved. Choral festivals in the area and the Forest of Dean Schools' Eisteddfod all necessitated a holiday being given, as did the school choir outings to Weston – because the teachers invariably went as well.

Temperance was also a Forest tradition as well as music and if there were a Band of Hope or Temperance demonstration locally the school would declare a holiday in the hope or expectation that the children would attend. The log book for June 1907 states proudly that over 100 children took part in the Temperance procession at Cinderford.

Sunday school could also, at certain times, generate holiday time for the children. Periodically the Sunday school teachers held a local meeting and, since many of them also taught in the National School, this necessitated a holiday being given. Sunday schools also created holidays in June and July each year. This was the 'treat season' when every Sunday school organised a games, tea and prizes event for their children. Bream schoolchildren benefited considerably from the treat season because there were four Sunday schools in the village, St James, the Primitive Methodist chapel, the Bible Christian chapel and the Wesleyan chapel. To be scrupulously fair to church and chapels the school managers awarded a half-holiday on each of the four treat days with the result that sometimes the children had four afternoons off school in a very short space of time. At one point in 1890, the managers had the temerity to suggest that the four treats be all held on the same day to reduce the children's time off school. The suggestion was not taken up. What had been was still to be and the children still got their four half-day holidays, irrespective of whether they attended Sunday school or not. It is interesting to speculate whether any of the children, with an eye for the main chance and modelling themselves on the 'vicar of Bray', acquired two free teas, or even three or – fantastically, four.

Finally, and to go from the sublime to the humdrum, the children were given a holiday every year when the school chimneys were swept.

School Attendance – to Go or Not to Go?

In the late nineteenth century it was a long hard slog to establish widespread and regular attendance for the majority of Bream's schoolchildren. From the early days of the Eaves schools teachers after 1862 were very keen on high attendance rates, if only for the reason that attendance figures and exam performance determined the grant to the school and thus their salaries.

It is however doubtful if staff enthusiasm was fully shared by parents and by pupils. For parents, attendance at school was a fairly new development and one that they themselves may well not have experienced. It also cost money that they could probably ill afford. For many of the children school was where they went if they had nothing better to do. And they often did have something better to do and their parents colluded in their absence.

Bream was a rural village and many residents lived at or near subsistence level and supplemented their diet by keeping a pig and growing their own vegetables. Bream Flower Show has a long and distinguished career and when it first began in 1865 it was known as the 'Cottage Garden Society.' The competition for prizes was severe because there were many 'cottage gardeners' in the village.

Because of the rural nature of the village the log books contain many references to absence for agricultural and horticultural reasons. The girls' log book for October 1865 states that some girls were absent because of fieldwork; nowadays we would assume that this was a geography or history-related curriculum visit, but in 1865 it was, quite literally, fieldwork. The August holidays were known as the harvest holidays and if for some reason the harvest was late many children would not attend school until it was 'in.' In spring, the garden needed planting, flowers needed collecting to decorate the family grave on Palm Sunday and the church on its reopening anniversary. In summer, fruit needed picking and crops harvesting; in autumn, potatoes needed digging out, acorns needed collecting from the oak woods to feed the family's pig, cider needed to be made and finally the wood needed to be gathered in for winter fuel. Children in the village had always done these jobs and school was not going to get in the way of them.

There were also other reasons for absence. Bream Fair was not always given as an official holiday, in which case many children would vote with their feet. Many would also rather attend Lydney Fair or Coleford Christmas Market than attend school. Attendance would similarly be badly affected if a visiting show came to the village – a wild beast show (1870, 1872), a circus (1873, 1904) or a waxworks exhibition.

Various clubs and feasts and anniversaries could be held elsewhere in the village – for example at The Rising Sun or New Inn – which some children would attend, probably with their parent's blessing. Additionally some of the girls would be absent for domestic reasons – helping prepare the home for Christmas or Easter or minding the baby. Spectacular local events could have an impact too. On 15 September 1879 most of the schoolchildren were absent. They had gone to see the opening of the Severn Railway Bridge.

The authorities' campaign against absenteeism at Bream schools was a mixture of rewards and punishment. Prizes were awarded to the boy and girl with the most attendances and would consist of items such as a bat or a draught board for the boy and a work-box for the girl. In February 1875 the Reverend Gosling, in an act of largesse, which came I suspect from his own pockets, gave 6d. each to thirty-six infants who had made over 250 attendances. Perhaps this was to induce good habits of attendance at a young age. Later, in May 1905 the managers decided to instil a collective responsibility for attendance by deciding that, if the attendance at the mixed and infant schools was 93 per cent or over during a four-week period, then the schools would be awarded a half-holiday. This seemed to work well and the monthly high attendance half-holiday became a regular feature of Bream school life. By this stage the authorities were on top of the attendance problem and any persistent absentees would be isolated, reported to the attendance officer who operated from Cinderford and he would then serve summonses on the parents. Pupils in 1907 were far more regular in their attendance at Bream school than their parents or grandparents had been in 1862.

Children and their Doings

Albert Carey became head of Bream School in the summer of 1867 and in the October he made two entries in the log book on events that he may well have found privately amusing. On 10 October the log records that Mrs Burgham brought her son to school 'and denounced him.' A few weeks later Carey had another visitor, James Webb's grandmother, who 'called about him (James) and all his doings.' Many of us have heard an adult say of a child 'I can't do a thing with him/her' and both of the October 1867 events seem to be along those lines. Unfortunately the log does not give details of the Burgham denunciation or James Webb's 'doings' but it does raise the fascinating question of how well-behaved (or otherwise) children were at the time. Were they 'seen and not heard'? Were any misdemeanours they committed different to any committed today? What punishments were used and how did parents react to the way the school dealt with the child?

In terms of punishment it is important to point out that different attitudes prevailed in the nineteenth century. Now corporal punishment in state schools is illegal. Then it was part of everyday school life and was accepted as such by all sections of society. It was administered formally by the use of the cane and it could legally be used on boys, girls (on the hand) and even infants. The most strokes or 'cuts' I have seen in the Bream records was four – Albert James, an infant, for 'telling an untruth', but I have no doubt that on occasion 'six of the best' was administered to older boys for serious offences. When a head wrote in the log book 'punished severely' that may well have been a euphemism for six strokes of the cane.

What kind of offence was the cane used for? The following list is a summary of misdemeanours where the use of the cane is a reasonable assumption even though it may not be specifically stated. The words 'punished' and 'punished severely' have been used.

1868 July   Punished three girls for bad behaviour in church on
             Sunday.
1868 Nov.   Frank Dobbs refused to put away the maps because he
             was kept in for being late. After having the cane and
             again refusing he was sent home with the understanding
             that he must do it in the morning or be expelled. [The
             following day] Frank Dobbs grown wiser during the
             night, the maps were put away.
1869 Oct.   Boys punished for throwing stones at gypsies.

1870 May   Boys punished for muddying water in the well on the Green [The forerunner of the Jubilee Well?]

1871 June Tom Jenkins and Enoch Kear punished for pilfering Master's premises.

1874 Dec. Punished Eliza Bradley for disobedience.

1877 May   Punished some infants for throwing stones at the girls' school door at 4 p.m. (infants finished earlier) and for throwing their caps up trees. [This was 1 May and the infants probably wanted their elder sisters out of school so they could go 'Maying']

1878 Sept. Punished Edwin Bird and Randal Web (*infants*) for scratching and hitting Lucretia Williams.

1880 Oct. Punished Matilda Williams and Eliza Ward for being dirty.

1880 Nov. Seven boys punished severely for driving Mr Williams' pigs on to the ice.

1881 Apr. Punished G Watkins for indecency.

1881 Dec. Albert James four cuts on the hand for 'telling an untruth.'

1883 Oct. A boy punished for molesting girls.
           Punished Esther Jenkins severely for refusing to hold out her hand for the cane.

1883 Nov. H Brooks punished for 'being saucy.'

1883 Dec. Punished Ernest Jenkins for committing a nuisance in the closet. Also Tom Morgan for telling an untruth about it.

1884 Mar. Fred Beech punished for loitering.

1884 Apr. R Ruck punished for throwing stones at a female teacher.

1885 Sept. Sam Brain punished severely for trying to kick master.

1887 Apr. Albert Bradley punished for defacing the reading books with paint.

1888 Nov. Three punished for stealing vegetables from the school garden.

1891 Oct. Three punished for calling after the pupil-teacher.

1896 Nov. Three punished for cursing – Alfred Wix, John and Tom Phillips.

1901 Jan. Willie Jones flogged for insubordination and kicking the head [the pejorative use of the word 'flogged' rather than caned is perhaps indicative of the head's, Mr Mullan's, anger at the time].

The use of the cane was however not the only way of dealing with serious misbehaviour. Expulsion could be threatened (as it was with Frank Dobbs) and actually enforced. In 1868, Marianne Carey found 'improper letters' on Clara Preest. The offence was reported to the  vicar and the girl was expelled. George Masters, as previously mentioned, was expelled by William Mullan soon after his arrival as head. George Masters also appears in my corporal punishment list as being one of the seven boys who drove the pigs on to the ice.

If serious misbehaviour involved theft or damage to property the schools had no hesitation in involving the police. In October 1878, two policemen came into school and cautioned some of the boys who had been swinging on the railings of the school house garden. In December 1888, somebody had stripped all the trimming off Harriet Frowen's hat; the police constable was called in to investigate. He ascertained it was Thomas Watkins who had recently left. Mrs Watkins was notified. She replaced the trimmings and undertook to correct the boy. In July 1896, four boys entered the school garden and stole fruit. They were cautioned by Sergeant Haggart of Parkend Police Station.

Perhaps the ultimate deterrent, and used on really intransigent disciplinary issues, was not to use the cane or call in the police but to involve the vicar. In the nineteenth century, to stand before the vicar was probably only one step removed from being interviewed by Saint Peter. He was seen by parents, teachers and children as the ultimate authority in all matters spiritual and temporal. In March 1871 two of the girls, E Panting and E Merry, were punished by the vicar for bad language – had they been boys they would probably have been caned by the head. In the same month the vicar cautioned some of the boys 'on dirty habits in the offices (toilets).' In January 1878 two shawls went missing from the girls' porch – it was left to the vicar to make enquiries. In 1879 a school map was torn – the investigation as to who was responsible was left till the vicar's return. When Clara Watkins was to be punished for rudeness in 1879 it was left to the vicar to speak to her. Similarly Jeanette Blower who defied the pupil-teacher in 1880 and Margaret Kear who had been 'very saucy' in 1881 were 'spoken to' by the vicar. Apart from a 'speaking to' the vicar did have other sanctions he could impose or suggest. In 1868 a girl who had done poor work and had refused to stay in was made to apologise, at the vicar's suggestion, in front of the whole school. A similar public humiliation was used in 1885 when the head stopped the whole work of the school for one of the girls, B Treherne, to apologise for 'breaking the rules.'

No doubt most children were in awe of the vicar but being a member of the cloth did not necessarily generate respect. Reverend Henry Williams became Curate of Bream in 1869 and encountered difficulties, certainly in the early years, if he tried to teach a lesson. There are a number of references to the lower classes being very unruly when he was in charge and in December 1870 some of the girls even complained to the head that boys had been swearing during the curate's scripture lesson.

From the early days of the Eaves school, keeping children in seemed to be a standard punishment for offences such as being late (the detention in 1868 being twice the length of time lost) and to learn spellings that should have been learnt in class. No doubt on a regular basis children would receive a good old-fashioned 'telling off.' This would rarely be recorded in the log book unless, as in 1867, the head recorded that he had administered a formal telling off which he called 'a caution' to show the vicar that he was doing his duty (the vicar as a manager did check the log book). The caution in 1867 was to the choir boys for their behaviour before choir practice.

Collective punishments were rarely recorded. In 1882 the girls were punished by Mary Newman for 'lack of order' by being made to stand still from 11.20 a.m. to 11.50 a.m.

Public humiliation could be used to punish children apart from making them apologise to the whole school. In November 1867 three girls were sent for lessons from the top class into a junior class because of their behaviour in church on the Sunday before.

Then, as now, a very common method of disciplining children was by involving the parents. Sometimes the children themselves were sent home, the assumption being that the parent would want to know why they were home early. Sometimes a note or letter from the head would go home. Sometimes – and probably if the parent could not read – it would be an oral message that would be sent home. In practice involvement of the parents tended to be in respect of the boys more than the girls and included a range of offences.

> 1868 Dec. Hubert Jenkins came to school at 2 p.m. Drunk from drinking cider at his uncles. His mother later promised to go to Woodside and get them to refrain from giving him cider *in the dinner hour.*

1869 Jan. Charles Preest sent home for bad conduct. Punished by his father and brought back.

1870 Jan. Edwin Morgan. Sent home for not lighting the fire in his turn. [At the time the boys took it in turn to be fire lighting monitor].

1886 Jan. Albert James sent home for swearing and kicking the head.

1886 Sept. Peter Nash sent home for leading a gang to attack the monitor Napier Williams.

1888 Dec. Three boys smoking. Notes sent to parents.

1890 Nov. The James boys [Harry and Edwin] were sent home to wash.

1892 Jan. Sent a letter to John Baker and Andrew Jenkins parents about their bad language.

1893 Feb. Eli Wintle, John James and John Watkins were disturbing the school by throwing stones through the ventilators under the floor. Notes sent to their parents.

1894 Mar. Esther Neal was searched and a ball of wool was found on her that belonged to Kate Hook. She was sent home until her parents had seen the managers.

The reaction of parents to school discipline can be quite illuminating and will be considered in the next section.

Occasionally accidents and disciplinary issues occurred that were so rare they were unique. In December 1868, Edwin Kear (Haines) was shot in the face with an arrow fired by William Nelmes. I do not know what punishment was meted out to William Nelmes – if at all – it may have been a freak accident. In June 1868 there was something of a drought in the village. So scarce was the water supply that the headmistress noted that many girls were coming to school 'soiled' [dirty]. In stark contrast, the same month Sarah Merry and her four sisters came to school wearing 'fine necklaces.' I would assume that very few of the girls would possess jewellery in 1868 and, as such, the Merrys were presenting something of a challenge to the headmistress (Marianne Carey). She handled it with a mixture of velvet glove and iron fist telling the girls that they would look better without necklaces and if they were wearing them tomorrow they must find another school. The girls got the message.

In summary, there is some variation across time in respect of children's misdemeanours and similar variation in respect of how teachers dealt with them, but we are left with the conclusion that if we judge both against the context of the time the similarities outweigh the differences. Children are children, and teachers are, on balance, judicious professionals.

Parents and Their Doings

The log books contain some evidence of how parents reacted to the above disciplinary actions of the schools and also some references to parents as a body and their attitude to the schools.

We may well start from the hypothesis that parents were very accepting, supportive and unquestioning of how the schools were handling their children but, on the evidence of the log books, we would be wrong in this assumption. The log books contain far more evidence of parental criticism than parental support though it may well be that most parents constituted a silent majority and that the criticisms voiced on the log books were the exceptions rather than the rule.

Reference has already been made to the father of Charles Preest who, in 1869, when the boy was sent home for bad conduct, punished him again and sent him back to school. This was exceptional and, three months later, it was the self-same parent who had an issue with the school over the payment of the pence and withdrew both his sons.

Many parents did take exception, in some cases strong exception, to school discipline. A summary is as follows:

1874 Dec. Elizabeth Bradley punished for disobedience. Her mother threatened to remove her.

1875 July Mrs Wilcox complained Kate is not getting on very well but her attendances have been 40/130 and 13/120!

1878 Jan. Thomas Whiting (*infant*) was kept in to learn his spellings. His mother came and fetched him out.

1880 Apr. Lucretia Williams taken home by her mother who seems to think she has the right to do this.

1881 May Pupil-teacher kept Eliza Beach in. Her elder sisters fetched her mum who abused the pupil-teacher and took the child away.

1881 Nov. Caned Louise Meek for disobedience. Mrs Meek was very insolent to me.

1882 Mar. Lucy Jenkins went home instead of in to infants class as she had been ordered. Her mother complained to the vicar.

1882 July Mrs White took Eliza out of school because I'd kept her in. Will not readmit her till I've seen the vicar.

1882 Oct. Jane White of Woodside came to school and beat the monitor.

1883 Dec. Mrs Preest complained to the vicar about my punishing Minnie Hughes. She took Minnie away.

1884 Oct. Mrs Wasley came up during playtime and assaulted Mary Dobbs for keeping her little boy in. Mary was only obeying my instructions.

1888 Mar. Mrs Baker came to take her son from school. I told her if she did so she must take him away altogether.

1888 July R Ward left school without permission. Attendance cancelled. Mother very abusive. Will not return him to school.

1889 July Mrs Williams did not want Harry punished for truancy. She took both her children to another school.

1889 Nov. Received a letter from Mrs Taylor. She believes her son and accuses me of injustice.

1892 Apr. Punished John Baker and Arthur Jenkins for swearing. Sent letters home. Mrs Baker replied that John should not have been punished.

1903 July Richard Beach [father of Maud] entered school and threatened Mr Meek stating he had struck his daughter. Mr Meek denied it. I took him from the room where a dozen children were present and pointed out that he was trespassing and if he did it again he could face prosecution.

1904 Sept. Mr Parker took Sam away to another school. He objected to the punishment Sam received (one cut, never more than two). Sam is always fighting and playing truant.

1905 Feb. Mrs Price accosted Mr Meek on his way to school and used insulting and threatening language towards him and accused him of beating her girl. I investigated – she said she hadn't been touched. Mrs Price did apologise. She was told by other children and had not questioned her daughter herself.

Some parents certainly did not seem to 'take prisoners' and teaching at Bream did have its challenges. The worst recorded incident occurred on 25 March 1891; as follows:

'Yesterday afternoon after school, one of the parents Mr Jabez Carpenter entered school accompanied by a large dog and assaulted one of the pupil-teachers Napier Williams alleging that he had kicked his son Willie.'

A summons was taken out against the parent and six days later he was tried at Coleford Police Court, convicted and fined 5/- with costs awarded against him of 14/- (using an Average Earnings Index the 2005 equivalent of these figures would be £108. 50p and £303. 80p). He was also severely reprimanded. Judging by some of the other incidents, he may have got away with it if he'd left his big dog at home. One of the truly remarkable things about this case is how quickly the judicial process was completed – less than a week between incident and conviction.

In one respect, children were the same then as now in that on occasion they were reluctant to attend school – a difficult problem for both school and parents. Victorian parents seemed to have a no-nonsense approach. In October 1868 six-year-old Joe Davies was admitted for his first day at school – his mother got him there by literally dragging him. In November 1873 Tom Bradley had to be carried to school by his mother but had already run home by playtime.

As to whether school/parent relationships are more harmonious now than then I could not possibly comment, except to state that I would hope that Jabez and his large dog is a thing of the past. Such direct action has long-since been replaced by a complaints procedure.

I cannot resist finishing this section on parents with a 'school gate' story. In 1869 Tom Kear complained to his mother of John Shingles' mother taking and claiming his ball. Both mothers met and were 'very pointed' in their remarks to each other. They finally withdrew in a great passion threatening each other with 'law.' The issue was resolved the next day by the next best thing to 'the law' – the vicar. Could such a scene possibly happen now at the school gate?

School Links with the Community

Situated in the centre of the village, the schools at the Eaves have always been at the heart of the community. As previously mentioned, the schools' premises were extensively used by local clubs and societies though sometimes such events could be an inconvenience to the schools if things were not put back correctly or if damage had been done. For example, in October 1898 a complaint found its way into the log book that flowers had been picked following the previous night's band practice and choral society meeting. In November 1903 a Friday evening dance had resulted in a broken window and on Monday morning the school floor was still slippy from the wax put down for the dance, with the result that the desks were sliding across the floor – no doubt with a bit of teenage encouragement.

Prominent members of the community were also regular visitors to the schools. One such was Lady Campbell, wife of Sir James Campbell of Whitemead Park. Sir James was deputy surveyor of the Dean and had been a key player in the schools' acquisition of the Eaves site in 1862 and was one of the managers named in the 1860 Deed. His wife, Lady Caroline Campbell, seems to have very much adopted the school and was a weekly visitor for some thirty years. She helped with the clothing club, occasionally took lessons and became heavily involved in the sewing and knitting work that was done by the girls. Knitting and sewing became almost a community business for the girls at school. All sorts of fabric were ordered in – winsey, calico, print, holland, canvas and cheesecloth. Orders were taken for shirts, socks, chemises, pillow slips, aprons, pinafores and so on, and periodically there would be a sale of work where the community bought the items that had been made in school. Lady Campbell seemed to do a lot of ordering of the fabrics and when the sale of work was completed the proceeds went to the vicar for the schools' accounts. I have no doubt the business ran at a profit. Since the 1980s there has been a drive within secondary education to bring the world of business into the curriculum by means of 'mini enterprise schemes' whereby pupils manufacture, market and sell certain commodities – yet another curriculum wheel that has been reinvented.

It may be of interest to know some comparative prices of these 'school factory' goods. The annual order for fabric from Marshall and Snellgrove in 1887 cost 14s. 3¾d. (RPI 2005 £53) and in 1882 a pillow slip was being sold by the school for 1s. 2d., a chemise for 1s. 1d. and a print pinafore for 1s. (RPI 2005 equivalent £3.91, £3.63 and £3. 35).

The schools seem to have been positive in developing community responsibility. Reference has already been made to older boys lighting the school fires but there were also monitors for the porch, clearing out the grate, the closets and even sweeping or cleaning the school. At one stage girls in the 1860s seem to have been paid for sweeping the schools but this seemed to have been changed for a sweeping rota whereby the senior girls took it in turns to sweep. They were issued with gloves and pinafores and the girls who did the best sweeping were given prizes. It was probably not a very popular job – in September 1875, three of the four sweepers on the rota refused to sweep and were punished by being given an extra week of sweeping duty. Resentment of the sweeping duty got worse. In 1878 Gertrude Phillips ran home after having been told to stay in and sweep and the following day Gertrude was sent home after refusing again. A couple of weeks later Mrs Brooks fetched her daughter Annie out of school when it was Annie's turn to sweep and was also exceedingly insolent to the mistress in the process. The troublesome rota consisted of four girls, one of whom swept the girls' school, one the infants' school and two the boys' school – there's a comment on cleanliness if ever there was one. It was probably soon after the 1870s sweeping disputes that the school started to pay cleaners to do the job.

With the school being at the centre of the community the log books record events of local note. The schools declared a holiday on 13 May 1864 when the first sod was turned on the Worcester, Monmouth and Dean Forest Railway. The erection of the new Bream Maypole on Thursday 1 May 1884, whilst not a holiday, was still an event worthy of record in the school log. No doubt some children did go because it was certainly an impressive monument. A local newspaper tells us it was made of oak and stood some 43 feet high. When it was erected there was quite a crowd gathered to watch. They witnessed a dramatic event. The attempt to run up the Union Jack encountered difficulty when the wire got tangled in the pulley at the top of the pole. Several tried unsuccessfully to climb up. Eventually Andrew Vaughan became a local hero when he managed to shin up to the top and untangle the wire.

Schoolchildren were also involved from 1865 in Bream Flower Show. Posters to advertise the event were produced by the older children and no doubt many of them attended. The schools were proud of village events in just the same way as the village was proud of the schools.

School Links with the Church

Henry Poole had affiliated Bream School to the National Society in 1819 which, in effect, made it a Church of England school. This gave St James' and particularly the vicar of Bream the lead role in the development of the school throughout the nineteenth century. Thus, four outstanding clergymen inspired four major building projects that transformed Bream schools (Henry Poole, Cornelius Witherby, John Frederick Gosling and Francis Eales).

The vicars of Bream were not only involved at the strategic level of the schools but also in their day to day operations. All of Bream's vicars were managers of the school. They checked the registers and log books, they took classes and supervised exams; if the master or mistress was ill or there was an interregnum between heads, the chances were that the vicar would step in as acting head. The vicar often had a role in the administration of the school accounts and was responsible for placing the schools' orders and seeing that they were delivered. He was also often used as an ultimate authority for the schools in dealing with parents and children, could be used by parents in any appeal against a decision made by the schools and could also double up as an attendance officer by visiting families where a child was suspected of truancy. He would also host the schools in church when they came down for special services such as on Good Friday or Ascension Day. At times, the vicar was so busy with the schools he probably barely had time to be a vicar.

The schools were not just costly on the vicar's time but costly on his pocket. The log book for 1869 records Cornelius Witherby paying the pence for ten poor or fatherless children. Similarly John Frederick Gosling, as well as paying for the extension of the schools from his own funds, also paid for and presented each child with a shawl, scarf or comforter.

Nor was it just the vicar who was involved in a central role in school. Like Lady Campbell, Mrs Witherby the vicar's wife was involved, particularly with the girls' school, as were Miss Gosling and the Misses Eales.

By the end of the nineteenth century the Church was finding the financing of ever expanding schools a burden it could no longer carry and the 1902 Education Act led to Gloucestershire County Council becoming increasingly involved in Bream schools. Even so, to this day, the Church has a major part to play in the life of the school.

Inside the Classroom

The core curriculum in Bream National School in the nineteenth century consisted of the three Rs (reading, writing and arithmetic). We may well assume that infants started on this curriculum from the age of five when they first went to school. In fact children started at Bream School at the age of three. There are several references in the log book to the 'babies class' as the three-year-olds were known. Their hours per week were reading (3 hours), writing (3 hours 20 minutes) and arithmetic (3 hours 20 minutes). They also had 'object' lessons for 1 hour 10 minutes per week. The 'object' lesson was based on the teacher's 'object' box which contained a variety of items, or pictures of items or animals on which the teacher would deliver a lesson. 'Object' lessons might be given on a knife and fork, an umbrella, a needle, a pair of scissors, sugar, a lead pencil, a honeycomb, sheep, cows and swans.

As children moved on up the infant school the curriculum had more variety in it. A typical top infant class timetable time per week was:

Reading	3 hours 50 minutes
Writing	3 hours
Arithmetic	3 hours 30 minutes
Singing	55 minutes
Spelling	30 minutes
Varied occupations	99 minutes
Needlework (Girls)	3 hours
Drawing (Boys)	3 hours
Recreation	2 hours 5 minutes

The list of songs that the infants learned in 1882 is as follows:

See Our Hands
The Peasant
March Away
Oh Dear! What Can the Matter Be?
Time to Work
The Bee

'Varied occupations' sounds as though there was some degree of pupil choice in their curriculum time. History and geography topics would probably be included in the last quarter of the nineteenth century as part of the children's reading and writing work.

Religious teaching began with the youngest infants when they learnt 'prayers and graces.' A survival of this is in a 'corrupted' version of the phrase when we speak of 'airs and graces'. Thus, younger children learnt 'prayers and graces', older children who had acquired 'attitude' put on 'airs and graces' instead. As they grew older, children learnt the stories of the Bible, their catechism in detail and what were called 'scripture proofs.' A scripture proof was a lesson based on a religious question which then is answered, the answer being proved by a biblical textual reference. Scripture proofs and catechism would be taught by the clergy. A copy of the Gloucester diocesan syllabus has fortunately survived in the log book c.1870 and is here produced in full. (see page 137) Division I was the infants.

The children in the mixed school did study history and geography as discrete subjects and, after 1872, the managers consented to literature being an integral part of the work of the school. The children also studied recitation – the learning of poems or prose by heart and being trained to speak them aloud in public. The recitation list changed every year. For 1896-7 it was:

standard I and II (infants)	*The Ballad of the Sailors Children*
standard III	*The Level Crossing*
standard IV	*Llewellyn and his Dog*
standard V to VII	*Julius Caesar* [presumably Mark Antony's funeral oration]

There were also more songs to learn in the mixed school and – as with recitation – the list changed every year. The songs for 1892-3 were:

The Midshipman
The Four Jolly Smiths
The Bay of Biscay
If I were a Sunbeam
The Sleigh Ride
Catch the Sunshine
At my work I'm always singing

Homework seems to have been a feature of school life for the older pupils from the early days of the Eaves schools. In 1863 the top class boys were allowed to take their slates home for 'home lessons' on the life of Solomon. In January 1877, the girls' mistress, Emma Wall, bemoaned the fact that she was having great difficulty getting the girls to do 'home lessons' because the children were losing their books and pencils and breaking their slates. Homework has always been a challenge to a teacher's discipline.

Some children found education very hard. In the 1880s Bream schools drew up a 'Children for Exception' list which categorised children who found education difficult under labels such as 'dull and defective', 'weak in body and mind' and 'defective intellect.' Such children were unlikely to make progress in an academic curriculum consisting basically of the three Rs and were allowed to leave school at ten if they could produce a certificate of regular attendance for a specified period of time. This device was known as 'The Dunce's Pass.'

In researching this book, I have been very fortunate that Jennifer Hancocks has kindly made available to me a collection of nineteenth century exercise books from Bream National School that have been passed down in her family. These give a real insight into what did actually go on in the classroom at that time and enable us to make comparisons with present day school work. If we believe that nineteenth century elementary education was very basic, and that twenty-first century education must, of necessity, be superior in every respect, the evidence from these exercise books would challenge that simplistic conclusion. Education was different in that the society it served had different requirements of its educational system. At heart, Victorian society wanted to educate its working class to be mechanical, to manufacture, to have basic literary skills and to be competent at basic book-keeping and ledger work.

The oldest of Jennifer's exercise books belonged to her great grandparents, John Phillips and Emma Phillips (née Watkins). John Phillips was born in Saunders Green c.1843 and would have attended the school at the Tufts. Initially he would have been taught by William and Sophia Webb and, at the end of his school career, possibly by Joseph Augustus Lewis Littlewood. It is also possible that, as an adult, John attended night school at the Eaves. The 1881 Census lists John as an agricultural labourer. By 1901 he is running a grocery shop at the Maypole. The copied extracts from John's book (see page 138) gives a definition of numeration and one of subtraction with examples of the same showing difference and proof. All his writing is 'copperplate.'

Emma Phillips (née Watkins) was born c.1853 and probably attended Bream School at the Tufts and then transferred to the Eaves. The example chosen from her copy book (see page 139) is a humorous example of copy writing. Unfortunately she ran out of time on the exercise and it was unfinished. I found it fascinating that Emma's copy book also contained Tennyson's poem 'The Charge of the Light Brigade' which occurred during the battle of Balaclava during the Crimean War. Clearly Bream teaching was very up-to-date – the battle had only recently happened (October 1854) when Emma was a baby.

The other examples of work chosen are from Bessie Phillips. Bessie was born in 1883. She was the daughter of John and Emma Phillips and was Jennifer's grandmother. Several of her exercise books have survived (see pages 139–40) and samples chosen include:

1. An essay on a male dominated Flower Show, dated 1896.
2. An example of a letter dated 6 September 1897 when Bessie was in standard VII and her last year at school.
3. A St James Sunday school exercise book with a prayer composed by Bessie and marked by the vicar, Francis Eales.

I suspect Bessie left Bream National School in 1898 and St James Sunday School at approximately the same time, and after the Sunday school had finished preparing her for confirmation by the bishop.

When she left school, the 1901 Census tells us that Bessie, aged seventeen, was working at home as a dressmaker. No doubt her stitching skills had been learnt at Bream mixed school. A sampler Bessie produced, dated 7 March 1899, has survived and it bears testimony to those skills. (see page 141)

In conclusion, what went on inside Bream schools' classrooms in the late nineteenth century was very different to what goes on today. As to why this is, it is very tempting to argue that context drives curriculum; that the determinants of what is taught and how it is taught are the political, economic and moral expectations and pressures of the time. Education for its own sake has little to do with it.

It is now time to look at the schools following the erection of the state-of-the-art infants school in 1907.

A very early photo of some Bream infants, c.1898. The infant head at the time was Clara Jane Brain. *Photo courtesy of Dave Rudge*

Bream infants c.1902-3. The teacher on the left of the photograph is possibly Annie M Williams, head of the infant school 1902-13.
Photo courtesy of Ruth Hirst

Bream junior standard 4c 1906. The staff are Mr W F Mullan and Annie Williams (Annie/Nanny Parrot/Parry). The boy on the back row is not necessarily tall for his age – at one time the school was criticised for holding back a ten-year-old boy in the infants. Note the broken window – ball, stone, marble or sturty bird?

Photo courtesy of John Marchant

Diocese of Gloucester & Bristol.

INSPECTION OF SCHOOLS IN RELIGIOUS KNOWLEDGE.

The following Syllabus is recommended for the use of Church Schools in the Diocese as supplying a systematic course of Religious Instruction. But any other List of Subjects, which the Managers may prefer, can be adopted for particular Schools.

DIVISION I.—Comprising generally Standard I.

The Catechism to the end of the Commandments.

Outline of the life of our Lord, with more particular knowledge of his early years.

Outline of the Book of Genesis, with the lives of one or more of the Patriarchs.

DIVISION II.—Comprising generally Standards II and III.

The Catechism, with simple explanation, to the end of the Lord's Prayer.

The Creed illustrated by the History of our Lord's Life; and the Course of the Christian Seasons.

A fuller outline of the Life of our Lord, with more particular knowledge of at least two Miracles or two Parables.

Outline of the historical portions of Genesis or Exodus.

DIVISION III.—Comprising generally Standards IV, V, and VI.

The Catechism, intelligently explained, with some Scripture proofs.

The Order for Morning and Evening Prayer.

Outline of New Testament History, with accurate knowledge of One Gospel; or Acts, chap. I to XIII.

Brief Outline of Old Testament History to the death of Solomon, with more particular knowledge of the *Biographies* out of *one* of the following Books—Joshua, Judges, Samuel I or II.

Division I will be examined *viva voce*.   Divisions II and III partly *viva voce*, partly on slates or paper.

The Children in each Division should be able to repeat, *intelligently and distinctly*, Hymns and *Private Prayers*, also some fixed portion of Holy Scripture, the portion varying in the different Divisions.

Infant Schools will be examined generally as under Division I.   They should also learn Texts and Hymns suited to the Christian Seasons.

The Biographies of the Old Testament should be taught, not as Facts only, but in connection with Christian duties.

Particular attention will be paid to the manner in which answers in Religious Subjects are given.

Gloucester and Bristol Diocesan Syllabus c.1870. Standard I was older infants.

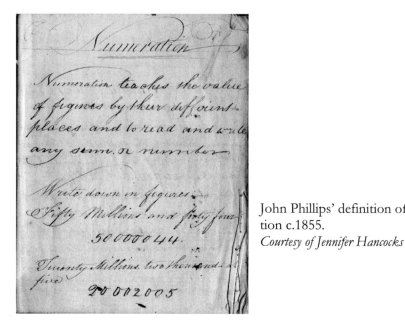

John Phillips' definition of numeration c.1855.
Courtesy of Jennifer Hancocks

John Phillips' definition of subtraction with examples c.1855.
Courtesy of Jennifer Hancocks

Curing the Measles *july 20th*

A lady had her two children sick with Measles. She sent to her friend to ask for the best cure. At the same time the friend received a letter from another lady asking her how to make certain pickles. In answering she sent the letters to the wrong ladies. The lady who asked about the pickles had the answer concerning the measles. The mother of the sick children read with horror the following
" Scald them three times in very hot vinegar sprinkle them with salt, and in a few day

Emma Phillips' (née Watkins) copy book work describing a 'cure' for measles. c.1865. Unfortunately the exercise was not finished.
Courtesy of Jennifer Hancocks

July 22nd the man's name.

An essay on
A Flower Show.

A Flower show is an exhibition of Flowers, Fruit, Vegetables and herbs.
It is usually held in a field in tents, or in a large hall.
The object of holding flower shows is to encourage men to be industrious in their gardens, to cultivate the best kinds of flowers and vegetables and to take the greatest care in their cultivation. Men strive hard to rival each other for the honour of taking the first prize.
If we go to a flower show we see tastefully laid out on long tables, the best of all kinds of vegetables, fruit and flowers. Each collection is ticketed with a number which is in a book against

August 26th

Two Great Preachers

About 1730 John Wesley began a religious revival at Oxford. On account of the strictness and regularity of their lives Wesley and his followers were spoken of sneeringly as Methodists. In 1735 he went out as a missionary to America where he met with but slight success. On his return to England in 1738 the Wesleyan movement was fairly set agoing George Whitfield and Wesleys brother Charles were among his most earnest supporters. Meeting with opposition from the clergy they separated from the church of England and built chapels of their own.

Bessie Phillips. An essay on a flower show, dated 22 July 1896. Bessie would have been in Mr Mullans class.
Photo courtesy of Jennifer Hancocks

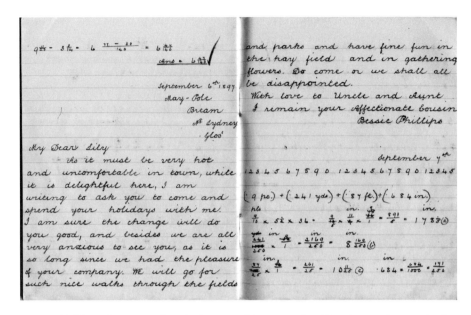

Bessie Phillips. An example of a letter writing exercise. Bessie was in standard VII, her last year at school.
Courtesy of Jennifer Hancocks

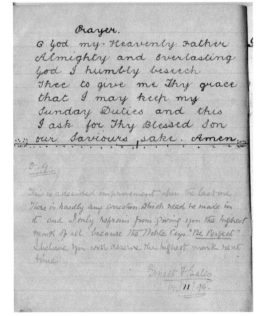

Bessie Phillips. A prayer written by Bessie in her Sunday School exercise book in 1896 and marked by the vicar Revd. Francis Eales.

A sampler produced by Bessie Phillips, 1899.
Courtesy of Jennifer Hancocks

CHAPTER SIX

1907–27: On to the Next Crisis: A Very Public Row, A Black List and a Court Case

Head Teachers 1907–27

Mixed school heads
William F Mullan 1885–1918
Edward William Sylvester 1918–24
Cecil E. Buck 1924–25
William Watson 1925–1953

Infant school heads
Annie M Williams 1902–13
Eliza Young 1913–1941

Premises and Organisation

Overcrowding had been an endemic problem at Bream schools through-out the latter half of the nineteenth century. The increasing overcrowding at the Tufts school had led to Cornelius Witherby building a new school at the Eaves in 1862. That in turn had quickly become overcrowded and been extended by John Gosling in 1873 and again by Francis Eales in 1900. Even when the Eales extension was under way it was apparent that, owing to the limited finances available to the Church, it was too little too late and that the schools would again suffer from overcrowding. And so it was. Hence the new infants school in 1907.

One would have thought that building a new school would resolve the overcrowding issue for at least the foreseeable future. It did and it did not.

In respect of the infants there was not a problem at all because the new school had plenty of spare capacity to cope with any reasonable increase in infant numbers. The overcrowding issue was, however, still a problem in the 'old' or mixed or National School across the road. This school was still overcrowded even without the infants. What is more, the building was now forty-five years old and needed money spending on it to bring it up to standard to avoid being classified as 'defective educational premises.' But where was the money to come from? The Church had had to work very hard to even raise the cash for the Eales extension. Further capital building funding on that scale was not a realistic option.

In one sense the building of the infant council school in 1907 was bad news for the Church, in that it lost its monopoly on education in the village. This had been threatened on two previous occasions but both times it had survived intact. On the first occasion, the Witherby building at the Eaves saw off the nonconformist rival school in Parkend Road. On the second occasion, John Gosling's funding of the 1872–3 extension protected the Anglican monopoly in Bream by making a board school unnecessary. But now, in 1907, the monopoly was finally broken and the Church's future stake in education was looking precarious. The National School was overcrowded, not very well equipped and with very limited funding. Across the road was a brand new school with up-to-date equip-ment, spare capacity and – via the LEA – access to considerable funding resources. Logically, if the Church school was overcrowded and the council school had spare capacity, it was only a matter of time before more pupils were transferred from the one to the other. Thus, after 1907 the Church was on the back-foot in terms of village education. Some possibly even saw 1907 as the beginning of the end of Church influence on the schools. What Henry Poole had started, Gloucestershire Education Committee could well finish, had they a mind to do so. They certainly had the opportunity in the 1920s. They did not, however, take it.

The 1909 HMI report on the mixed school spelled out the premises situation in stark terms. The school was 'still seriously overcrowded.' It had accommodation for 298 pupils but the average attendance was 342 and there were 364 on roll – a notional sixty-six above capacity. The inspector also found an uncertificated teacher in charge of a class of sixty-three.

In August 1909 the LEA decided that standard I should stay in the infant school instead of transferring across to the mixed school. This affected fifty-nine pupils and the LEA kitted them out with new desks and books. Two years later a similar decision was taken in respect of standard II. By this stage the council school itself was approaching capacity and the LEA decided the school needed to extend its buildings to cater for 100 extra places. In response to this suggestion the Forest of Dean Group of Council School Managers stated that, in their view, because of the number of new houses being built in Bream and the prospect of further mining developments in the area, the LEA should consider 150 extra council school places rather than 100. The LEA agreed to this and put the scheme out to tender. Eight building firms submitted quotes ranging from £1,310. 10s. to £2,117. 2s. 7d. The lowest tender, from Orchard and Peer of Stroud (who had been the 1907 builders) was accepted. A separate tender of £84 from R E and C Marshall of Cheltenham was accepted for the extension's 'heating apparatus' (central heating). The LEA also decided that, given the number of pupils now on site, it would be sensible to fill in the pond that had been left intact in 1907 and cover the playground with ashes. This was duly done in August 1914.

The rate of expansion of the council school had been truly remarkable in a very short space of time. When it had opened as an infant school in 1907 there were just 119 on roll but six years later in 1913 the school had become, with the acquisition of standards I and II, a junior and infant school, much as it is now. What is more, in 1907 the 119 on roll had risen to 272 pupils and, for the first time, the numbers in the council school exceeded those in the mixed or National School. 272 as against 252, a total of 524 pupils being educated in Bream schools. By 1915 the mixed school had dropped to 213 and the council school had correspondingly risen to 310. If the LEA were to consider possibly moving standard III across to the council school and maybe consider extending it still further, then the future of the mixed school would really be in doubt. Both courses of action were proposed in 1923 and led to a major row.

Managers versus the LEA

1. The Enlargement Plan
In February 1923, HMI reported on the mixed school, noting again that it was overcrowded and recommended that the April admissions – the standard III children, should be accommodated elsewhere. This was done and they consequently remained in the council school.

At this point the LEA began serious consideration of a fundamental reorganisation of both schools. Their first proposal, made to the managers of the mixed school on 13 November 1923, was that the council school should be used for senior scholars and that the junior scholars should be educated in the Church school. There was a certain logic in the proposal, in that the council school had domestic science and handicraft facilities already on that site, courtesy of a wooden 60 feet by 20 feet ex-army hut that had been installed against the back fence of the council school in 1920 at a cost of £565.

The vicar of Bream, Reverend William Joyce, responded to this proposal at a meeting with Horace Household, Secretary to the Gloucestershire Education Committee. The vicar, as a manager of the Church school, was not happy with the proposal to limit that school to juniors only. At this point, Horace Household came up with an alternative proposal – that the council school should educate infants and girls and that the Church school should educate all the boys above infant level. The vicar did not really see that anything had to change at all, but, of the two proposals, he was more inclined to accept the second.

Following this meeting, Horace Household firmed up the proposal in writing. Joyce then discussed the proposal with Canon Sewell, the chair of the Education Committee in Gloucester, and with the Bishop of Gloucester. Both supported the boys only proposal for the Church school. On 29 November Joyce wrote to Household, stating that the managers 'seem disposed to agree to the Church school becoming a boys' department.'

This letter seemed to be the green light for the second proposal. Horace Household then wrote formally on 10 December 1923 to advise that the LEA would proceed with this proposal 'as soon as additional accommodation had been provided at the council school.' The following day, 11 December , Joyce confirmed the managers' position in a letter to the LEA stating that, while they preferred matters to stay as they were, they did wish to work in harmony with the LEA and would, with reluctance, accept the reorganisation plan.

At this point matters started to go wrong. It is possible that the crucial letters of 10 and 11 December 'crossed in the post' and that when the managers gave their consent on the eleventh they were unaware of the letter of the tenth and its key reference to the need for 'additional accommodation.' Certainly, the managers appear to have been unaware of the scale of building involved in the reorganisation and, as 1924 progressed, they became increasingly alarmed at what they had agreed to and were trying to reverse it.

Meanwhile, the LEA was proceeding as per the proposal and began arranging a loan to finance it. The estimates were prepared by April 1924 as follows:

	£
Cost of extra land (70 perches) with standing timber (32 oak trees), frontage of 78ft by 280ft and all legal costs	130
Buildings: three classrooms, cloakroom and corridor for 150 girls	3,630
Heating £150; Sanitary Conveniences and Play Sheds £450; Boundary Walls and fencing £175	4,405
Cost of furniture and fittings: 75 dual desks £132; three cupboards £18; three blackboards £24; three teachers' desks and chairs £16; Blinds etc., £10	200
Surveyor's fees	100
Clerk of Works salary: 24 weeks @ £5 per week	120
Total	£4,990

When the loan was finally sanctioned it was for a total of £4,860 whereby the county council agreed to repay £200 for the furniture in ten years, the remaining balance over a period of thirty years.

As a footnote to the estimates, the drinking water for both the girls' and infant schools was to continue to be filtered from rain collected in a storage tank on site. When the plans were first put out to tender in 1925 the lowest of the five bids received was £1,300 above budget and the plans had to be scaled down. A separate heating system was abandoned; the infant boiler would have to heat the entire site. The girls' entrance doorway was much simplified. It was originally planned to be on a similar scale to the infants' entrance. The girls' offices (toilets) and play sheds were to be in brick, not, as originally intended, in stone. Finally the teachers' room (staff room), instead of being on the ground floor, was to be relocated at the top of the steps and above the cloakroom.

The managers of the infant school, as joint users of the site, were also presented with copies of the plan and their observations were invited. They imposed two conditions. Firstly, that the infant teachers should also have a staff room. Obviously such facilities were 'de rigeur' in the 1920s – and secondly, that the playground should be divided for the girls and infants. This condition was the origin of the famous 'white line' or 'Berlin Wall' as it was known in the latter years of its history.

The problem of getting the project within budget postponed it by one year. The revised plans were drawn up in the spring of 1926. The lowest tender received was from Mr H J Walker of Bream who submitted a costing of £3,157. 16s. It is hardly a surprise that his bid was the lowest –

his building yard was literally a stone's throw from the school, being sited where the Cross Keys car park now stands.

2. Reaction to the Plan

And what of the reaction of the vicar and the Church school managers to all of this? In April 1924 the LEA informed the managers that they were submitting enlargement plans to the Board of Education. The managers did not respond. In fact they were, initially unknown to the LEA, working to overthrow the enlargement plan. Joyce wrote to the National Society to ask if they could rescind their consent given on 11 December 1923 to the proposal. The National Society advised that they could appeal against the LEA enlargement plan and offered to send an inspector down, provided the managers paid for his travel and hospitality. The managers declined the offer; they did not have the funds. However, what they did do was, on the advice received from the National Society, write to object to the plan in July. This was, I think, the first inkling the LEA had of the managers' objection. The LEA had been working on the plan for several months at this stage.

In August the dispute became very bitter when a ratepayers' petition against enlargement was organised in the village. It was addressed to the Board of Education in Whitehall and worded as follows:

Ratepayers Petition
The West Dean Bream Council Public Elementary School

We the undersigned ratepayers resident in the Parish of Bream beg to appeal against the proposed enlargement of the West Dean Bream Council School. We are assured that there is ample accommodation in the council school and Church school as they stand, and we must respectfully and strongly appeal against the contemplated unnecessary expenditure of nearly £5,000 at a time when strict economy is absolutely essential.

The petition was signed by 139 local people, amongst whom was the vicar. I do not know how active the vicar was in the petition but I think it highly likely that he was one of the leading lights in it and, quite possibly, personally organised it. Having had advice from the National Society that he could appeal the enlargement decision a petition would be an emphatic way of doing so. Furthermore, the petition mirrored the views he had already expressed to the National Society that the Church school, contrary to the view of HMI, the LEA and the Board of Education, had the capacity to house 315 pupils. His National Society letter gave details of his allocation:

Junior Library (32)
Main Library (56)
Room 1 – aka Witherby Room (72)
Rooms 2 or 3 – aka Eales Room (107)
Café – aka Gosling Room (48)

The self-same letter by the vicar contains a thought which he probably believed would never see the light of day. At this distance in time I think it is fair to release it. He wrote 'In Bream Nonconformity is very strong. I am inclined to think they object to the Church school having the teaching of all children above ten or eleven years of age, and that the action of the LEA is due to pressure from them.' Had that sentiment been publicly aired at the time I suspect it would have created very deep divisions in the community.

3.   The Gloves Come Off
Once the petition was delivered the gloves were well and truly off between the Church school managers and the LEA. Unfortunately for William Joyce and the other managers, this meant they were now up against Horace Household and, as the dispute with the Office of Woods over the site for the 1907 school illustrated, he could be a formidable opponent when roused.

On 16 September 1924 Horace Household wrote formally to the Board of Education in Whitehall demolishing the managers' and petitioners' position and putting an irrefutable case for enlargement.

At that point the LEA did not know the names of the 139 petitioners and Household makes the point that it is impossible to verify if all were ratepayers and, even if they were, they would represent only a small proportion of the 7,000 ratepayers in East and West Dean. He thought that possibly the petitioners were under the impression that most of the cost would fall upon 'The Parish of Bream' but, as he pointed out, there is not in fact a Civil Parish of Bream and one half of the cost would be born by the parishes of East Dean and West Dean anyway, both of whose councils had offered no objection to the LEA's plan. The other half of the cost would be carried by the County council.

Household further pointed out that the managers *did* know of the enlargement plan prior to their letter of consent of 11 December 1923 and that it was very remiss of them not to notify the LEA of any objection until July 1924. He also by implication suggested that the managers had organised the petition. Finally, in respect of numbers, he stated that the vicar seemed unaware that the Board of Education would not tolerate classes of fifty or sixty, that the proposed boys-only Church school should house only about 230 boys, that at present Bream was educating 127 infants and 453 older pupils and therefore extra classrooms were a necessity. The Church school could not afford any capital expenditure on their own admission and that the enlargement of the council school was therefore necessary. The case was well and truly put and he finished with an authoritatively damning condemnation of the Church school managers:

> 'I am instructed to say that the Authority are not prepared to tolerate the permanent accommodation of Children in the unsatisfactory manner suggested by the managers of Bream Church school.'

4. New Year Resolution

In response to the petition and the various written submissions received, the Board of Education offered a public enquiry with costs being the responsibility of the two respective sides in the dispute – the managers and the LEA. It was now time for the managers 'to put up or shut up.' They capitulated. It was hardly likely that, if they could not afford to pay the expenses of a National Society inspector, they could foot the bill for a barrister for a public enquiry. On 24 November Joyce wrote to the board that the managers were content to leave the final decision to the board and mentioned a further worry the managers had, which perhaps was the real reason for their public campaign of opposition. They were worried that if the plan did go ahead and the council school was expanded to ten classes with consequent capacity for 500 children then, if the population in the area did reduce, the closure of the Church school would be a probability.

The Board of Education found in favour of the LEA on 23 December 1924 and communicated their decision in a diplomatic letter to William Joyce dated 1 January 1925. They thanked the managers for the 'reasonableness' of their attitude (in leaving the decision to the Board), stated the Board's decision in true legal jargon 'that the proposed addition to the council school is not unnecessary' and, to reassure the managers on the issue of Church school closure, that, if such an action were ever to be considered, public notice would be required under Section 16 of the Education Act 1921.

Building work on the new Bream girls' council school took place during the spring and summer of 1927. It officially began life as a separate school under a new headmistress on 1 September 1927. It was effectively the second school that Horace Household had built in Bream in the space of twenty years.

5. Blacklisted

In the mid 1920s, the managers of the Church school clearly felt that the enlargement of the council school made their school vulnerable to potential closure. They had every reason to feel vulnerable. Not only did they not have the funds for any capital developments but in 1926 they were also blacklisted at the Board of Education for defective premises. The blacklisting was as a result of an architect's report dated 13 October 1926 which had been commissioned by the LEA on all schools for which it had some responsibility. Bream National School was blacklisted in category B, meaning that it could be made suitable for education if money was spent on it. The report stated that the school needed £230 worth of work doing on it to bring it off the blacklist, (£8,993 RPI 2005 equivalent). Prominent among the modifications would be a new gateway, the breaking up of large stones in the playground, a new urinal, a concrete sloping entrance to the cloakroom to replace the high steps, a new window in the south side and a partition in the schoolroom (now rooms 2 and 3).

The managers now had to try and raise the necessary £230. By June 1927 they had the full amount: £55 in their funds, £91 from local subscriptions and collections, a grant from the diocesan board of £65 and one from the National Society of £20. The work was done in the summer of 1927 and in 1928 the school was removed by the Board of Education from its category B blacklist. This was much to everyone's relief – probably not least Horace Household's and the LEA who were keen to keep as many of the voluntary society schools on board as possible, if only to prevent their own financial outlay from increasing any further.

Within a few years however, problems with the Church school premises were to reappear.

Staff

Infant School Heads

Annie M Williams who had been head when the school opened its new buildings in 1907 continued in post until her resignation in October 1913. I have not met anyone who personally knew her but her record speaks for itself. Her thirteen years in charge of the infant school were characterised by good HMI reports. To isolate just one as an example – in 1909 the report states 'This is a good school. The classes are well taught on the whole and much of the work is very creditable indeed . . .'

The head who succeeded Annie M Williams in October 1913 was Eliza Young. Miss Young, as she was known to the pupils, was the longest serving head of Bream Infant School. She retired in February 1941, having served a total of over twenty-seven years. In her early days at Bream there was a big question mark over her suitability. She had previous teaching experience, having worked at Soudley School and St White's in Cinderford but, as the managers' minutes in November 1915 record, her experience of infant teaching was very limited and 'she had seen little or nothing outside the Forest of Dean.' The Education Committee in Gloucester had doubts about the appointment and sent Horace Household on an official visit to the school. His report stated that the school was not inefficient and her removal 'could not be required.' Common sense had prevailed. The committee decided to remedy the lack of experience by sending Miss Young on a week's visit to Kingswood High Infants School.

Horace Household's report on Miss Young contains a phrase that admirably sums up Eliza Young in the recollections of many past pupils. He wrote that the Education Committee 'fully appreciated Miss Young's kindly and motherly way with the children.' Many past pupils speak of her with affection. Margaret Addis described her as 'short and dappy and very patient – I remember her spending hours trying to teach a boy to write his name.' There was a lovely atmosphere in the school and she was, as Peggy Baynham said, 'quite a poppet with a good way of handling children.' Infants felt at home in her school and enjoyed being there. She could, if the need arose, be strict – as evidenced by Len Wildin's account of his life at school (later in this chapter).

It is fair to say that her twenty-seven years in charge of the school saw many changes and upheavals. She led the school through the First World War, the beginning of the Second World War and the arrival of evacuees. She also had responsibility for the expansion of the school in its first twenty years with the arrival of older children, to the point where, in 1927 when the new girls' head arrived, she was not just head of an infants school but effectively a council elementary school as well. These changes caused some difficulties and criticisms, particularly over how the older pupils were taught in the 1920s but, on the whole, standards were very commendable. One inspector wrote in 1938:

> 'This Department maintains an efficient standard under the competent headmistress who has been here for many years. The children are fearless and friendly . . .'

The other infant teacher from this generation who was well remembered was Miss Annie Williams. She was remembered for being strict and, because she had a loud voice and talked a lot, she was known as 'Annie (or Nanny) Parrot', which in time became shortened to 'Annie Parry.' In fact, the nickname took over from the name and some infants at school at that time would not respond to the name Miss Williams but would know full-well who was meant if you referred to Miss Parry. Generally speaking, she was not a popular teacher but the recollection of her did produce one lovely story from Angus Cooper. Angus learnt the lesson at an early age that teachers have eyes in the back of their head. When he had been a naughty infant at Bream, Miss Parry told him off and explained that she knew what he had done because she had eyes in the back of her head. Angus believed that teachers always told the truth. Miss Parry had her hair in a bun and next time Angus was at the teacher's desk he examined the bun to see if he could see the eyes.

Occasionally staff were transferred from one school to the other according to local educational need. Annie Williams fitted into this category. She had started at the mixed school in 1893 and was transferred to the council infant school in 1923. There could be difficulties however in the transfer market. Possibly her reputation went before her but the infant managers would only accept her transfer 'under protest.' Another problem with transfer had occurred the previous year, when the LEA wanted to switch Mrs Morris from the infants to the mixed school. She refused to go and her contract therefore was terminated.

Mixed School Heads
The career of William F Mullan has already been described in chapter four. When he retired in July 1918 there was a brief interregnum before a new head took over. Edward William Sylvester began as head on 11 November 1918 and revived a tradition at Bream that was in danger of lapsing by having his wife, Mrs Augusta A Sylvester, on the staff. The Sylvester years at Bream were uneventful, the school carrying on along the lines so successfully laid down by William Mullan.

When Edward Sylvester left at the end of January 1924, the school was again without a head. During February and March, Mr T H Hancock, a county supply head, took charge of the school until a new head took up post.

The new head was Cecil E Buck. He took up the headship on April Fools' Day, and for those who believe in omens it was a sad day for the school and for him. Thirteen months later he left in disgrace.

The Scandal of a Court Case

During Cecil Buck's time at the school there appear to have been some ominous signs. The numbers in school declined – 268 on his arrival, 233 by September 1924 and only 201 by February 1925. Children, or parents, appeared to be voting with their feet and going to other schools such as Pillowell. On 13 October there was an ugly situation between Cecil Buck and one of the parents, Mrs Lucas, the mother of Ivan Lucas. There was a row in school (over Ivan's detention) which took place in front of twenty or so children. Cecil Buck warned Mrs Lucas she had no right to enter the school and cause such a disturbance.

A far worse incident was to follow which ended up at Coleford Police Court on Tuesday 7 April 1925. Cecil Buck was summoned by a parent on a charge of assaulting one of his pupils. The pupil was eleven-year-old Horace Albert Watkins. His father was Albert Watkins who had died in the battle of Passchendaele in 1917. His mother, Kate Louisa Rudge, had remarried after the war.

On Friday 20 March, Horace had been sent to the headmaster for talking in Mr Fernley's lesson. Mr Buck gave Horace a choice, to have the cane or write out a thousand words. Horace opted for the cane and duly held out his right hand. As the cane came down he pulled his hand away and was then caned once on the left hand. The prosecution case was that Cecil Buck used a notched cane which he raised above his head and hit Horace so hard as to constitute an assault. Overnight the hand began to swell and the boy had a sleepless night. The following day Kate Rudge went with Horace to school to challenge Mr Buck's conduct. The head defended himself by arguing that it was only one stroke and the boy must have had a chilblain for it to react so. He suggested a visit to the doctor. Before doing this Kate told the headmaster that he was 'not fit to teach pigs.'

There were two visits to the doctor because, after the first one, an abscess developed on the hand. This necessitated a second visit six days after the caning.

The crucial issue was whether the caning had caused the abscess. Doctor O'Driscoll was to be the key witness. Apparently the hand which was struck was operated on three years previously leaving it scarred and vulnerable. Crucially, the doctor gave evidence that when he first saw the hand there was a black and blue streak on it but the skin was not broken. The skin broke later as the abscess developed.

The case now collapsed. The fact that the skin had not been broken by the cane did not make it an unlawful blow. Following the doctor's testimony the view of the Bench was that the injury might have been caused by a blow which was within Mr Buck's lawful power to administer. Prosecuting Counsel accepted the case could go no further. At this point Counsel for the Defence went on the offensive suggesting that Kate Rudge's sole motive in bringing the case had been to blackmail the head into paying compensation. He therefore asked that costs be awarded against her. The chairman of the Bench ruled against that request and the case was dismissed with no order as to costs.

In consequence of the case Kate Rudge transferred Horace to Pillowell school. Three weeks later Cecil Buck left Bream School and a new headmaster had to try and pick up the pieces and restore the school's reputation in the community. That task could not have gone to a safer pair of hands. The new head of Bream School was Willy Watson. His headship will be dealt with in the next chapter as will the career of two of his staff, Doris Worgan and Herbert Davies.

In defence of Cecil Buck it could be argued that, in the days when corporal punishment was the norm, it was a case of 'there but for the grace of God went any number of headmasters.' There were certainly other cases of assault being brought against heads and some of them locally.

During this period of the schools' history there were two events that impacted on the school, the village and the nation; the First World War 1914–18 and the General Strike of 1926.

The First World War and the Schools

Britain entered the First World War on 4 August 1914. On a tide of patriotic enthusiasm, by mid September half-a-million men had volunteered for active service. In their first meeting following the outbreak of war, the Forest Group of Council School Managers decided that any teacher responding to the country's call to arms should have their position kept open for the duration of the war and that neither they nor their dependants should suffer any financial loss from the fact of their military service. In other words, the salary was to continue to be paid.

In schools the war became a part of the curriculum. Maps were displayed showing progress of campaigns and no doubt teachers gave explanations of what was going on and where. On 25 October 1915 the LEA decreed a holiday for the mixed school to allow the older boys to do paid work for a day so they could donate their earnings to a local fund for the purchase of a new ambulance wagon for the Western Front. On 31

May 1916 Mr Eaton left the mixed school to join the Army, his place being taken by a female supply teacher. At that stage of the war however, he was told to return to teaching – ominously he was not required yet. He was in fact called up during the German offensive at the end of March 1918. By then, because of the war, both schools had an all female staff with the exception of William Mullan who was far too old for active service.

Occasionally, staff were given compassionate leave to visit relatives. Miss Hill from the infants school was allowed a day to go and see her brother prior to his departure for the Front. Similarly, in December 1916 Miss Morgan, also from the infants school, was given a day's leave to visit her wounded brother in London.

In 1917 the boys of the gardening class in the mixed school were 'doing their bit' for the war effort by digging the gardens of soldiers who were away on active service. Elsewhere, I have already told the story of how the infants school celebrated the entry of the USA into the war, also in 1917, with a marching rendition of *'Yankee Doodle'*. In 1918 the U-boat campaign had begun to have an impact on the country's food supplies and in May of that year there was no school for one week because the teachers in both schools were asked to do clerical work in connection with the meat rationing cards that were being introduced. One other disruption as a result of the war was the arrival at the school of Graham Nelmes as a certificated assistant master in May 1917. He had been invalided out of the Army. He was at Bream mixed school for six months before leaving in November 1917 for a headship in Rutland.

Finally in the summer of 1919, when peace was at last officially declared, all Bream school children were given an extra week's holiday in celebration. No doubt it was gratefully received.

The General Strike

During the First World War the Government had taken over control of the mines, the railways and basic heavy industry. Once peace was declared there were many in the Labour movement who wanted those industries to remain nationalised and under government control. Equally there were many others who wanted them returned to private ownership as they had been before the war. The latter argument prevailed. This was to have enormous consequence for the Forest of Dean where coal mining was the principal occupation at that time.

In 1921 the coal mines, therefore, returned to private ownership. On the argument that the mines needed to be profitable, the mine owners then announced a reduction in wages. Miners everywhere resisted. They were 'locked out' from work and, after a bitter dispute lasting several weeks, they had to face the choice of going back to work on the owners' terms or face starvation. After much hardship they returned to work.

The same scenario occurred in 1926, only this time the owners wanted a longer working day as well as a reduction in the wage. On this occasion, however, the miners were better prepared with promises of sympathetic strike action from many other Trade Unions if required. The miners' attitude was symbolised by their slogan 'Not a penny off the pay, not a second on the day.' On 30 April 1926 the coal owners again locked the miners out, except for those doing essential maintenance work underground. At midnight on 3 and 4 May the Trades Union Congress (TUC) came to the miners' assistance by calling a General Strike.

Initially matters looked promising for the miners. The Trade Union movement was solid in its support and for over a week the country was virtually at a standstill. On 12 May however, riddled with doubt about the course of action it had embarked on, the TUC itself was the first to blink. It called off the General Strike.

As in 1921, the miners were now on their own. They hung on with increasing desperation until November. Throughout the strike the Government supported the mine owners. They repealed the Seven Hours Act of 1919 which had limited working time underground. Also, by full use of the Emergency Powers Act, miners' pickets were arrested and the Boards of Poor Law Guardians found it increasingly difficult to use public money for the relief of strikers or their families. The argument used was that work was available and if miners opted not to do it they thereby disqualified themselves from any financial benefit. The miners, therefore, were almost literally starved back to work.

The Strike had a catastrophic effect on the local community. In June 1927 Reverend William Joyce wrote a description of the effect both of the 1921 and 1926 strikes on Bream as part of his application for funding from the National Society.

He wrote:

- The Parish has a population (1921 Census) of 3,226.

- The men find employment in the mines.

- They are practically all colliers.

- We have no wealthy residents.

- The Miners never really recovered from the 1921 strike and money is still due to local tradesmen for goods supplied at that time. There has been considerable unrest since then. The men were locked out from 1st May 1926 until the end of November. A number are still out of employment.

- Where possible the Poor Law Authorities are demanding repayment of monies loaned during the Strike.

- Each summer there are certain weeks when men only work four or three or even two shifts per week.

- It is well-nigh impossible to carry out all the work demanded by the LEA without financial support from outside

Between May and November 1926 most families in Bream suffered hardship which in many cases was severe. The children at school invariably suffered and particularly so if they were members of large families. The LEA had power under Section 84 of the 1921 Education Act to provide food for the needy if the situation required it. Both Bream schools took action soon after the middle of May. On 17 May the mixed school provided dinner and tea for 121 children – most of the school. The infant school did likewise on the same day. The following week was Whitsun week but by then the situation was so serious that the holiday was cancelled (except for Whit Monday) and the children were kept at school so that they could be fed. A similar pattern was continued throughout the long summer holiday with children coming to school just at meal times.

Those who were at school at the time remember the food arrangements. Hylton Miles remembers the school meals being served in the wooden ex-army hut, that had been put in the infants playground in 1920. The boys were fed in the woodwork room and the girls in the cookery room next door. Each child had to take his own knife, fork and plate. The food was cooked and served by members of Bream Labour Party.

Inevitably, there were issues concerning the emergency feeding of children. Usually the food was cooked but, to cook it, coal was needed for the kitchen stoves. This was the Education Committee's responsibility but because of the strike the Gloucestershire Education Secretary felt he could not order a supply of coal to fuel the stoves. The managers decided to order a ton of coal from Princess Royal Colliery on their own initiative. The problem then arose when the official correspondent (clerk) could not sign the order because like the Education Secretary he was a member of a union. Eventually the order was signed by Mr Rowlinson, chairman of the managers.

Feelings ran very deep. Hylton Miles tells a story of how his father, Jesse, and two other miners, Albert Brookes and Sonner Hoare, argued with the under-manager of Princess Royal Colliery, Mr Burdess, over the feeding of the children. Mr Burdess, who was coincidentally one of the school managers, wanted to reduce the number of cooked meals for the children and feed them with corned (or bully) beef sandwiches. When the three miners tried to return to work after the strike had ended they were told 'There's no work here for you three buggers.' A similar fate awaited Mavis Brain's (née Hewlett) father. Before the strike he had collected the union dues down at Princess Royal. During the strike he lit the cooking stove fires in the domestic science room at school to cook the children's lunch. After the strike he was blackballed and was never employed at Princess Royal again.

The community was solidly behind the strike but not universally so. A few of the smaller pits remained working and, in some of these situations, the atmosphere between picket and 'blackleg' became ugly. Three pits local to Bream stayed open – Shutcastle near Clements' End, Fryers Level on the road between Brockhollands and Whitecroft, and Parkhill Pit at Saunders Green. At the end of June a crowd of about 200 was waiting at Fryers Level for the two o'clock shift to surface. When the miners emerged they were greeted by a 'tanging' crowd who were rattling and banging old kettles, tins and other instruments and continued with this 'tanging' as they followed the miners home. The cry 'blackleg' was constantly used and one of the men was assaulted. Similar treatment was meted out as the nine o'clock shift surfaced (at this stage the Seven Hour Act was still in force) and turfs and other missiles were thrown. At this point a troop of mounted police was drafted into the Forest from Cheltenham to protect miners who were back at work or still at work. They were based behind the Feathers Hotel in Lydney.

'Blacklegs' were persistently followed and booed whenever they were in public. The longer the dispute dragged on the worse it became. Many men and women were taken to court for assault and intimidation. A typical example occurred at Saunders Green when one woman in a picketing crowd threw a tin at a miner; it knocked his pipe out of his mouth and cut his lip. His son, in the process of putting his bag over his shoulder to try and go home, hit a woman with it. The usual outcome of this kind of situation was being bound over to keep the peace and being required to pay costs.

The worst local situation involved Mr Burdess the under manager of Princess Royal Colliery. He was hated by the striking miners. One of the Bream men, 'Deany' Richards, who worked at the pit and a Welsh miner who also worked there plotted to blow up Mr Burdess' house in White-croft Road. They stole gelignite and fuses from the stores and laid the charge at the house with the fuse going down the road near to the Methodist chapel. Once the deed was done they agreed to run in different directions and meet up in Knockley afterwards. They lit the fuse. As they ran off, the miner from Wales, thinking that Mrs Burdess and the children might still be in the house, changed his mind. He returned to the house and put a wet sod over the lighted fuse just short of the gate. All hell then broke loose and both miners were arrested. Subsequently, Deany was sentenced to nine months in jail and the Welsh miner six months. Deany did eventually get his job back at the 'Parr Gutter' but on short time. He subsequently left the village and later died in a Luftwaffe bombing raid in Coventry in the Second World War. I am indebted to Hylton Miles for this story.

I am also indebted to Hylton for informing me of another sad story to do with the strike. If we were to ask a question 'What do you know about evacuation?' some would answer that child evacuation happened in 1939 and 1940 when children were taken out of cities such as London to be housed in country areas such as the Forest of Dean, so that they would escape the expected Blitz. In fact 1939–40 was not the first evacuation in this country. There was one in 1926 because of the strike and this time the evacuation was in reverse, from the Forest to London.

The Board of Guardians in Monmouth issued a 'meal ticket' to each mining family. The ticket did not provide for the striking miner, merely his destitute wife and children. In terms of value, the 'ticket' amounted to 10/- per week for the miner's wife and 3/- for each child. Using the Retail Price Index (RPI) this would be £19 and £5. 80p respectively in 2005. The maximum allowed per family was 25/- (RPI equivalent to £48 in 2005). Clearly this figure was well below any modern 'poverty line.' By August, as the strike was dragging on and the Board of Guardians' poor-relief money was becoming scarce, it was decided to set up an evacuation scheme for families with more than three children. The proposal was to evacuate the fourth child to London and foster them into a family there.

Hylton was the eldest of four children. When the evacuation offer was made his sister Phyllis begged Mum and Dad to allow her to go. Phyllis was just nine and a half years old. On 31 August 1926, the Bream evacuee children were assembled and taken down to Whitecroft railway station to catch a train for Paddington. On arrival in London, Phyllis and the other children had a label tied to their coats with their name on. Hylton writes 'Each child was viewed up and down, placed on a pedestal, then one of the organisers would shout 'Who wants this child?' Phyllis was very lucky being fostered by a Lewisham police sergeant and his wife (Mr and Mrs Tarrant), and they still thought of her as their daughter until the day they died. Phyllis attended a school in Catford for a few months. When the strike was over she was brought back to Bream. During the Second World War Phyllis became a nursing sister and saw service as a Queen Alexandra Nurse in North Africa, Europe and the Far East.

Some of the evacuated children never returned to Bream. Evacuation was a feature of every Forest town and village during 1926 and Winifred Foley has written a delightful account of her own experience of evacuation in *A Child in the Forest.*[6]

Other recollections of the strike come from Molly Williams and Angus Cooper. Molly's father was Ben Bath the Baker and everyone in Bream in the 1920s and 1930s remembers his famous alliterative slogan 'Ben Bath baker Bream bakes best brown bread.' Molly remembers her father talking about the 'slate' system by which families got goods on credit. Apparently only one family managed to pay Ben Bath back for what they had had 'on the slate' in 1926.

Angus' story concerns Russia. As a Communist country in 1926, Russia was very sympathetic to the miners. Russian money was sent in support of miners' families. Aid was also sent in the form of boots for the children. Parents could not afford to buy new boots as the old ones wore out, so many children's boots had material such as cardboard inserted to help them last longer. No doubt the Russian boots were a godsend at the time but Angus and his friends did not like them. For one thing they had a brass toe cap but, even worse, they came too high up the leg and the boys thought they looked like the girls' gaiters that they wore over their boots.

The contribution made by the schools and the LEA in 1921 and 1926 to relieve the hardship in the village was considerable. Eligibility for free school meals is still used today as an educational indicator and certainly in 1921 and 1926 could be used to show the degree of hardship in the

---

[6] *A Child in the Forest,* originally published by BBC Publications in 1974, has been re-published by Douglas McLean Publishing, Coleford, 2001.

community. Courtesy of the head, Mr Sylvester, I have the figures for the free school dinners served at Bream in 1921. During that time 11,459 dinners and 7,285 teas were served, a total of 18,744 meals. The cost of this was £179. 16s. 0d. (RPI equivalent to £5,313 in 2005). It worked out at 28p per child per meal in today's money.

The comparable meal totals for the 1926 strike would probably be triple the 1921 figures. We know how badly families suffered in this village during those two 'lock-outs.' Without the free school meals the suffering would have been far worse.

Standards of Health

Chapter five detailed how vulnerable children were to infectious diseases. During the 1907 to 1927 period there was a gradual improvement in health among schoolchildren. Even so, they were still vulnerable. In the infants school alone there were nine closures between 1907 and 1927. The usual culprits were to blame – diphtheria, scarlet fever, measles, mumps and influenza. Fatality arising from such illnesses became less likely, though there was still an average of one death per year of five to fourteen-year-olds in the parish.

Inevitably accidents continued to happen. We may think that traffic accidents did not occur in those days when we assume that roads were far less busy than now. That was true but accidents could still happen. In July 1909 a little girl called Dulcie Stephens was knocked down and run over by a cart on her way home from school. She was taken to Gloucester Infirmary with a fractured skull. The following day the head of the mixed school, Mr Mullan, again cautioned the children to be careful on their way to and from school. Fortunately Dulcie survived. Almost ten years to the day, in July 1919, Doris Lewis was knocked down by a car in the mixed school playground. Luckily no bones were broken. In January 1927 a potentially far worse accident happened at the mixed school. A slate fell off the roof and hit one of the boys, Dennis Morgan. But his injuries were not as serious as they might have been and he escaped with minor damage to his arm. I would point out that at this stage the school was blacklisted because of dilapidation. The makeover to be done in the summer of 1927 obviously could not come soon enough.

An entry in the infants school log for 1927 is a forcible reminder of how tough children were expected to be. Reopening after the Christmas holiday it was found that the boiler had burst and the heating system was not working. A supply of oil stoves subsequently arrived to heat the different classrooms. Each of the classrooms had a thermometer and with the stoves at full power the thermometers were registering from 42 °F to 48 °F (6 °C to 9 °C) in the various rooms. The school did not close because of these temperatures. It stayed open. Nevertheless attendance was well down the following week, many of the children suffering from coughs and influenza.

This particular time also saw efforts being made by Gloucestershire to institute a system of medical and dental inspection for children. The 1907 Education Act made medical inspection a statutory requirement. The inspection was carried out by doctors appointed as school medical inspectors for the county accompanied by two nurses. The nurses, in the course of time, acquired the graphic title of 'nit nurses.' In 1908, the year in which infestation records were first kept for Gloucestershire schools, 23.4 per cent of school children were infected.

School meals could also help to improve the health of children but the Education (Provision of Meals) Act of 1906 conferred only permissive powers to provide meals to LEAs. They could provide meals but they did not have to. Consequently, they usually only acted to provide in emergency situations such as the 1921 and 1926 coal strikes. A pioneering attempt to set up a regular school canteen at Ruardean Hill council school in 1919 came to an end in 1922, because the teachers were struggling to run it on their own. At lunch time in Bream schools, as elsewhere at this time, children either went home or brought lunch to school in a 'tommy' bag. Angus Cooper tells me the typical content of his 'tommy' bag was sandwiches and lemonade made with crystals.

Holidays

The pattern of the school year continued much as it had been prior to 1907. With the exception of the years 1907 to 1910 the school year officially began on the 1 May. In 1921 this was changed to 1 April, with children going up a class or school at the beginning of that month. The summer holiday lasting usually for four weeks was the longest of the holiday periods for children, but they also now had one or two weeks for Christmas and Easter, one week for the Whitsun holiday and, first recorded at Bream School in 1914, a half-term week off at the end of October and beginning of November.

In 1916, in an innovative move, the British Government set up British Summer Time to operate with effect from midnight on 21 May. The fact was duly recorded at Bream schools where the clocks were advanced by one hour on the morning of 22 May. I wonder how many children (or staff) were late on that day, the first time ever British clocks had been advanced. British Summer Time lasted that year till the end of September.

Also during the First World War the schools introduced a summer and winter timetable system. The school day invariably started at 9 a.m. but from 1915 onwards the winter school day was shorter. In 1915 during the winter months morning school ended at 12.45 p.m. and afternoon school was timed from 12.45 p.m. to 2.50 p.m. This varied in later years but as a general rule winter school finished around 3 p.m. and summer school finished at 4 p.m. Both schools at this stage were still lit by oil lamp.

The children's basic holiday entitlement continued to be boosted by a wide variety of events. In June 1909 the schools had a holiday on the occasion of Edward VII's visit to Gloucester. A similar holiday occurred to celebrate Princess Mary's wedding in February 1922. Best of all the royal occasions from the children's point of view was the coronation of George V in June 1911. The whole of Coronation week was given as a school holiday throughout the country 'by request of His Majesty.' This actually made 1911 a good summer to be a pupil at Bream schools – they were on holiday more than they were in school. The Coronation week followed closely on their Whitsun Holiday. Between 29 June and 20 July, they had the usual circus of four Sunday school treat holidays. Then on 4 August, they began a four week summer holiday.

Empire Day, which had started in 1904 was a half-holiday during the first part of this period. The children attended school, saluted the flag in both playgrounds, sang patriotic songs and then had the rest of the day as holiday. Empire Day celebrations took rather a knock during the First World War and seemed to be replaced by both schools rigorously observing the two-minute silence at 11 a.m. on 11 November.

22 July 1912 was a first for Bream schools in that both schools were closed so that all the children could go on a day's outing to Weston Super Mare. Outings were already a feature of church and chapel treats, usually to Sharpness, but this was the first occasion, to my knowledge, that both schools had been on an outing together.

Temperance days and travelling circuses as being a reason to close the schools seemed to be on the decline, but other events could create a reason for holiday or – if one was not given – truancy. For example, in 1927 there were separate holidays for the Dilke Hospital Bazaar, the Forest of Dean Sports at Coleford and the Dilke Sports and Carnival. Musical events, national and local elections (with schools being polling stations) and bonus half-holidays for a high attendance rate all boosted the number of holidays, as did the enforced closures due to epidemics and bad weather. This period also saw the beginning of the scholarship system by which children could take an exam to see if they could get a free place for secondary school. Possibly because of the need for quietness, the rest of the mixed school could be given a holiday on these occasions, and in 1920, when Una Macey won a scholarship, the whole mixed school celebrated with a half-holiday. I should think Una became very popular.

To a child, I suspect the unexpected holidays were the most well received. The best such that I have seen in the Bream records occurred on impulse on Friday 27 September 1918 in the mixed school. William Mullan had retired at the end of July and until a new head was appointed the managers asked two teachers to take charge of the school when term began on Monday 2 September. Both were new to the school – Mrs Milborough Esther Young–Jones had started in April 1918 and Miss Elizabeth Gertrude Davies had started in the June. I do not know why they did what they did – almost certainly it was a beautiful September day and possibly there was a 'feel-good factor' because the Great War was as good as over. At lunchtime on that day they shut the school and took all the children blackberrying. What a wonderful thing to do. I wonder if a long-established head would have dared. I bet the children remembered it though.

Children and their Doings

During the period 1907 to 1927 the log books are not as profitable a fishing ground for children's misdemeanours and how they were punished. It is usually only matters that the head regarded as serious or out of the ordinary that found their way into the record. That is not to say that common or routine misdemeanours were less frequent or that the cane and other sanctions were used less often. In these respects I am sure matters continued much as prior to 1907. Indeed the cane was clearly still a regular feature of even infant school life, as Len Wildin's account at the end of this chapter bears witness.

Certain 'major' incidents have already been described in connection with Cecil Buck. Other incidents that are recorded are as follows. In June 1908 one of the classrooms in the mixed school was broken into and 1½*d.* 'abstracted' (stolen). The culprit was identified – George Hancock – and the police were informed. I do not know what the final outcome of this incident was but I do wonder how we would react today to a similar incident. The sum involved would now be worth around 45p. Would we call the police for that? It may be that the police were called more for the break-in than the theft.

In October 1910 an ugly situation developed outside the mixed school. Two small boys had been fighting and had been separated and brought back onto the premises. An older boy, who had been encouraging the fight, was also brought inside the school gate whereupon two of his friends in turn tried to rescue him and pull him away. The teachers concerned were then threatened with stones. The school managers were informed of this but I do not know what action they took. Len Wildin's account of his school life at Bream describes a playground fight and any conversation with the pre-1939 generation will certainly tell you that schoolchildren fighting was a not uncommon event in Bream. Usually, however, a fight was arranged to take place away from the prying eyes of adults and teachers, down at 'The Jube' (Jubilee Pool) – to give it its official name. These matters were 'sorted out' without adult interference.

One of the less serious situations that did find its way into the record occurred in January 1923 when George Benson and Ken Howard were each given one stripe of the cane for 'throwing mud in the playground' – a useful reminder of the fact that the playground was years away from a tarmac surface.

A more serious situation was recorded in June 1913. Mr Barlow had been teaching at the mixed school for six years. He rode to school by bicycle and stored the machine in the cloakroom. On 9 June 1913 the tyres were slashed. Two particular boys were suspected and the police were promptly called in.

Having spoken to a number of school children from this generation of Bream pupils, I was intrigued by what several of them said about starting school, specifically the age they began and how the decision to start school was arrived at. Many of them started at what we would call a pre-school age and some of them even seemed to take the decision to start school by themselves.

Hylton Miles started me off on this line of enquiry when he told me that his younger sister Megan started at Bream Infants before she was three. As previously mentioned, Hylton was the eldest of four children, Hylton, Phyllis, Megan and Tom. Hylton's story is that Megan used to follow himself and Phyllis to school and was several times escorted back home to mother. Eventually the headmistress, Miss Young, gave up sending Megan home and she started school at the age of two years and ten months.

Fortunately, the admission register for Bream Infant School has survived for the 1920s giving us details of date of birth and date of admission. The register confirms that Hylton, Phyllis and Tom all started school at the tender age of three and a half. It records Megan as starting at three years and two months, but I am sure Hylton's memory is the correct one, because children were not allowed to start before the age of three, and he remembers Megan being in school unofficially. Megan subsequently won a scholarship to Lydney Grammar School at ten, became head girl there and went on to college. On returning to the Forest she taught for a year at Double View School. She was then recruited by Ivy Drabble, the Head of Bream girls' school. In Bream she taught the scholarship class. During the Second World War she was persuaded by the evacuated Rochford teachers to go and teach in Essex.

An analysis of infant enrolment in April 1919 when Hylton himself started school shows a total of twenty-nine children joining the school. Eight of them were three years old. The eldest was six. The average age of entry was four.

Molly Williams (née Bath), like Megan, seemed to have taken the lead herself over when she should start school. Molly was born on 8 April 1914 and lived at Bristol House. On her fourth birthday she was allowed out on her own, to go to Williams and Cottons Stores at the end of Blue Rock Crescent to buy herself a hair ribbon for her birthday. It was playtime at Bream Infants when Molly was out and, when someone invited her to go in the playground, she did. She then went into class. The head wanted to know what Molly was doing there and sent Margaret Burdess to tell Mrs Bath what had happened. In the subsequent conversation between Molly, Mrs Bath and Miss Young, Molly said she wanted to start school and Miss Young (and presumably Mrs Bath) agreed that she could. The admission register duly confirms that Molly's first day of school was 8 April 1918, her fourth birthday – no doubt ribbon and all.

The admissions procedure at Bream School in the 1920s was an interesting one and permitted a certain amount of economy with the truth. When a child was enrolled at the infants school the head was required to ask for evidence of date of birth. Three different types of evidence were permitted and listed on the record by the initials B, CB and D. B signified that the head had seen the birth date recorded in the family bible. CB indicated the head had seen the birth certificate. D meant simply that the parent had made a declaration as to when the birth was. In Bream, as probably in most schools, D was the standard option adopted by parents. The D category is obviously the one where parents, should they wish, could indeed exercise some economy with the truth.

Thelma (otherwise known as Peggy) Baynham (née Wildin) told me an interesting story about her admission to Bream Infants. Entry was never refused at four years of age but could be at three. Peggy's mum Helen (or Nellie) Wildin took Peggy along to enrol at school before she was four. When Nellie told Miss Young that Peggy 'would be five next birthday', Peggy nudged her mum because she knew she was only four next birthday. Mum then nudged Peggy back to make sure that Peggy kept quiet about the fact. To this day Bream school records give Peggy Wildin's date of birth as 11 June 1920 when it was in fact 11 June 1921. The grapevine tells me that this was probably not the only such erroneous declaration made by a Bream parent. The moral of this story for genealogists is, do not use school admissions registers as sole evidence for a date of birth. No doubt Peggy would now be happy to have the process reversed. Instead of having a year added on to her age, she would prefer having one year taken off – if not more.

Parents and Their Doings

As with the children 'and their doings', comments about parents are very limited in the log books for 1907–27. The major events during Cecil Buck's headship concerning Mrs Lucas and Mrs Rudge have already been described. One other incident is worthy of note although I do not know whether the gentleman concerned was actually a parent of the school or merely a member of the public who happened to be a neighbour. He lived in one of the houses adjoining the mixed school playground. As such he was very much in the front line whether the yard itself was a school playground or, for that matter, a community centre car park. He deserves everybody's sympathy. His right to peaceful existence could be disrupted by trespass, damage to boundary fence, noise and even the odd broken window. There could also be verbal abuse.

The gentleman concerned was called Mr Payne. In June 1914 he called into school to see the headmaster concerning a window which had been broken by a cricket ball during playtime. Before William Mullan could even reach the door Mr Payne had acted. He pulled the four cricket stumps (one for the bowler, three for the batsman, I assume) out of the ground, took them home with him and refused to return them. The vicar had to be called in to mediate on this one. Consequently the window was paid for and the stumps were returned.

Periodically parents did get the opportunity to go into school in a supportive role, for example to buy items that had been made by the children. In December 1925 in what I think was a 'first', parents were invited in one afternoon to see children's work in the mixed school.

Thirty parents attended. At the time there were around 212 children on roll. I doubt that the school would consider its 'open afternoon' much of a success.

In terms of parents giving financial support to the school, concerts were organised in 1926 and 1927 to help pay for renovations to get the mixed school off the blacklist. One such concert in February 1926 raised just over £13 (£505 RPI 2005 equivalent). The mixed school repair fund continued after the school was off the blacklist. In a two-night concert at the Miners Welfare Hall, held in December 1927 the sum raised was just over £10 (£399 RPI 2005 equivalent).

School Links with the Community

Both schools continued in their long established roles as community centres in the early twentieth century. True to custom and practice, damage could occasionally occur as a result of a let. On Saturday 15 October 1910 an entertainment company hired the main room in the mixed school. On the Monday morning when the school opened, three desk castings had been broken and other desk surfaces had been 'roughened and scratched' by being used, unreasonably, for standing on.

The council school across the road was also hired for community events but, possibly because it was ultimately controlled by the County, the regulations surrounding the hire of rooms may have been stricter. The council school managers, at their February meeting in 1925, received a letter written by the school head, Eliza Young, requesting the use of the school premises on behalf of Bream Tennis Club, who wished to hold a dance there on 20 February, from 8 p.m. to 2 a.m. The tennis club probably thought they were on a winner with the head making the booking. They were not. The managers turned the request down. They could only allow public use from 6 p.m. to 10 p.m. and they could not make an exception for the tennis club, which probably meant they could not make an exception for Miss Young.

With the council school we actually know the hire charge. In February 1922, the choir applied to use a room for Bream Male Voice Choir to practise in. The fee was 2/6d. per occasion and a further 2/6d. if the school piano was used. The choir also had to pay for the room to be cleaned. In September of that year Mrs Phipps of Highbury Villa booked part of the ex-army hut for WI meetings. Again the charge was 2/6d. with the WI providing the heating and lighting and paying for the cleaner. They were allowed to put their piano in there – but at their own risk.

Prominent locals continued to be associated with the schools. The Bowles family at Priors Mesne appear to have been particularly generous at this time. In 1908 Miss Bowles presented a cricket set to the infants school (I assume these were not the stumps Mr Payne confiscated in 1914). In 1909 Doctor Bowles redressed an imbalance that existed between the two schools. The infant school had a new flag pole when it was built in 1907. Doctor Bowles bought one for the mixed school in 1909. The school could then celebrate Empire Day in the appropriate fashion. The flag was hoisted, saluted by all the children on parade, the vicar and other gentlemen made speeches, patriotic songs were sung and then the children had a half-day holiday. The following year Miss Bowles presented twenty-two tennis balls to the mixed school. With her gift of cricket equipment and tennis balls I wonder if Miss Bowles were responsible for any broken windows near the schools?

Sale-of-work activities continued in both schools, much as before 1907. The range of goods seem to have broadened a little – as the practical curriculum was enlarged – cane baskets put in an appearance in the 1920s. The one big difference, post 1907, was in where proceeds from the sale went to. In the mixed school it continued to go to the vicar for school funds. In the council or infant school, now fully controlled by the LEA, it went to Gloucester.

Links with the Church

With regard to the mixed school, links with the Church continued to be as strong as ever. The vicar, as evidenced by Reverend Joyce's role in the school reorganisation crisis of the mid 1920s, was always in a central position in the management of the school. If a letter needed writing on behalf of the school the vicar would write it as 'official correspondent.' When funding needed to be raised the vicar would play a key role. In 1924, soon after Cecil Buck became head, the vicar wrote to the National Society to request a grant for Bibles and prayer books. He pointed out that there was an average attendance of 248 children and only twenty Bibles in the school and no prayer or hymn books, which was deplorable in a Church school. He wanted to purchase 200 Bibles at 1s. 3d. each (a total of £12.10s.) and fifty prayer books at 9d. each (a total of £1. 17s. 6d.). The Society gave a grant of £5 towards this overall expenditure of £14. 7s. 6d. (RPI 2005 equivalent of 1s. 3d. and 9d. is £2.37p and £1.42p). The clergy were also regularly in the mixed school, taking RE lessons and assemblies and supervising exams.

With the infant or council school, the links with the church were still strong but in a less formalised way. For one thing the management of the school was different. After 1907 the school was part of the Forest of Dean Group of Council Schools. There were local representatives on the managers meeting but the meetings took place at Cinderford and the official correspondent who serviced all schools in the group was a Mr Bradstock. If anything went wrong in the school, such as the heating breaking down, Mr Bradstock, in his office in Cinderford, would be the first to be informed. If the Church school had such a crisis a message would be sent to Bream vicarage.

That said the vicar was regularly in the council school. He would carry out the RE inspection every year and, as in the Church school, take RE lessons and assemblies and even supervise exams.

Inside the Classroom

If we were to think that children were taught the same subjects in the same way in 1860 as in 1900, we would be wrong. The school curriculum has always changed. What is perhaps different about it over time is the rate of change. The three Rs curriculum of the mid-nineteenth century had, over the next forty years, been gradually modified by the addition of subjects such as English literature, geography and history but the pace of the change remained slow.

The 1902 Education Act speeded up the rate of educational change in that it led to a local organisation, the Local Education Authority (LEA), with expertise that could act as a catalyst to drive change in schools within its area. In schools such as Bream National School this resulted in a broadening of the curriculum, which was facilitated by the ending of payment by results in 1904. Subjects that Horace Household and the LEA were keen to promote included handicraft, gardening and cookery.

On 20 September 1909, Nurse Blackburn began a series of six lessons in domestic science to the top class girls from three till four o'clock every Monday. A couple of days later Mr Elison from Lydney began handicraft classes for a dozen top class boys. These lessons took place in ordinary classrooms because specialist facilities were not yet available, but at least a start had been made.

The LEA was keen for as many elementary schools as possible to acquire a small patch of land where gardening could be taught. By the outbreak of war in 1914, 117 Gloucestershire elementary schools had gardens. Bream school was one of them. In March 1912, the managers 'at last' procured a garden from Mr Ralph Williams for the boys. It was reckoned that a class of fourteen boys could do gardening at any one time.

Another change in curriculum was the emphasis on drill as part of physical education. In November 1911, the mixed school timetable laid down three, twenty minute lessons per week for drill. It will be remembered that the plan for the 1907 infant school insisted there should be 'adequate provision for marching' and that Margaret Addis and the rest of the infants sang *'Yankee Doodle'* as part of their marching drill in 1917 to celebrate America's entry into the War. Drill was organised on military lines and it is not difficult to imagine children marching on Empire Day onto the playground or parade ground a class at a time, being stood in rank and file and saluting the flag. The military association with school drill was a close one and in February 1923 one Captain Parker accompanied an HMI on a visit to the mixed school to inspect the drill.

Specialist provision for handicraft and cookery teaching had to wait till after the First World War. Mention has already been made of the fact that an army hut 60 feet by 20 feet had been purchased in 1920 for that purpose and installed on the infant playground against the doctor's fence. The hut itself cost £265 and the surveyor estimated a further cost of £300 to pay for foundations, hauling and erection, lining with match-boarding and providing drains and water supply – a total cost of £565, half of the cost coming from Gloucestershire, the other half from East and West Dean. The building became known as the 'special subject rooms'. Because of its location, trouble arose between the two schools over how children from the mixed school should gain access to these rooms. In 1923 the Forest managers ruled that the Church school children should use the double gateway near the rooms. Under no circumstances should they use the infant gateway.

The concept of 'special subjects' helped create a climate in which teachers of older pupils started to specialise in specific subjects. This happened in the top three standards of the Church school in 1926. Mr Davies took classes in geography, history, drawing, boys' hygiene, bookkeeping and boys' physical training (PT). Mrs Jones took all the arithmetic, observation lessons, music, general knowledge and girls' PT. Miss Worgan took all the English and helped with the music.

During the First World War, Gloucestershire began to introduce a new approach to teaching in elementary schools which was known by its initials PNEU. I had come across the initials a number of times during my research but was uncertain as to how the scheme actually worked in practice. Fortunately, in 2004, I had the opportunity to ask Cecily Leach about it. Cecily had been head of Bream Infants from 1955 to 1969 and had actually operated the scheme. PNEU stood for Parents National Educational Union. Cecily described it as a curriculum scheme that underpinned an emphasis on learning rather than teaching, based on a motto for the children *'I am, I can, I ought, I will.'* Cecily particularly remembered two features of the scheme – that it supplied sepia copies of masterpiece paintings for the wall and that it so encouraged children to develop their skill in narrative writing.

PNEU was an educational creed based on the ideas of an Ambleside spinster, Charlotte Mason. In Gloucestershire, Horace Household became an ardent convert and argued for its introduction to as many Gloucestershire schools as possible. On the basis of Mason's philosophy that 'self education is the only possible education', Household wanted the emphasis in Gloucestershire on learning rather than on teaching, with the child being the unit in the classroom rather than the class.

Before PNEU, a lot of elementary school work was dull. Reading-books in most Gloucestershire schools were few-and-far-between, well - worn and uninteresting. When children wrote composition it was little more, in Household's phrase, than 'reproduction of the teacher's words.' Above all, he castigated 'teachers who talked too much.' The emphasis, he thought, should be on enjoyment and self activity. Great works of literature, Shakespeare, Scott, Dickens and so on, were to come into schools, as were lots of history books – historical novels as well as text books. As Household himself stated in 1927 'Our children are brought up on and inspired by great masterpieces of living literature, and in eager fancy they will stride along beside Mr Greatheart, roam the taverns with Prince Hal, adore Di Vernon, sail round the world with Francis Drake, thrill with emotion as Nelson lies dying on the *'Victory'* and as Scott writes his last letter in that splendid tent of *Death in the Antarctic.'*

The magazine *'Punch',* in a famous sonnet on the PNEU Gloucestershire scheme, wrote:

'O happy County, foremost in the van
of culture, where two-thirds of all its schools
Are now conducted on the kindly plan
Laid down by Charlotte Mason in her rules . . .'

The final two lines emphasised to the teacher what needed to change:

'Abandon arid text-books, blackboard chalking,
And cease as far as possible from talking.'

In January 1924, Bream Infants School became the first Bream school to adopt PNEU. In the Church school it was under consideration in 1926 and the PNEU syllabus books and exam system was finally adopted in 1928.

I am convinced the scheme had a major impact on Bream schools. Several people I have spoken to who were at school between the World Wars have confessed to a lifetime love of literature. That, I am sure, was due in no small measure to PNEU.

It could be argued that PNEU still echoes down the generations. Perhaps more modern teaching agendas such as 'child centred learning' and even 'every child matters' have a pedigree stretching back to Charlotte Mason.

Given Bream School's current excellence at sport, it is interesting to investigate whether the school had any school games fixtures against other schools. Gerald Vaughan remembers cricket being played in the sports club car park and fixtures against other schools such as Parkend being played on 'The Lonk.' Each team had one innings and there was no over-limit per side, or per bowler, involved. Ron Watkins remembered playing for the school team at football. In a game against the Craft School at Lydney, Bream School team walked there, changed, played at Bathurst Park, changed back and walked home. The team also walked to other local fixtures – Elwood, Pillowell and Parkend.

Playground games popular at the time among the boys were a whipping top, sturty bird[7], marbles, quoits (played with stones and probably very similar to the French game 'boules') and 'strong 'osses and weak donks.' Strong 'osses and weak donks was a team game where four or five boys would form a line and all get into a collective leap-frog position. The other team with the best vaulter going first would then start to jump on top. If the line was still in position when everybody had jumped on, it was a 'strong 'oss', if it had collapsed, it was a 'weak donk.' Not a game for today's playground, nor a game that was popular with mothers either. As Ron Watkins says, 'it really was a game that stretched the jumpers.'

---

[7] 'Sturty bird' is the name of a children's game that appears to be unique to Bream, although variations of the game were once played throughout Britain. The game, which required some skill, was played thus: A piece of wood, about as thick as a man's thumb, four to six inches long, and tapered to a point at both ends was the bird. This was placed on the ground and whacked with a stick to make it rise spinning into the air. The skill was to then swing a hit at the spinning bird so that it 'flew' into the distance. The champion was the one who could most accurately estimate how far the bird had flown in lengths of the stick.

A number of ex-pupils of Bream schools have given me invaluable information on life in the schools and the village when they were young. I am particularly grateful to Gordon James who, with his twin brother, was evacuated from London to Bream during the Second World War. Gordon's uncle, Norman Schlosberg, was born in 1907 and grew up in Schlosberg's shop opposite the Cenotaph. Some years ago Norman wrote down his recollections of Bream in the early years of the twentieth century. I am grateful to Gordon for allowing me to read those recollections and to use some of them in this book.

Extracts From The Recollections of Norman Schlosberg:

The Coming of War in 1914, Nits and Wages

The clouds were gathering for war between England and Germany. I in my young way did not fully understand it and it was the general topic of conversation between my parents and to me was a little frightening. The Colliers were gathered on the Sun Green corner and me in my little way did listen to them talk before the pub opened.

I was already going to the Bream infant school and the teacher was called Nancy Parrot. Other teachers were Miss Hill and Billings. It was cold classrooms and forms to sit on with a little desk with an ink pot and a little hole for it to be placed in with pen and nib. I looked forward to writing in our exercise book for inspection by teacher who marked it accordingly.

We had inspection of our heads for nits and lice now and again. If someone was found to have some, the dreaded part was to sit by the ones who had them. My father done all the cutting of heads and it was close to the scalp with a little tuft of hair left in the front. If one grumbled about the scalping, as we knew it, he gave us a crack with the scissors and maybe the stick for he could use it with gusto, as he had a quick temper. I never knew him to fight with any men. My mother was the one to come and sort troublesome drunken men customers. She hated the drinkers and it was cider that had them unsteady on their feet with or without a purchase of boot or clothing.

Wages were at a low premium and my brother(s) got a pittance for their shift in the collieries. One pound would have been the wage and the man with kids would only be getting 30/- (£1.50) for five shifts, which were an eight hours stint. Their fists were really hard with the handling of the pick and shovel. They had big families too – eight, twelve and thirteen kids were the outcome of their ardour, yet they managed to keep going a good vegetable garden, a pig in the cot and in a lot of cases fowls open running in a wire enclosure, fed with Indian corn and now and again barley meal mixed up in small pots and with a Kerswood spice.

I used to listen to the laughter and cursing while they guzzled the cider, about 2*d*. a pint then. Not many women entered the pub then. A dog which if it was kept under the bench they sat on had an occasional kick in the ribs if it got in front of the owner. A spittoon was on the floor with sawdust in it! to take the accurate spit when chewing black loose tobacco and the Woodbine fags at 2*d*. a packet of ten. Rarely did they miss the spittoon, that would never have done, for the boards or stone floors were scrubbed daily.

Corporal punishment

The war had been raging for a year and I was eight years old. School was to me unpleasant and I only enjoyed writing and music lessons and playtime. Now and again blooded fights developed between rival gangs or two boys who could not agree. I believe they got a beating during the fight and one from the headmaster when they were hauled up before him.

There was a good five foot of cane given to the boys who misbehaved, also many times to me for laughing during lessons and caught by the teacher. It was a tingling sensation and I often wonder why the tips of my fingers did not drop off with the force that dropped from shoulder high by the head and maybe a good whack across the back when leaving for the route back between the classes, with all eyes focused to see if the tears were falling, which very often was the case.

Looking back I believe we deserved the cane, for misdeeds were many. I look upon it all in this way, beat up not brought up for we had plenty of stick at times. Boys I knew then were severely beaten by their fathers with the buckle end, brass fastening is the word. Weals were always in view when a boy took his shirt off, cruelty is the word that fits. A policeman to others and me was not a familiar sight but when he was around we stayed clear for his eyes were enough for me. If we were caught in the hours of darkness around the street, we could expect the thwack with a cane he carried and a command to get indoors at once. He knew gangs of boys were only making the tempers of people we chose to act the fool with, tapping windows and tying cotton to door knockers to see them come out there. If we were caught there was always a good cuff around the ear holes and a kick up the rear. There were so many things we done for a laugh but I don't recollect doing wanton damage to any property.

Our lives were centred around the season. We [would] scrump apples when the orchards were producing the apples and plums. We went through the small places in the hedges and filled our jerseys with a lot to eat on the way home. We were caught at times. A whip was then used by the owners and a warning by the police was going to be the end result.

Life as a schoolboy, the nicknames boys had and the story of Hoppin Potter

Although we felt free to go wherever we chose and exploration was upper most in our minds the different places were unlimited. The Devil's Chapel so called held most of interest, the caves and rocks and woods that stretched all round could tire the best pair of legs. Many card games were held mostly by the older boys. There was always a look out at these circles, for if the village bobby had got wind of the goings on, he could creep up and try to catch the culprits. Someone had to be the winner and he would be lucky to get two or three shillings after it seemed, hours of play.

The linings of our pockets would never wear out if we had any more than sixpence. Mostly nuts or apples would have done more damage for we could stuff to over flowing and find room under the jersey we all wore sometimes. On our escape from the raids on chosen orchards, we lost a few and got a good lashing from a horse whip if caught and that could happen any time if one was up a tree picking the best.

Most of us would have a nickname for it was one way of identifying most names, Jones, Evans or Smith were the most common. Whenever my parents spoke of going to see the individual it was mostly a nickname that was the clue. We had a good laugh when they said certain names for I always found out the true description would have been the easiest way of meeting the person or a clip around the ear would have been the end result by saying the wrong name.

A few worth mentioning were these:

Chick Morgan

Bog Whiskers Worgan

Stonewalker Walker

Slasher Wicks

Parrot Williams

Duddle Watkins

Twister James

Bowy Camm

Poller Rollins

Dick Runner Beech

Tully Beach

Farmer Elsmore

Scriggle Lewis

Whacker Brain

Bunny James

Snerf Thomas

Roller Croome

Rooky Downham

These are a few of the many and mostly got their nicknames of how they acted in walking, working, speaking , or playing.

I well remember a certain lady who was called Hoppin Potter. The hats that adorned her head were always to me a laughable moment for some were easily a foot high and she could balance same in hail, wind and sunshine. A good hat pin would be required to join hair and hat. Another boy with a handful of lard was chasing me and his arm was pretty accurate for on this occasion he took the hat off her head, after I dodged the throw and the result was I got a good whack across the face for the complaint to the manager after it had happened. We all got what was deserved and if we complained to our parents that called for further punishment so a still tongue was a wise head. We never did anything wilfully to cause too much trouble, for people then took the law into their own hands and gave a good hiding to the offender. If at times ones parents could see there was justification in their taking action, in such cases then that was the send of the story. I was never happy if I got the treatment for I knew I should not have done it.

Naturally some parents took the matter further and a fistfight could have developed and many a time I have witnessed the same. If a good stick came into use and sometimes it did that was the weapon to be feared. A cracked head or the body was black and blue before the fight ended. It could be years before any conversation ever was transmitted between the families concerned. I once witnessed a fight between a bobby and a drunken collier who had gave his wife a beating. The copper donned helmet and tunic and the end result was the cider drinker getting the full treatment in bare fist arresting. It was a long walk to Coleford or Lydney police court and only the very bad ended up there and then a full day could be wasted as nobody was taken by a policeman there. His word was law, he could be good, bad, or indifferent so it was a wise person who steered clear. But they did not forget and an instant dislike was war as long as the years came and went. Of course it was a wise man that never showed fight for that could have a different ending. For instance fist or court and the story splashed all over the *Weekly Gazette*.

Norman probably attended Bream schools between 1911 and 1920. I particularly enjoyed what Norman had to say on the subject of nick names. It was a question I asked Angus Cooper and he came up with the following list:

	Real first name
Bubs Carpenter	Harry
Spuddy Baker	Harry
Slasher Wicks	Clifford
Sammy Sheerpig Wilding	Edgar
Fatty Henderson	Sid
Nobby Baker	Norman
Dipper Davies	Leslie

I am not sure how politically-correct some of these nicknames would be viewed now or even how the recipient viewed them at the time, if they even knew. It may well be that Hoppin Potter did not know she was called Hoppin Potter. But that is another question.

The second account is specifically about Bream schools and was written for this book by Len Wildin. He was enrolled at Bream Infants on 3 March 1919, transferred to the Church school on 31 March 1924 and left school in 1929. Thank you Len for this account.

Recollections of Bream Schools by Len Wildin:

I was born in 1915 and in 1918 was admitted to the reception class at the infant school It was a comparatively new school, warm and inviting. Life was idyllic.

One day it all changed. I must have been about five at the time. Frank Cannock and I were having a great time chasing each other around the cloakroom during playtime. When of course we should have been in the playground. Our glee was terminated by the arrival of the headmistress, Miss Young, a formidable lady. We were marched to our classroom door, lectured and told to wait. The bell went, the children marched to their classrooms. Things looked ominous. Yes, Miss Young appeared complete with a cane and a look of determination.

Like criminals we were hauled, inside and the errors of our ways made clear to all my class mates. There was no caution, no second chance, retribution was the order of the day. When the cane came down with a swish, I chickened out and took my hand away. That did me no favours because the strikes that followed had extra venom. Frank, of course had the same treatment. The rest of the day was a blur, did I deserve such punishment? Lesson No. 1.

As I grew older, the realisation came that learning was not all fun and that grappling with sums, especially shillings and pence and halfpennies was a serious business. Even to this day I've not come to terms with numbers – they are elusive things! I suppose really I'm a dreamer.

But all this time I was learning about living, absorbing life and the ways of the world. The playground was surrounded by railings and one day I put my head through them. As my ears are prominent, you've guessed right, I couldn't get it out again. Rescue eventually came after soaping the railings and my ears. Lesson No. 2.

On another occasion I returned to school after lunch when I was asked by some girls what I had for dinner. I told them, 'spotted dick.' They obviously had never heard of this dish before and rushed to tell teacher Len Wildin had been rude. For the rest of the day I had visions of more cane, but nothing transpired and sanity prevailed. Lesson No. 3.

By this time I must have been near completing my stay in the infant school and reading was top of the agenda, but there were few books to be had. The teacher introduced a scheme whereby each child should bring a shilling to school and she would buy 30 books with the sum collected. We then borrowed each others books making a mini library. We were allowed to take the books home for extra reading and the scheme worked for a while, but I never saw my book again!

Finally, one day George Sillett and I were leaving the school when we decided to enumerate all the boys in the class we could fight. We decided we could fight each other, but where's the proof?

Yes, let's sort it out. Fists were flying like windmills and no quarter was asked nor given. By this time the boys from the senior school surrounded the playground railings and their furore alerted the teacher on duty to explore, I'm glad she intervened because I'd had enough. Again I had visions of the cane but as I'd taken a bit of a battering, she considered that enough. Lesson No. 4 – Don't boast.

The day came when I was no longer an infant but a junior. That meant the boys had to transfer across the road to the C of E school. The girls continued their education where they were. It was a rude awakening! It was an old school, a cold school, a draughty school. Of the six classrooms two were heated by open fires and the others by 'tortoise' stoves. If you sat at the back of the class they provided little comfort.

We were allocated 'houses' which were Romans, Grecians, Trojans and Spartans. I never felt like a Grecian but that was my destiny and the only time 'houses' seemed to play a part was sports day!

Gone were the comfortable dual desks of the infants' school, now five to a long desk with no back. You learned never to lean back. For the first two years this was the kind of desk we experienced.

And where were the exercise books? No such luck, slates in wooden frames were the order of the day. Some were plain and others had lines on one side and squares, like graph paper on the other. If you were given a cracked slate by the monitor your problems increased.

As you progressed up the school you had the luxury of dual desk, pencils and pens. Nevertheless, each day the pens and pencils were given out by the monitors and meticulously collected again at the end of the day.

Mr William Watson was the headmaster and in my opinion not only a good headmaster but a good teacher as well. In those days there was no school secretary, no telephone, no computers. It was a full-time job and he brought enthusiasm and fervour. Enthusiastic teachers breed enthusiastic pupils. He helped to dispel some of my dread of numbers and while much of this was rule of thumb, he hadn't the time or resources to use apparatus or models to make understanding complete. The blackboard was his only visual aid and the squeaky chalk of course. He had no office and his desk was on a raised platform which could overlook two classes if necessary. Normally, there was a partition dividing the room but this could be pulled back for school assemblies, concerts, whist drives etc.

His predecessor, Mr Buck, spent a short time at the school. He was invited to resign or resign voluntary because he was brought to book for being over zealous with the use of the cane. I don't know details, after all, I was only just finding my feet as junior – sad though!

And the toilets, horrible, dirty and smelly. There were four cloakrooms, but only one had basins and running water. The water was provided by a large tank, fed by ran water from the roofs. During a hot spell when there was no rain, the tank and taps ran dry.

The playground was a jungle. In one corner there would be strong 'ossies and weak donks'; in another corner quoits with stones as big as fists flying about; sturty birds, darting hither and thither and perhaps a more discreet game of marbles. Health and Safety were unheard of. There were so many broken windows, wire netting screens were fixed to the windows. Miraculously, nobody got seriously injured.

All, in all, the school provided a sound basic education working under conditions that would not be tolerated today. Although pupils left at 14, they had a sense of responsibility and maturity to be admired.

1927 had been a landmark year in the history of Bream schools with yet another new school.

The next thirty years or so at Bream schools were to be dominated by two heads – Ivy Drabble and Willie Watson.

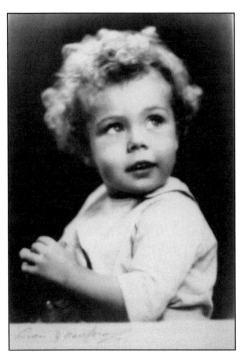

This is the only photograph I have seen of Miss Eliza Young, infant head 1913-41. It was found in some school papers. Possibly even in those days baby photos were used in school for 'guess the teacher' competitions.

'Doing her bit for the war effort'. Emma Blower of Bream School was awarded these two certificates in 1915 for helping to provide parcels for serving soldiers and sailors.
Photo courtesy of Jennifer Hancocks.

Football team, season 1921-2. Staff are Lancelot Billings (camera left), Edward Sylvester (headmaster 1918-24) and Robert Wintle.
Photo courtesy of Roy Haviland

Rugby team, season 1921-2. Teachers are Lancelot Billings (on left), Edward Sylvester (centre, headmaster) and Robert Wintle.

Photo courtesy of Roy Haviland
Hylton, Megan and Phyllis Miles
c.1923. Younger brother Tom has
not yet started school.

Standard IV girls with Annie/Nanny/Polly/Parrott/Williams c.1925. At this
stage Standard II, III and IV girls were being taught in the infant school.   *Photo
courtesy of Ella Dawe*

Senior boys c.1925. Staff are Willie Watson (left) and 'Sergeant' Davies.
Photo courtesy of Ella Dawe

A class of forty-five infants in 1926, the year of the General Strike. The teacher is believed to be Miss Gladys Howell.
Photo courtesy of Hilary Wood

CHAPTER SEVEN

1927–1958: All Change

Headteachers 1927 – 58

Church of England School	Girls School to 1951 –	Infants School
Mixed school till 1927	Secondary School 1951 – 1973	
Boys school 1927–51		
Junior school 1951 – 1986		
William Watson 1925–1953	Ivy Drabble 1927–58	Miss Young 1913–1941
Ken Pritchard 1954–1977		Miss Vater 1941–48
		Miss Alford 1948–54
		Mrs Leach 1955–1969

Premises and Organisation

On 1 September 1927, a truly formidable schoolma'am became head of the new girls' council school in Bream – Miss Ivy Drabble. The rest of her teaching career, over thirty-one years, was spent in Bream. For over twenty years she was girls' school head, then, in a reorganisation in 1951 when boys were admitted to the school, she was head of Bream Secondary School until her retirement in 1958.

Across the road in the Church school the head was Willie Watson. In career terms, he was very nearly an exact contemporary of Ivy Drabble. He replaced the discredited Cecil Buck as head of Bream mixed school in 1925. In the 1927 reorganisation he continued as head of Bream boys' school and in 1951 changed role again to be head of Bream Junior School.

Same head, same site, but three different schools. Willie Watson retired in 1953, a few years before Ivy Drabble.

These two heads dominated the educational scene in Bream for several decades and are still very well remembered by many of the village's older inhabitants. They are however remembered in very different ways. Mr Watson is universally held in high regard by ex-pupils and is usually referred to as *Willie* Watson. Miss Drabble is remembered very differently. She is never referred to as Ivy Drabble, it is always *Miss* Drabble and she still has the capacity even now, over fifty years after leaving the village, of sending shivers of recollected fear up and down people's spines.

The mid 1920s to 1950s saw further changes in the national picture in education. The Hadow Report in 1926 made a case for abandoning the elementary system of education whereby all children were entitled to a basic education up to fourteen and only a minority received any secondary education. Hadow argued that all children should transfer to secondary school at aged eleven or twelve. Such schools would be centrally placed (hence the label 'central school') to serve wide areas. Many children would need to attend such schools by bus and the curriculum would change to include woodwork, metalwork and domestic subjects.

In Gloucestershire, Hadow was difficult to implement fully because the county had many small rural schools for five to fourteen-year-olds that would be costly to modernise. Furthermore, many of these small schools in Gloucestershire were National Schools and the diocesan education authorities would not want the church schools to be passing all the children on at eleven to secondary education in council schools.

Local constraints on implementing the Hadow Report were reinforced by national problems. The 1930s saw 'The Depression' in which there was no spare cash for education. From 1939 to 1945 the country was involved in the Second World War and again educational spending was at a virtual standstill.

It was only towards the end of the war that the wheels of educational change began to move again. In 1944 the Butler Education Act finally fulfilled the promise of the Hadow Report. The word 'elementary' disappeared and all children were to receive a form of secondary education suited to their aptitude and ability. It was the Butler Act that created the 1951 Bream reorganisation. In that year Bream had a secondary school for the first time, with children actually being bussed in from as far away as Yorkley!

The 1927 Reorganisation

Bream girls' council school officially opened its doors on 1 September 1927. As previously stated the head was Miss Ivy E Drabble. Initially, there were six members of staff teaching the following standards:

standard II	Miss Meek,
standard III	Miss Miles
standard IV	Miss Williams
standard V	Mrs Ferley
standard VI	Miss Lawrence
standard VII	Miss Howells.

Standard I was still the responsibility of Miss Young in the infant school.

When Mrs Ferley, who was a supply teacher, left on 30 September the school was reorganised into five classes. A further change took place in January 1928 when the last seven standard VII girls were transferred from the Church of England school across the road, which now became exclusively a boys' school. The symbolic last link with the mixed school was finally and emphatically severed when the Singer sewing machine was sent over the road on 18 January.

The girls' school finally reached its full complement at the beginning of April 1928, when the older standard I's came up from the infants with Miss Wright. The girls' school now reverted to six classes and were allocated the nearest of the infant classrooms so that each class had their own separate room. The number of girls on roll on 1 October 1928 was 192 and they were taught by six teachers including the head.

At this point it is worth digressing for a moment to examine the layout of Bream's three schools. The National School had been built in 1862, the infants school in 1907 and the girls' school in 1927. As buildings, all three were products of their time and reflected the educational architectural designs that were then in vogue. Thus, the three buildings highlight the evolution of the corridor in education. The 1862 building has no corridor (which results in a current problem for the management committee of the community centre) and all children's lessons were in the same room. The 1907 infant school was transitional between the 1862 and 1927 design, in that it has an entrance hall (or marching hall) off which all classrooms could be accessed. The 1927 design for the girls' school was different again in that all rooms could be accessed off a long corridor. Eventually this led to a situation where different rooms (some not in the main building) could be devoted to special subjects and children would go there for particular lessons.

Inevitably the new school had teething problems. One was the toilet facilities. These were not flush toilets but operated on an earth-sprinkler system which then fed into a receptacle that had to be emptied fortnightly. This system was notoriously inefficient. In 1932 septic tanks were fitted and in 1938 flush toilets were finally installed for both the infants and girls' schools. Such luxury was not, however, the end of the story. The girls' new toilets came into use on 26 September 1938. On 23 November 1938, the roof blew off – presumably due to weather conditions. Pipes were torn from cisterns and part of the roof ended up in a neighbour's garden. As if that was not enough, on 19 December the cisterns froze.

Another modernising issue concerned the provision of electricity in the council schools. In 1929, two years after the girls' school had been built, the Forest of Dean Council School Managers asked Gloucestershire LEA why electric light had not been installed at Bream, if the Board of Education in London considered the same to be an essential requirement of any new school building. This was a contentious issue. The school was lit by oil lamps at the time, leading to the fact that evening classes could not be held and the school's lighting arrangements, particularly during the dark winter months, were criticised by HMI. The LEA attitude to the installation of electricity was a piecemeal one because they could not afford to put it in every school at the same time. However, this approach led to much criticism because every school where it *was* installed created further complaint from those that were still waiting. Having missed out in 1927, when the new build was going on, Bream council school had to wait till the Christmas holiday 1937–8 for the installation of electricity.

Another improvement in facilities to the council schools was the tarring or asphalting of the playgrounds. This was done in the June of 1939.

A further change in the council schools at this time, was a modification to the boundary to the rear of the infant school. A strip of land about five feet wide and representing some 72 square yards on the western boundary of the site, was sold for £5 in 1938 with a covenant that the purchaser was responsible for the erection of a fence. The sale enabled the extension of the doctor's house on the crossroads side.

This western boundary of the site is still something of an anomaly. The 1907 school railing, somewhat dilapidated, is still in existence here with fencing for Lindum House, erected along part of its length – in effect comprising a double boundary.

School

In 1927-8 the Church school had been reorganised as a boys' school. At the time it was blacklisted as 'defective premises.' As mentioned in the previous chapter, considerable maintenance work was done in 1927 and the school was taken off the blacklist by the Board of Education in 1928. Nevertheless, problems continued with the premises. The building was after all some seventy to eighty years old and the Church was finding it difficult to raise funding for improving the premises. Invariably the church school was the poor relation in Bream's schools and lagged behind the infants and girls' schools in terms of improvements such as tarring the playground and installing electric lighting and flush toilets.

It was not only lack of money that blighted the school. There was also a decline in school numbers. In 1943, Mrs Jones was made redundant leaving a teaching staff, including the head, of only four. There was real uncertainty over the future of the school. One of the options was closure and so what would be the point of creating considerable expenditure by trying to modernise the site? It all helped to create an atmosphere of uncertainty that was not resolved until the decision to reorganise as a junior school in 1951.

Documents in Lambeth Palace testify to how serious the situation was. The £230 spent in 1927 to get the school off the blacklist, had merely papered over the cracks. By 1935 it was clear that a further £800 was needed to be spent on basic repairs, drainage and tarmac work in the playground. In the then climate of reorganisation however, the work was deferred. By 1937 the vicar was writing to the National Society to inform them that the managers had now decided that the work 'can no longer be delayed.' But it *was* delayed and the LEA were the reason why. They had pledged £239 towards improvements but they had not yet decided 'whether the school will be required as a junior mixed school or as an infant school.'

By 1940 the managers, the Diocesan Council of Education and the National Society itself, were alarmed at the state of the school. Henry Herrick, vice-chair of the Gloucestershire Diocesan Council of Education, summed this up in a letter to the National Society dated 3 October 1940, 'The school has been allowed to get into a state of serious neglect. We are advised that, on external and internal work, an expenditure is urgently required of about £600–£700. It is a very serious matter indeed, because it is most important that no further Church school should be closed in the Forest of Dean area. . . '

The major expenditure was tarmac work on the playground. This was eventually done between December and February 1941–2, more than two years after the council schools had been done. In respect of electrification and flush toilets, it was even more a case of 'catch up.' The council schools had electric light in 1937–8 but with the church school the process was a piecemeal one. It was not finally completed (by Price Lighting of Lydney) until 1955. Up until that point, parts of the school were still lit by hurricane lamps. The situation was as laggardly in respect of flush toilets. The school had been connected to the mains water supply in 1932 but was still using earth closets instead of flush toilets as late as 1949. It was only when a decision was finally taken to reorganise the school as junior mixed, from January 1951, that flush toilets arrived. The boys' earth closets were replaced in 1950 by a new toilet block, complete with running water and flush toilets. Recently, this toilet block has been demolished to make way for the parish office.

Prior to the school being designated as a junior school in 1951, its official classification was modified in 1948 to clarify its position as a Church school. The 1944 Education Act had created two types of voluntary (church) school; voluntary controlled and voluntary aided. Under the seal of the Minister of Education on 1 February 1948, Bream Church of England School was officially given voluntary controlled status. It still is a voluntary controlled school to this day and that status determines, for example, such issues as the composition of the governing body in terms of the balance of its various elements – parents, staff, LEA, community and foundation governors.

At the request of the managers in 1952, Gloucestershire Education Committee agreed that the official name for the school, should thereafter be Bream County Primary School.

Further Reorganisation 1947–51

The Butler Act of 1944 created a spate of plans for secondary reorganisation in Gloucestershire. An additional complication in any planning was that in 1947 the school leaving age, for the first time in nearly fifty years, was raised to fifteen. In December 1947, a meeting of local managers was held to discuss the possibility of educating all thirteen to fifteen-year-old girls from Yorkley, Pillowell, Parkend, St Briavels and Bream schools at Bream itself. This plan was modified in June 1948 by a proposal to put all eleven plus non-grammar school girls at Yorkley school.

Reorganisation plans finally crystallised in 1948, when the decision was taken to make Bream Church school into a junior school. This then created the problem of what would happen to the eleven to fifteen-year-old boys needing non-grammar school education in Bream. The solution was to transform Bream girls' school into a boys' and girls' secondary modern school, to cater for eleven to fifteen-year-olds from Bream, Parkend, Pillowell and Yorkley.

The crucial date was 8 January 1951, the first day of the Easter term. Bream Junior School, under Willie Watson, began on the church school site. Across the road, on the same day, Ivy Drabble became head of Bream Secondary Modern School, which occupied the former girls' school site. Also, Bream children were transferred in both directions across the High Street. Sixty-four eight to eleven-year-old girls were transferred from the former girls' school to the junior school. In return thirty-seven, eleven to fifteen-year-old boys were transferred from the former boys' school across the road to the tender loving care of Ivy Drabble.

As secondary modern schools went, Bream's was a small one. This was to make it vulnerable in any future reorganisation scheme. At the time it opened there were 173 pupils on roll, taught in five classes. The teachers were Miss Drabble (head), Mr B James (senior master), Gordon Gwilliam, Gerald Hill, Marion Watkins, Miss D Head and Miss E Wright. By September 1952, 209 pupils were on roll and the staff complement had risen to ten. By this stage Miss Parry (domestic science) and Mr Lane (woodwork and metalwork) were officially Bream school staff and no longer classified as peripatetic teachers. In terms of the 209 on roll, the balance of the sexes was very even – 104 boys and 105 girls. As regards geographical distribution, of the fifty-six new arrivals to the school in September 1952, twenty-four were from Bream, eighteen from Pillowell, ten from Yorkley and four from Parkend schools.

Inevitably, there were problems with transporting the children to the new secondary school. Initially the LEA had laid on one bus and one car to transport children from Yorkley and Pillowell. Not surprisingly, the bus became overcrowded. The managers wanted two buses to be provided. The LEA, mindful of cost, was reluctant to accede to this demand. A further complication arose because of the ribbon settlement of Pillowell. According to the regulations, free school transport was only available to children who lived over two miles away from the school. Technically, some parts of Pillowell, for example Phipps Bottom, could be considered within the two-mile limit. The parents protested about this by organising a strike. On the first day of the new school, seventeen out of twenty-five

Pillowell children were absent. This protest continued for some weeks. Eventually the LEA agreed to subsidise travel from Parkend as well as Pillowell. Victory to the parents. Later that year there were two school buses feeding the school – one from Pillowell and one from Yorkley and Parkend. The LEA carcass was still twitching however, and early in 1952 they suggested that they could provide bicycles to enable pupils to travel to school. The managers immediately condemned that idea, pointing out that the journey was steep (Whitecroft Hill), winding (Pillowell) and beset with dangerous level crossings (Whitecroft and Parkend). The LEA accepted these arguments and the transport war was finally over.

There were other teething problems with the new secondary modern school. Obviously the switch from being a girls' to a mixed school required provision for boys' toilets. Eventually, although classes were mixed, the school operated two entrances, one for boys and one for girls. Both entrances are still in use in the current primary school.

A further problem was overcrowding. The new school had more pupils than the previous girls' school. What is more, there were no playing fields on site. To counter these problems plans were drawn up in 1951 for a new secondary school complete with playing fields at High Beech. By 1952, this scheme had been deferred indefinitely and cheaper options were being explored. In 1950, a HORSA[8] classroom had been erected to cater for domestic science but pressure from growing numbers (221 on roll by September 1953) created an urgent need for yet more classrooms. In June 1953, the managers approached the United Methodists in Parkend Road with a view to hiring their schoolroom. The chapel trustees refused. The possibility of using the Wesleyan schoolroom was then considered but the managers decided against this. Instead they opted for art and science classrooms in the playground. Work on these was begun in the summer of 1954 at the same time as the outside entrance to the girls' toilet block was completed. The art classroom and the science classroom became finally operational in January 1955. In the same year, plans were drawn up for the new kitchen, dining room and woodwork/metalwork room along the western boundary of the school.

Perhaps the new secondary school finally came of age on 21 June 1955 when the fish were delivered to stock up the school pond. The following year, by means of a loan of £42 from the LEA, the school ordered a gross

---

[8] In 1947 following the decision to raise school leaving age by one year to fifteen, an additional 168,000 pupils had to be housed throughout Britain. To cope, pre-fabricated buildings were set up in many schools under the 'Hutting Operation for the Raising of School-leaving Age' (HORSA) programme.

(144) of school badges to sell on to the pupils at 5s. 9d. each. Bream Secondary School now had a uniform. The school had well-and-truly arrived. It now had its uniform as well as fish in its pond.

Staff

Infant School Heads

Eliza Young ceased to be head of Bream Infants School on 28 February 1941. Unusually this was not the end of her connection with the school. She was, by this time, held in such high esteem that she was invited onto the board of managers of the Forest of Dean Group of Council Schools. This was an honour indeed – she was the only woman on that committee at the time. Her successor as head was Miss Vater who took up post in August 1941.

Miss Vater died, aged fifty-five, in the summer of 1947 with the result that the managers appointed Mrs Morris as acting head in temporary charge of the school. In the subsequent interviews, Miss Alford was appointed head, with effect from the beginning of May 1948. Ironically she had been previously interviewed for the Bream headship in 1941, but had been passed over in favour of Miss Vater. Miss Alford resigned in December 1954, to take up position as head at Broadwell School. Until April 1955 the infant school again had a supply head. At that point the school entered a golden phase with the arrival of Cecily Leach. Cecily was to lead the school with distinction for the next fourteen years.

Church of England School (mixed school till 1927, boys' school 1927–51, junior school 1951 onwards) Staff

As a graduate of Durham University I was fascinated, on first moving into the village, to find a property on New Road that was named Dunelm House. Dunelm is an abbreviation of Dunelmensis, the Latin name for Durham. I was intrigued by this link, but not any more, for I found out the house was so named by Willie Watson who was born and bred in the county of Durham and was headmaster of Bream Church of England school from 1925 to 1953. Dunelm House had been built by Willie Watson just before the Second World War, when the Watson family moved out from the school house at the crossroads. At the time, the school house was lit by oil lamps, there was no electricity and water came into the house by means of a hand pump in the kitchen. A large modern house on New Road, some distance from the school site, would have had a lot to recommend it as a family home.

Willie Watson was born in the village of Hunwick some eight miles south-west of Durham on 1 April 1893. His wife to be, Lillian, came from nearby Crook. Aged twenty-one, on the outbreak of the First World War, he volunteered for active service and was allocated to the 18th Battalion of the Northumberland Fusiliers. The 18th, part of Kitchener's New Army, was a Pioneer battalion. It went to France in January 1916 and saw service during the horrific battle of the Somme that summer. The battalion only existed for the duration of the war and, on demobilisation, Willie Watson went to train as a teacher at St John's College, York. His first teaching post was at March in Cambridgeshire. He and Lillian married in April 1925.

Willie Watson's first day as head of Bream mixed school was Friday 1 May 1925, following Cecil Buck's discreditable departure the day before. At the time the school desperately needed his calm and reassuring leadership. He was to provide this for the next twenty-eight years. For the first two years he was head of the mixed school, educating all Bream boys and girls from eight to fourteen. In the 1927-8 reorganisation he became head of the boys' school. He held this position till January 1951, when his role changed to head of the junior school with responsibility for all post-infant eight to eleven-year-old boys and girls. On his retirement as junior head in August 1953, he did some part-time maths teaching at Cinderford Technical College. A few years later, he and Lillian moved back up north. He died on 17 November 1974.

As a schoolmaster at Bream, Willie Watson was held in very high regard. He could be strict if the occasion required, but it rarely did. Both Roy Hook and Don Wintle have told me that they remember an instruction from Mr Watson for boys to go and cut long sticks for his use in school. I am sure such sticks were not used as canes, more probably they were used as pointing sticks for the blackboard. If used in a punitive way such a stick could be used as a long-range device to touch a miscreant at the back of the class lightly on the shoulder or ear. The cane itself was used only rarely. Mr Watson had a natural authority which, allied to an understanding of children and a sense of humour, resulted in a well behaved and orderly school. As one HMI wrote in 1937, 'The happy relations existing between the headmaster and his scholars are a good feature of this school.' His qualities are well illustrated by the story of the lardy cakes. The lardy cakes were sold at Ben Bath's Bakery for 1d. and became very popular with the children. The bakery was only fifty yards from the school playground and many children were 'wagging' school to go and buy a cake. What did Mr Watson do? He did not issue threats or patrol the perimeter. He wisely appointed a 'cake monitor' to collect the pennies and purchase and distribute the cakes. Everybody happy.

Hylton Miles remembers Willie Watson's first day as head of Bream. At the time (May 1925), Hylton was aged nine and in standard IV. Mr Watson entered the classroom in Hylton's words 'looking like an under-taker' in full morning dress – black jacket, pin-striped trousers and with a hunter watch in his lapel pocket. He then held an impromptu quiz with the children of standard IV, saying that any child who could tell him where and when the Magna Carta was signed, could immediately go home. Hylton got both answers correct, grabbed his cap and disappeared. Would a nine-year-old today know those answers?

Len Olley, an eleven-year-old evacuee from Rochford in Essex who arrived at Bream School in 1940, also remembers the impromptu quizzes and Mr Watson roaming round other classes just before lessons ended for the day. Len had an evening delivery job and suspected that some ques-tions in the quiz were loaded by Mr Watson to enable those with jobs to leave school early – a very humane gesture. Len also narrates a funny story about one of Mr Watson's impromptu end-of-afternoon visits. Len's teacher, Mrs Evan Jones, was reading from *The Pied Piper of Hamlin'* by Robert Browning. She had just uttered the lines:

'Come in', the Mayor cried, looking bigger
And in did come the strangest figure.'

Cue, enter Mr Watson to great hilarity.

Mr Watson's sense of humour is well illustrated by a story from Hylton Miles. He remembers one of Willie Watson's regular sayings to the boys of Bream School – 'It's better to sit there and look a fool than to open your mouth and let the whole world know you are one.' Wise words – and not only applicable to children.

On the humanity of the man, Hylton remembers him organising a Christmas concert after the miners' strike of 1926 to raise money. He then found out what was on each child's Christmas list and went to Wool-worths in Gloucester on a motorcycle combination and bought a present for everybody in the school.

As a very young child, Joan Watson remembers a turtle shell on top of a cupboard in her father's classroom. When she was in school with her father, she was allowed to sit in the turtle shell on the floor and remem-bers being a pirate sailing the seven seas in it. A delightful image. She also remembers the bag of wine gums and eucalyptus gums always kept in his desk as a reward.

Willie Watson was undoubtedly one of Bream's great schoolmasters. When he gave the managers notice in 1952 of his impending retirement they universally expressed their regret that he was leaving and their sincere and warm appreciation of the excellent work he had done in his long period of service. I am sure they spoke for the whole village.

Two other staff at the school who were contemporaries of Willie Watson were Herbert 'Sergeant/Popeye' Davies and Doris Worgan. Both spent their entire teaching careers at Bream.

'Sergeant' Davies

Herbert Johnson Griffeth Davies began as an assistant teacher at Bream on 2 June 1921. He retired on health grounds, twenty-five years later in January 1946. Past pupils describe him as one of Bream's more unpopular teachers.

Like Willie Watson, Herbert Davies had been in the Army during the First World War and thus was a late entrant to the teaching profession. Angus Cooper believes that he was gassed during the war. During the 1920s his nickname at school was 'Sergeant', which not only reflected his wartime service but also his strictness with children at school. As wartime memories receded in the 1930s he was more frequently referred to by the nickname 'Popeye' Davies rather than 'Sergeant.' The 'Popeye' description was due to a starey-eyed expression.

Herbert Davies' manner with children was in stark contrast to Willie Watson's. Among the words used to describe Popeye that I have heard used are 'unpopular', 'vicious', a 'swine' or – a little more tempered – 'very strict.'

Ron Watkins recalls that Popeye 'would hit you with anything.' Dave Rudge suffered from this philosophy. When he got something wrong Popeye slapped him on the back of the neck. Unfortunately, Dave had a carbuncle there, swore at Popeye and ran off home. His mum was up at school the following day to give the teacher her opinion of what he had done.

A similar situation happened with Ron Watkins. Popeye hit Ron round the head with a book. Ron's mum reacted to this. She did not mind Ron having the cane but was very angry at his being hit with a book round the ear. She marched straight into school and let rip at Popeye in front of his class. On one occasion a boy from Clements End, Testy Baker, had a fight with Popeye in the classroom. The blackboard stand, the easel and Popeye went onto the floor and by the time they were separated, Popeye was decidedly getting the worst of it.

Willie Watson had control of children because he had their respect. Popeye did not. He ruled his classroom by fear and, perhaps because children made his life difficult, he was very hard on them in turn. One habit of his (as recalled by Len Olley) which we would now condemn out-of-hand was that of using the heating stove as a spittoon. I do not know whether this was a habit picked up in the Army. It may have been a means of testing the temperature of the stove. It may have simply been a bad habit. The story is corroborated by Hylton Miles who reckoned that if you sat on the front row you could get 'showered with spittle.'

The final word on the teaching of Willie Watson and Popeye Davies goes, as always, to Hylton Miles. Hylton writes: 'Willie Watson . . . was a wonderful character, so many pupils who attended Bream School during his time I am sure feel the same as I do, that we are extremely grateful for his tolerance which at times was sufficient to try the patience of a saint . . . Mr Davies never seemed to command the respect of the boys as some of the other teachers of that time. I can recall . . . HMI paid one of his visits and on this occasion he actually smiled and I never knew from that day to this if he had been congratulated or whether he had had a sudden attack of the wind.'

As time went by, Popeye suffered increasing bouts of ill-health. In December 1937 he was off school for two weeks with 'nervous debility.' In 1940 he was ill for over two months with 'general debility.' In 1941 occurred the tragedy, dealt with later in this chapter, which may well have had a further harmful impact on his health. In August 1945 he was off school with cardiac asthenia (weak heart). He never returned to work.

Willie Watson's log book entry for 28 January 1946 is succinct – 'Mr Davies ceased duty.'

Doris Worgan

Doris Worgan was as popular as Popeye Davies was unpopular. Like Popeye she never taught anywhere else than Bream. She was born in Bream in 1901, attended Bream schools and began as a student-teacher at the mixed school under Edward Sylvester in September 1919. The following July she left to train as a teacher at Brighton College. On 5 July 1923, she returned to Bream mixed school as a qualified teacher, a post she continued in for over twenty-five years. In the later 1940s she suffered from increasing ill-health and gave up teaching at the boys' school. Nevertheless, she continued to serve the school she loved in the less demanding role of clerical assistant. She did this for over two-and-a-half years, until ill-health forced her early retirement in April 1950, at the young age of fifty-two.

Anyone taught by Doris Worgan has fond memories of her. She was 'kind.' She was 'nice.' She was 'a lovely lady' and children, even adolescent and sometimes awkward boys, were responsive to her. To a very young Joan Watson she was delightfully known as 'Auntie Dor-Dor' with the 'Dor' standing for Doris. Alternatively, the name could be spelt 'Auntie Daw-Daw' with the 'Daw' standing for Doris' initials, Doris Annie Worgan.

Following her premature retirement, Doris Worgan lived on the Tufts. She died on 1 September 1968 and is buried in Bream churchyard, in the same grave as her sister Essie, widow of Gunnery Officer Walter Wildin.

Girls' School and Secondary Modern School Staff

Miss Ivy Drabble was a head in Bream from 1927 to 1958. In terms of length of service, her thirty-one years as a Bream head makes her second only to W F Mullan. As previously mentioned she had a terrifying reputation in the village. And yet she very nearly never came to Bream in the first place. Her arrival was due entirely to the obstinacy of the then Forest of Dean Council School Managers, who were at war with the LEA over her appointment.

At the time the new girls' school was being built in Bream in 1927, it was customary for the LEA in Gloucester to advertise for vacancies and then short-list the applicants who they deemed worthy of interview by the school managers. This could lead to difficulties. In March 1927, the LEA advertised for a head of Bream girls' school to start in September. In April they wrote to the managers to advise that they had not received any sufficiently worthy applicants and they intended to re-advertise in April, with a view to interview by the managers in May.

In May, the LEA wrote again to inform the managers that the re-advertisement had not produced any candidates that the managers would want and that they therefore intended to re-advertise a second time. At this point the school managers reacted to what they saw as interference from Gloucester. They insisted on seeing the applications and, despite – or because of – the LEA recommendation, decided to interview two candidates, Miss Nicholls of Muswell Hill, London and Miss Drabble of

Pitsmoor, Sheffield. Miss Nicholls then declined to attend the interview, leaving Miss Drabble as the only candidate who the school managers then proceeded to appoint.

Thus, it could be argued that Ivy Drabble became head at Bream by default. Nobody else was interviewed and possibly she got the job solely because the local managers wanted to assert their independence from Gloucester.

In 1949, when the girls' school was being re-organised as a secondary modern school, the reverse situation seemed to apply. The Education Committee in Gloucester decided to appoint Miss Drabble as the head of the re-organised school. When the LEA asked the school managers for their view of the matter they (the managers) were unanimous that the post should be advertised. They were, however, overruled by Gloucester.

During my research, I have spoken to any number of people who knew or were taught by Miss Drabble. She was fearsome. Some of the adjectives used to describe here were 'terrifying', 'vindictive', cruel', 'vicious' and 'very strict.' And yet she was small in stature. When I asked Phyllis Lewis how she could be so frightening, Phyllis reminded me that both Hitler and Napoleon had been small.

The punishments she meted out to children were typical of that era in education but it was the way that punishment was administered that earned her fearsome reputation. Children dreaded the phrase 'see me' on their work. A rollicking by Miss Drabble was a rollicking for life.

Particularly in the early days of her headship, girls would be caned on the hand in front of the whole school. Less formally, they would be told to roll up their sleeves and then they would be smacked on the wrist for their misdemeanours. Girls were sometimes humiliated by being sent into an infant class. Anyone sitting in an unladylike way in class with their mouth open was likely to get a piece of chalk thrown in it. Girls who spoke with a pronounced Forest accent would be roundly rebuked and even, as Alice Cook remembers, laughed at and 'made to feel like a dunce.' Another favoured punishment was to shake girls really hard while at the same time speaking to them to drive a point home.

She frightened everybody. According to Marian Rees, even officials in Shire Hall were frightened of her. Parents were frightened of her. Teachers were frightened of her, and children certainly were – particularly, if they were in her bad books. Mavis Brain (née Hewlett) who was a pupil at the school and then worked in the kitchen for thirteen years, told me that she either liked you or she didn't and she either trusted you or she didn't. There was no in-between. If she did not like you she could hound you to the point of destroying your confidence, even making you ill.

Not surprisingly, there were a number of complaints about Miss Drabble. Parents came in to complain about how their daughter had been treated on any number of occasions. There could also be problems with ancillary staff. In 1948 a cleaner gave notice after only two months. There was a 'nil response' to the subsequent advert. The same lack of applications occurred again in 1952. In April 1951, the managers set up a sub-committee to consider complaints by the canteen staff against the head. The sub-committee ruled, in May 1951, that the head was in charge of the school and the canteen was an integral part of the school, therefore the head was also in charge of the canteen. Managers *hoped* the canteen staff would carry out Miss Drabble's instructions loyally.

Clearly this row rumbled on. Three special meeting of managers were held in September and October 1952 to try and resolve the issue. Miss Drabble gave assurances to try and 'meet the criticisms.' Subsequently one member of the canteen staff resigned.

Joyce James told me a story that puts a human face on the relations between Miss Drabble and the canteen staff. Miss Drabble had her lunch taken to her, by a monitor, to the staff room at the top of the stairs. Miss Drabble complained when it was jam tart every day for a week. The monitor took the complaint to the canteen. The reply was then sent back 'she should yut what she's put and be thankful she's got it.'

In defence of Ivy Drabble it could be argued that she brought very high standards to the school or, as June Hardman said to me, 'she tried to make us better than we were.' In the sense of broadening the curriculum she was somewhat ahead of her time. Strong emphasis was placed on music and on drama. How special it must have been to have watched a theatre group playing *Romeo and Juliet* under the oak trees on the far side of the playground? How unusual it must have been for a school in those days to be taken up to Westminster and be shown round Parliament? How many school choirs could claim the distinction of performing live on the BBC as Bream Girls Choir did?

A defence could even be mounted for Ivy Drabble's attack on Forest dialect and pronunciation. She reflected – albeit in her own abrasive way – a missionary zeal for Oxford English that was common in education at the time. The 1920 HMI report in the mixed school had condemned 'indistinctness of speech.' In 1933 another HMI had written 'many of the children speak badly and it would be worthwhile for the teachers to make more persistent efforts to secure improvements.' Clearly, Ivy Drabble was trying to deliver on this.

John Hale has told me an amusing story illustrating the uphill nature of her task. One day she asked her class a typical 'catch' question; 'What is the plural of sheep'? Back came the answer in a delightful Forest accent 'Ship, Miss.' I think we can all guess what her response to that would have been.

For some pupils their relationship with Ivy Drabble was a love-hate one. As Phyllis Lewis said 'I loved and admired her but I also feared her.' Joyce Vahsholtz echoes that theme 'I hated Miss Drabble until I was in her class and then I grew to love her.' At heart, Ivy Drabble wanted the best for her school and wanted the best for her girls. If that led to a lifelong love of Shakespeare or music or a career that exceeded parents' expectations then perhaps one could understand, if not forgive, the means that delivered that end.

Miss Drabble, for all her reputation as a dragon, did have a human side. June Hardman remembers being taken on a bus all the way to the Malvern Show so she could see a dress that she (June) had made. Nancy Hoare remembers being escorted north on the train at the end of term. Miss Drabble was returning to Sheffield on holiday; Nancy was going to see her parents in Rotherham. Outside school Miss Drabble was convivial company. She also made sure that Nancy caught the Rotherham connection in Sheffield station.

Jean McPherson gives a human angle to Miss Drabble the iron disciplinarian. Jean had been part of the choir that had won a shield at the Cheltenham Music Festival. The shield was housed in Bream School for a year. Jean was becoming cross as the year-end approached when the shield would have to be returned because, as yet, it had not been engraved with the name of the current winners. Jean scratched 'Bream Girls' on the blank escutcheon with a pin. Miss Drabble noticed and demanded in assembly that the culprit own up. Jean did. When Miss Drabble asked why, Jean explained and Miss Drabble understood. She did not punish Jean and she did not announce in assembly the name of the guilty party, so nobody knew what had happened – till now.

The final comment on Miss Drabble's humanity comes from Peggy Baynham. Peggy remembers a Christmas party when all of the teaching staff turned up wearing gym slips, including Miss Drabble. Being short and plump she was apparently a sight for sore eyes. Well done Miss Drabble. Human after all.

As part of my research I have studied all the surviving log books kept by Bream heads. I have to report that Ivy Drabble kept the most voluminous records of all of them. And as time went by they became more voluminous. This is unusual. With time one would expect the record to become more sparse. Not so with Ivy Drabble. In the first twenty years or so of her headship her log book entries averaged some fourteen pages per year. The last ten years saw that average rise to fifty-nine pages per year. She certainly kept her eye on every aspect of school life, right up to the day she retired.

There is rumoured to be a ghost in Bream school. Its presence has been felt several yards down the corridor, from what used to be the girls' schools entrance. It is most noticeable in the area round the foot of the stairs leading up to the old staff room. Could the ghost be Ivy Drabble? Those who have sensed the presence of the ghost are convinced that it is female and short in stature, as Miss Drabble was. The stairs, near where the sightings have occurred, led at one time not only to the staff room but to Ivy Drabble's office. She was known to be a stickler for stopping girls running in the corridor and was frequently at the bottom of those stairs and in the nearby cloakroom (currently the staff toilets and cleaners' storeroom) to make sure everyone was behaving.

The ghost's behaviour has similarities to Ivy Drabble's behaviour when she was head of Bream Girls School. Yet those who have sensed the ghost's presence have never felt threatened by it. It is a friendly ghost. It is a benevolent ghost simply keeping an eye on the place. Could this possibly be the terrifying Ivy Drabble? Who knows? Underneath that crusty exterior was there a well-meaning person who cared passionately about the school . . . and possibly still does?

Ivy Drabble tried to give her girls 'class.' Once a Drabble girl always a Drabble girl. The girls who had been through her school would always carry the Drabble mark. Her impact on the school was considerable and lasting.

Ivy Drabble finally retired in December 1958. To commemorate her long service to the school she was presented with a gold watch and case at her last Speech Day on 9 December, at the Miners Welfare Hall, thirty-one years after she was the only applicant for the headship of Bream Girls School.

The previous chapter described the impact of the First World War on the village. Barely twenty years later a similar tragedy was to strike.

The Second World War 1939-45

Arguably, the Second World War had more impact on the village that the war of 1914–18. For one thing, there are more fatalities listed on the Cenotaph – twenty-five as against twenty-one. For another thing, the village and the schools hosted a considerable number of evacuated children.

Child evacuation in this country was not unique to 1939-45. As I pointed out in *Retrieving Wenty's Sturty Bird*, in July 1917 Bream hosted thirty children from London who came on holiday to gain respite from the Zeppelin raids that were hitting the capital that summer. A further evacuation took place during the 1926 General Strike, as described in chapter six, when a number of miners' children were evacuated from Bream to London.

The Second World War evacuation, however, was very different in scale to that of 1917 or 1926. Far more children were involved. Also the evacuation period was considerably longer – some arrived in September 1939 and the last evacuees did not leave the village till 9 July 1945.

The war began on Sunday 3 September 1939. By Friday 8 September, the end of the first week of term, seventeen evacuees were present in Bream's schools. Eight were in the girls' school, six in the boys' and three in the infants' (James Duff, Yvonne Enright and James Minor). However, the anticipated bombing raids on British cities did not materialise in the winter of 1939–40. It was well-and-truly the 'phoney war' and by Christmas 1939 most of the evacuees had returned home.

The war 'proper' began in Western Europe in the spring of 1940. France was invaded on 12 May, and within a few weeks the British Expeditionary Force was being evacuated from Dunkirk and then on 22 June France capitulated. Britain now stood alone against a potential German invasion.

In such circumstances, evacuation began in earnest all over again and on a larger scale. On Sunday 2 June, 127 children left Rochford in Essex for Bream. They travelled via Paddington to Gloucester railway station, where they then were conveyed by coach to Bream. They arrived at midnight, were shepherded into the Miners Welfare Hall (now Bream Rugby Club) and then allocated to the families who had volunteered to take them in. What a long and emotional day that must have been.

After a few days to acclimatise, the evacuees began school. Twelve went to the infant school, with Miss Baker as their teacher. Fifty-eight went to the boys' school with their own two teachers and were taught as separate classes until January 1941, when they were integrated with the Bream classes. In the girls' school there were fifty-seven evacuees taught separately by two Essex teachers, until they were integrated in May 1941. Courtesy of Miss Drabble and her log book, we know the schools from which the fifty-seven came – eleven came from Sutton School, twenty-three from Rochford juniors, twenty-two from Rochford seniors and one from a private school. In September, the twelve evacuees moved up into the senior schools and a further twelve evacuees arrived in the village.

As the Blitz spread from London to other major cities, further evacuation became necessary. Bristol, because of its port facilities and its aircraft industry, was a prime target for the Luftwaffe and, in May 1941, Bream received a further major evacuation, this time from Filton. The total number was sixty-two children, fourteen infants, twenty-two boys and twenty-six girls. Again, courtesy of Miss Drabble, we know the Filton schools involved – Shields Road and Charborough Road. The accompanying teacher for the girls was Miss Shepherd. Again they were taught in a separate class. On May 2 1941, Miss Drabble, in her wisdom, devised a creative solution to the problem of integration. She closed the school for the afternoon and sent the girls out on a nature ramble in three groups. The composition of each group was determined by age only, thus Bream, Filton and Rochford girls were forced to mix. A check on numbers in June 1941 reveals that sixty-one of the 202 on register in the girls' school were evacuees – over 30 per cent. It was a slightly lower percentage in the boys' school, forty-seven out of 194 (24 per cent).

After the summer of 1941, bombing raids on British cities decreased and the threat of invasion disappeared entirely. Thereafter, evacuees gradually returned home. By May 1942, all Filton evacuees had left the boys' school. By February 1943, the last evacuee had left the infants school although some were in the village for the duration of the war. On 9 July 1945 following a farewell picnic at Prior's Lodge, the remaining three girls and one boy were taken back to Rochford by Miss Burnham.

In the early days of the evacuation there were a few skirmishes and fights in the boys' school playground – Bream versus Rochford – but that soon settled down and the evacuees were made to feel at home in the village. They were on the whole supported in their foster homes. They had their own teachers, the Women's Voluntary Service (WVS) set up a daily after-school evacuee club and some teachers ran a weekly home-letter-writing session. In return, village children were enriched by having regular contact with other children from different parts of the country. Many made lifetime friendships. Many in the village still remember the wonderful concert staged in January 1941 by the children of Bream and Rochford, as their contribution to Spitfire Week. It was one of the highlights of the war years.

It is gratifying to know that since '*Retrieving Wenty's Sturty Bird*' was published in 2001, there has been an annual reunion of Rochford evacuees which started in 2003.

In 1939, there was a widespread assumption that there would be massed bombing raids on Britain's military installations, ports, industrial sites and possibly major centres of population. Rural areas such as Bream were comparatively low-risk. Indeed, Bream was part of a designated 'reception area', safe enough to host evacuated children from major cities. Even so, the village was in the vicinity of any bombing flight path to Bristol and the South Wales ports. Consequently, air-raid precautions were being put in place before the war began in 1939.

Heads were already attending briefing meetings on air-raids as early as February 1938. When the war actually started in September 1939, none of the schools had blackout facilities, thus the timing of the school day was altered. In the winter of 1939–40, children left school at 3.15 p.m. rather than 3.30 p.m., so that they could get home while it was still light. In the winter of 1940–1 this was amended to a 4 p.m. winter closure.

In July 1940, the county architect visited Bream to discuss safety provision in the schools in the event of an air-raid. He decided against building air-raid shelters on site but did make arrangements for all school windows to be made shatter-proof. This was done by treating them with cerrux varnish. In 1941, schools were kitted out with fire buckets, sand and stirrup-pumps to put out any small fires. Crucially though, it was not until August 1942 that blackout was finally fitted in the schools and by then the worst danger had passed.

In 1939, all schools received Circular 352 with instructions on what to do when the air-raid siren blew. The circular instituted the 'five-minute rule.' A direct hit on the schools would have been catastrophic and all children, on hearing the siren, were to be ordered to disperse. They would go home – if home was within five minutes of the school. Those who lived outside the five-minute zone were, in a group of no more than two, to go to a home within the zone. When the 'all clear' sounded they were (in theory) to return to school. There were at least a dozen occasions according to the log books when the children were dispersed and sent home. The last recorded raid was on 28 August 1942 – around the time that the blackout curtains were being fitted.

At the beginning of the war, everybody was issued with a gas mask. Every child was required to take their gas mask to school and was shown how to put it on and take it off. The infants had special Mickey Mouse masks – I wonder if any of them has survived?

Education has always had a creative capacity to 'make do.' When the blackout curtains were removed from the girls' school in August 1945, Miss Drabble had them made into PT shorts. In 1947, eight Air Raid Precaution (ARP) warden's helmets were delivered to the girls' school as war-surplus. They were used as rounders bases.

School holidays changed significantly because of the war situation. The long summer holiday was split into two parts. The first part occupied the first two or three weeks in August. School then resumed until a further two-week holiday in September/October, designated as the autumn holiday. The Government then decided that schools should not fully close at the end of July at all. They designated the holiday as a 'special period', whereby the school had a skeleton staff and remained open to children for recreation and any emotional support they may need. Staff involved in the 'special period' were then allowed to take their holiday in lieu during term time. It appears that at Bream the children made very little use of the 'special period.' Perhaps term-time attendance was more than enough for them.

Both the boys' and the girls' schools were involved in war work. As part of the 'Dig for Victory' campaign, the boys worked three gardens; their own to the rear of the boys' school premises, a second by the searchlight battery billet at Devil's Chapel and a third under the trees in the girls' school towards Hang Hill Road. Both schools took part in government initiatives for specific collections, for example blackberries, rose-hips and horse chestnuts. The whole school would take part in these collections with different classes going to different locations in the neighbourhood. One of these expeditions was to have truly tragic consequences.

The rose-hips were sent to a collection centre at Coleford. The horse chestnuts were sent off to MacLeans Ltd. of Brentwood in Middlesex. On 1 May 1942, the boys' school was closed completely for ten days, as directed by a government memo, so that the older boys could assist farmers in planting potatoes. They also helped with harvesting the potatoes during their two-week autumn holiday. Even as late as 1945, boys were still helping out on the farms.

The war would be a very personal thing in a tight-knit community like Bream. Everyone in the schools would know someone somewhere on active service. In the boys' school, William John Norris was called to a medical board at Gloucester on 30 August 1940. He passed A1 – fit for active service overseas. His call-up papers arrived and he left the staff of the boys' school on 30 September 1940. Consequently, the school had to be reorganised from five classes down to four. Mr Norris returned to the school on 10 June 1943 having been discharged from the Army. Prior to that, one of the staff in the girls' school, Mrs Jenkins, was given four days compassionate leave – her husband had been granted embarkation leave before going overseas.

The news everybody dreaded, of a death in action, usually came by telegram. One such arrived at the boys' school on 25 October 1943. The log book entry for that day states 'Miss Worgan left school during the lunch hour having been informed by the Admiralty that her brother-in-law was missing, presumed killed, on active service.'

Doris' brother-in-law was Walter Wildin, whose ship *HMS Charybdis* had been torpedoed off the Channel Islands on the night of 23/24 October. Such was the dearth of teachers in the boys' school, that Doris resumed duty the day after the news came through. No doubt the school was very quiet that day.

The end of the war was greeted with great celebration. Tuesday 8 May 1945 was officially proclaimed Victory in Europe Day (VE Day) and all Bream children were given the Tuesday and Wednesday as holidays from school. At 3.30 p.m. on Friday afternoon 11 May, all three schools joined together in a Victory Tea Party in the council school's playground. An amazing 800 cakes were baked specially for the event. I wonder how many were left at the end of the evening? The following Thursday 17 May , the children were given a free cinema show, two tickets for free rides at the fair and 6*d*. spending money. On Friday 6 July, the girls' school held a party at Prior's Lodge to bid farewell to Miss Burnham and the four remaining evacuee children – they were to return to Essex on the Monday. In September, when Japan had surrendered, further celebrations were held including a young people's 'social' in the school.

At the beginning of the war all locational signs had been removed because of the threat of invasion. Thus, the place names on the signpost at the crossroads by the school, had been removed and put into storage. The theory was that if German parachutists landed in the village they would not know where they were. But the infants' school presented a particular problem in this respect because it had its name 'Bream Infants School' carved in stone letters a foot high, above the main entrance. The solution to this problem was to hide the giveaway 'Bream' part of the carving behind a board.

At the end of the war the crossroads signs could thankfully go back up and '"Nowhere" Infants School' could proudly revert to 'Bream Infants School.' The only reminders of this particular episode in the history of the schools are four screw fixing holes around the carved label 'Bream'.

Standards of Health

Infectious diseases continued to be a threat to schoolchildren during this period. Health was, however, improving and there were fewer epidemics and the schools were less likely to close. There was a serious measles outbreak in January and February 1940 and despite the fact that attendance fell to less than 50 per cent in the infants' school, the LEA instructed that the schools stay open even though the registers were not to be marked till the end of February. The major flu epidemic in October 1957 was dealt with similarly. The schools stayed open despite an attendance of only some 50 per cent.

Between 1927 and 1951, twenty-two five to fourteen-year-olds were buried in Bream churchyard. Children were still very vulnerable. One such entry in the girls' school log book states 'March 12th 1930. Death of a standard IV girl, Audrey Lucas.' Audrey was a vivacious ten-year-old who died of diphtheria. That particular disease was not part of an inoculation programme until the 1940s.

The LEA continued to promote healthy living among the school population. Dental and medical checks were now an annual event for every child. By the 1950s children were also being checked regularly for pediculosis (more commonly known as 'nits'), hearing problems and flat feet. Inoculations were administered by school medical staff and in 1953, for the first time, pupils were taken down to Whitecroft Memorial Hall to undergo an x-ray screening.

The previous chapter mentioned that in 1927 classroom temperatures were as low as 42-48 °F. In 1930 the managers resolved that if thermometers were not recording at least 56 °F (13 °C) schools would not open.

In June 1942 the Forest of Dean school managers decided to provide school meals in Bream. The following month the heads of all three Bream schools visited Ruardean Hill School, to see their meals service in operation. School meals for all in Bream began officially on 20 September 1943 when the pupils returned from the 'autumn holiday.' Willie Watson was in charge of the scheme. There were two kitchens – one in the boys' school, the other in the girls school. The dining rooms were in the infants' school and the girls' school. Thus the girls' kitchen cooked for the girls and the boys' kitchen cooked for the boys and infants. The food cooked in the boys' kitchen was taken across the road, to be eaten by the boys and the infants – a safer system avoiding the risk of infants crossing the road. Later, the boys ate in their own school and the infants' food was sent across by trolley. On that first day, Miss Drabble recorded 113 meals served for the girls. Willie Watson recorded 254 for the boys and infants.

Interestingly, until 1949, the girls' kitchen lit the cooking stove by using a match and a pint of paraffin. In 1949 staff decided to discontinue this practice as being too dangerous.

In 1945 the managers protested because the price of a school meal rose to 5d. In 1957 it rose to 1/-. The cost depended on circumstances and some were entitled to free meals. Milk (a third of a pint) by this stage was already being provided free of charge for all children.

The school meals system seemed to work well, although on occasion there could be tension. Mention has already been made of tension between Miss Drabble and the staff of the girls' canteen in 1951. On one occasion some staff refused to report for duty. Across the road there could also be tension and in the late 1950s the managers threatened the cook with dismissal for heating up pre-cooked meat. Whatever was left over from the kitchens was sold to Mr Teal of Sun Green as pigswill.

Then, as now, accidents continued to happen to children. During this time several infants had to go to the doctor with problems to do with their noses. It might be better for everybody concerned if noses didn't grow till the age of eleven – then they might not have things pushed into them! What's more they might not get picked. In 1939 the school took an infant to the doctor because of a bead up the nose. The doctor removed it. A few years later staff took a child to the doctor for a crayon up its nose. This time the doctor became 'Doctor No' and said that the child should be brought back for the evening surgery – although by then it had been sneezed out. A few years after that the school took another infant to the doctor, with an acorn stuck up his nose. This time Doctor O'Driscoll successfully played the part of a tree surgeon!

A fascinating sideshow on school accidents occurred in 1948 when the National Health Service was set up, funded by National Insurance contributions. At the time there was considerable uncertainty as to how the new system would work. In July 1948, a ten-year-old girl fell in the playground. A fracture or dislocation was suspected. The school and others were uncertain who was to do what under the new scheme. Over half an hour's phone calls then ensued. The head rang the doctor, then the Medical Officer of Health for West Dean, who advised talking to the School Medical Officer's Department, who advised talking to the County Education Department. Eventually, two hours after the incident, the child was taken home and the mother advised to take her to the doctor's herself that evening.

A more serious accident occurred to a member of staff of the girls' school in 1950. On Saturday 4 March, Miss Wright had been in the centre of Bristol. It was University Rag Week. She suffered serious burns to her face caused by a magnesium flare that had been thrown by a student. It was seven weeks before she returned to work.

The tragic description of 'Accidentally Killed While Blackberrying' was written by Arthur Parr, vicar of Bream, in the burial register on 24

September 1941. It referred to Alfred Mark Stanley Johns. Stan Johns was just twelve years old. He was a pupil at Bream boys' school.

Mention has already been made of government initiatives in schools to help the war effort, by collecting fruit from the countryside. One such initiative, Memorandum Number 27, concerned the collection of black-berries. Bream schools acted on this memorandum. class 3 of the boys' school went out collecting on the afternoon of 15 September 1941. The following afternoon, 16 September, class 6 went out on the same task. On the afternoon of Wednesday 17 September, it was the turn of class I, the top class in the boys' school.

The account of what happened next is derived from the school log book, a report of the coroner's inquest, conversation with three witnesses and a visit to the site of the tragedy itself.

On the day in question Stan had lunch at home in Oakwood Road. He told his father, Stanley Johns, that he was going blackberrying and nutting that afternoon. He left home at 1.15 p.m. to return to school.

At around 2.30 p.m. some twenty-one boys left school with their teacher, 'Popeye' Davies, to go to Noxon Park. Before they left, the headmaster, Willie Watson, gave them a general warning to the effect of 'no foolhardiness.' When the class arrived at Noxon Park, Popeye told them to split up. Some stayed outside the Park, blackberrying. Others went inside. Stan went inside. Noxon Park, in a phrase used at the inquest, is 'one of the most dangerous places in the Forest.' It contains a number of crevices, narrow at the top and deep and wide below – the result of old iron mine workings.

The spot where the accident happened was one of these crevices called 'The Joint' which, measured by the police at the time of the accident, was 38 feet deep. Across the top of it was a fallen ash tree. Using this tree as a bridge, it was possible to cross to the other side. Possible, but extremely dangerous.

Stan did attempt to cross. According to one eyewitness he ran across. In doing so he stepped on a loose stick which rolled under his foot, causing him to fall feet first down into the crevice. He suffered a fractured skull.

Popeye was immediately summoned. He, in turn, sent for help to the nearest house. This arrived in the persons of Ernie Johns and Henry Batten, both of whom knew where the entrance to the Joint was. They carried the badly injured Stan out and took him to the nearby house, where the village nurse and doctor were summoned as well as the head-master.

Stan was later taken to Lydney Hospital and then to Gloucester Royal, where he underwent emergency surgery. He died two days later.

At the inquest, the family argued that the boy should not have been where he was and that the school Authorities were responsible for his death. Nowadays in such a situation the case for negligence would probably be a strong one. But this was 1941, wartime and a different world.

Now a formal risk assessment would be carried out before any school trip takes place. In 1941 the only risk assessment was 'common sense.' Further it could be argued, and was argued at the inquest, that all of the boys were familiar with Noxon Park and its dangers. Also, this was the top class and boys such as Stan would be leaving school and entering the world of work in less than eighteen months time.

The Gloucester Coroner recorded a verdict of 'accidental death' and stated that he found no evidence of negligence on anybody's part. 'The boys knew where they were going and are accustomed to the neighbourhood. It seems that it is one of those unfortunate accidents that cannot be guarded against.'

No doubt the coroner made what he considered to be an objective judgement. However, it is worth speculating for a moment what might have happened if he had found 'negligence.' How would teachers have reacted to government requests for 'war work' by schools if there were a possibility of legal action? Would they be as co-operative? Would a negligence verdict have had some impact on the war effort? In the context of the time it would have had to be a very brave coroner who would have made any other decision. An 'accidental' verdict 'satisfied' everybody – except the family.

The father, Stanley Johns, did not agree with the verdict. He thought Popeye was responsible for what had happened and told him so. The evidence of classmates at the inquest showed that Stan had on a number of previous occasions jumped the Joint. Ken Lewis (aged thirteen) also testified that Stan's father had on several occasions warned him not to go to the Joint because of the dangers. It seems ironic now that the boy should be there on a school outing.

It must have been a very traumatic experience for Popeye Davies. Aged fifty-six at the time, he taught for less than four years afterwards and retired from teaching at the end of the war on grounds of ill health. One part of his evidence at the inquest came under scrutiny. He said he had not taken any boys to Noxon Park before. In later evidence, one of the pupils stated that he had previously been with Mr Davies to Noxon Park.

The funeral was held on Wednesday 24 September 1941. The bearers were Percy Brookes, Cyril Jenkins, Tom Yearsley and A. Hapsey-Jenkins. Some of Stan's friends were pall-bearers – Ken Lewis, Patrick Carson, Tony Lansdown, David McKinnel and Jimmy Birch.

The whole school attended the funeral.

Holidays

By the late 1950s the pattern that we know today of the six-week summer holiday from the end of July to the beginning of September had come into existence. Half-term holidays in October, February and May tended to be two days with Christmas and Easter holidays being at least two-and-a-half weeks long. Because local industry was largely based on coal, children were also, for a time, given a week off in early July for Miners' Week.

Royal events – visits, weddings, funerals and coronations continued to be celebrated with special holidays. Thus, all Bream children had the day off on 20 November 1947, for Princess Elizabeth's marriage to Prince Philip. They also had a three-day holiday on 1, 2 and 3 June, 1953, for the present Queen's Coronation. No doubt, for the former event, the flag-poles on both sides of the road would have flown the Union Jack. Sadly by the time of the 1953 Coronation, the infants' flagpole had been taken down (February 1948) for safety reasons.

Several former pupils have told me of an interesting 'royal' custom that prevailed in Bream schools at this time. On 'Oak Apple Day', 29 May , the anniversary of the Restoration of the Monarchy in 1660, it was customary to wear an oak apple in commemoration of Charles II's hiding in the branches of an oak tree from Cromwell's troops after the battle of Worcester in 1651. Apparently, in Bream, if you forgot to wear an oak apple on that day other pupils would whip you with nettles.

Annual school outings continued to be school holidays, going to places such as Weston, Cheddar, Oxford, Windsor, London and Bournemouth. There was also an increase in class-based trips and other groups going to a wide variety of events. Children now were regularly going on theatre visits and to musical events and films. In June 1948 both boys' and girls' schools took children to the Three Counties Show at Staverton. On Saturday 1 October 1951, as previously mentioned, Miss Drabble organ-ised a trip to London for sixty-six girls and parents, that went to Parliament, Westminster Abbey, the Tower and Regents Park Zoo. In July 1953, Gordon Gwilliam took eleven boys to Bristol to see Gloucestershire take on the Australians at cricket. Interestingly, the LEA approved this as an educational visit. Gloucester was very keen on promoting educational visits, even subsidising some of them by grant. In May 1952, thirty-six class 1 pupils from the secondary modern went on a trip to Gloucester Cathedral. The cost of the bus was £4. 10s. Gloucester paid £2. 14s. of the amount.

Attendance holidays were still being given, as were holidays for school and Forest sports days, eisteddfods, elections when the schools were used as polling stations and Sunday school treats. In respect of the latter, they had a reduced impact on the allocation of holidays. By the 1930s the schools would close early at 3.30 p.m. rather than give a full half-day holiday for a Sunday school treat.

Inevitably, bad weather continued to disrupt attendance at school. Willie Watson wrote in March 1947 that the weather was the worst he had known in his twenty-two years at Bream. There were snowdrifts five foot high in the playground. Amazingly, nine boys reported to school on 6 March 'after the worst snow storm in living memory in Bream.' At the end of January 1954 the secondary modern buses from Yorkley and Parkend could not reach Bream because of the snow. Surprisingly some children had actually walked to the school from Yorkley and Pillowell. One of the teachers, Mrs Walters, walked from St Briavels and arrived at 11 a.m. There were no local radio in those days to advise of snow closure.

On 25 November 1954, the secondary modern school had a partial holiday for an unprecedented special event – the first ever school Speech Day. This was held at Bream cinema at 2.30 p.m. and followed by tea at the school at 4.15 p.m. Cups were awarded to the three different school houses – Argyle, Dean and Snowdonia, named after National Forest Parks.

The winners were:

> The Harold Craddock Cup for Industry – Snowdonia
> The Percival Cup for Cricket – Snowdonia
> The Ralph Williams Cup for Football – Argyll
> The Arnold Rounders Shield – Snowdonia
> The Hockey Cup – Dean.

The cinema was an ideal venue for Speech Day – except it did not have a piano. In 1956 a piano was specially transported from the school to the cinema and back again so that it could be used to accompany the choir.

Children and their doings

In respect of children's misdemeanours and how they were dealt with by the schools, some discussion has already taken place of how Willie Watson and Ivy Drabble ran their schools. In terms of specific incidents in the boys' school, the caretaker found one of the boys in school at 6.30 a.m. on a January morning in 1945. The head immediately informed the police and the matter was in court within a week. In February 1951, an official complaint was received by Willie Watson about damage to a garden wall adjoining the playground. The long-suffering neighbours of the Church of England school, could probably compile a quite effective dossier of complaints made over the years.

A number of problems in the schools at this time occurred from out-of-hours activities. Permission had been given by the managers to set up a youth club in the infants' school in 1943. The catalogue of damage over the next few years was depressing. In March 1943, the curtain pole came out of its socket and the curtain was torn. In May, the piano had been roughly moved about and almost came off its legs. Both instances were reported to Mrs King the youth club leader. In June 1944, the partition was damaged in the infants' hall and at the Victory in Japan (VJ) young people's social in September 1945, the piano lost two of its notes. There was further damage to the piano in 1947 but this, according to the piano tuner, was caused by mice and not the youth club.

In 1948, the managers laid down that an adult should be present every time the youth club met. Finally, in 1950, the managers ran out of patience and gave the youth club an ultimatum – find alternative accommodation or use the girls' school rather than the infants' school. Managers thought the girls' school furniture would be more suitable. Perhaps too, many infants had been saying – along with Baby Bear – 'Who's been sitting in my chair and they've broken it?'

A further problem experienced by the infants' school in the 1940s was that older boys were coming onto the site to do woodwork. These senior boys were not just coming from the boys' school across the road, but from other schools such as St Briavels and Pillowell. The only male toilets available to them on site were those for the infant boys. In May 1946, the cleaner reported the manual instruction class had now broken all the seats in the infant boys' toilets. This was probably not a matter of renaming the manual instruction class as the 'toilet destruction class,' for I am sure it was not wilful – more of a matter of horses for courses.

A couple of stories told to me are well worth recording. The first concerned an infant aged about four who was in Margaret Burdess' class in the 1930s. Margaret Burdess was the daughter of Mr Burdess the under manager at Princess Royal. The infant had been primed by his mischievous uncle to ask Miss Burdess a question. He did. He asked, in all innocence, 'Miss can my uncle have a lend of your face to go ratting'? The infant very quickly realised that had not been a sensible question to ask. His uncle kept a low profile in the village, over the next few weeks.

The second story, as told to me by Dave Rudge, concerned Dave Hodges and Slogger (Gerald) James who were doing a test on capitals of countries in Mr Watson's class. Slogger was copying Dave's answers:

Mr Watson asked 'What is the capital of England?'
Dave wrote 'London.' Slogger wrote 'London.'
Mr Watson asked 'What is the capital of France?'
Dave wrote 'Paris.' Slogger wrote 'Paris.'
Mr Watson asked 'What is the capital of Greece?'
Dave wrote 'Athens.' Slogger wrote 'Athens.'
Mr Watson then asked 'What is the capital of Peru?'
Dave wrote 'I don't know.' Slogger wrote 'I don't know either.'

Parents and their Doings

During this period, the relationship between schools and parents became more of a partnership. Schools were keener to show parents what children were doing in class. Parents became more involved. Open days and parent's evenings became a regular feature of school life and Parent Teacher Associations (PTAs) were formed with a view principally of raising money to provide better school facilities.

No doubt there were still confrontations taking place between parents and school but either they were less frequent or were simply not mentioned in any record that I have seen. We know that a number of parents had arguments with Miss Drabble but very little of this seems to be documented. Ruth Hirst tells me that one parent actually pushed Miss Drabble into a cupboard but I have not found any written record of the incident.

One situation that is recorded occurred in the boys' school where in 1944 Mrs Bradley came into school, 'created a disturbance and used bad language.' She refused to leave and the police were called. They arrived two hours later. Mrs Bradley had already left.

An open day for parents was a regular event at the girls' school. Usually this involved a concert being given by the girls. This was usually well attended but because it was in the afternoon the audience was principally mums. In July 1948 the open day broke fresh ground. It was held at 6.30 p.m. 'to enable fathers to visit the school.' Unfortunately, it later reverted to the afternoon when the school became a secondary modern. Even so, the school open days were spectacular events. In July 1952, the school had displays of needlework, woodwork, basketry, laundry and other work done by school hobby groups. There was also a demonstration of singing and country dance and a boys versus girls rounders match. Parents were also fund-raising for the school.

This was also happening in the infants' school. In June 1950, an infant PTA was formed when Miss Alford was head. Among the early purchases was a playground see-saw, bought from Galt Toys in 1956, at a price of £9. 9s.

School Links with the Community

As in previous generations, the community continued to meet at the schools. The infant school for a time housed the youth club before it was transferred to the girls' school. In 1956 the youth club was given permission by the Church school managers to use the playground for the latest teenage craze – roller skating. However, they then started to use it for five-a-side soccer as well and were consequently reported by the managers to the Adult Youth Committee for breaching the terms and conditions of use. Other organisations regularly using the schools were the Girl Guides, the Brownies, the Horticultural Society and the Choir. In 1955, the Choir was officially recognised by the managers of the Church school as an educational class – thus the LEA would pay the cleaner's fees for them. The fees for normal hire of the Church school were 10/- for an annual meeting and 2/6d. for any other meeting.

Even wedding receptions were held in the schools. The infant room was used for this purpose until 1947, when the managers decided to discontinue such bookings because alternative accommodation was now available. Across in the Church school it cost £1 to hire the building for a wedding reception in 1949. This included 7/6d. for the cleaner's wages.

Links with the Church

In respect of the Church school the link with Bream Church continued to be as close as in previous years. The vicar was the 'official correspondent' and any letter that needed writing was written by him. When the school adopted Voluntary Controlled status in 1948, it was the vicar, Reverend Charles Vernon, who became chair of the new governing body. In the 1950s the new vicar, Reverend J W Davies, assumed that role. In terms of direct contact, possibly due to a conflict of interest issue, the vicar ceased to take the Scripture inspection in the boys' school in the 1930s. This was now done by an external examiner.

The vicar was regularly in the infants' and the girls' schools and usually undertook the religious education (RE) inspections. Relations were usually harmonious between the Church and the council schools. The only possible sour note to have occurred was in 1928, when the vicar, William Joyce, made a request for a half-day holiday in the council school. The managers refused. From one perspective this could have been sour grapes arising from the differences of opinion in the 1920s over building a new school in the village. From another perspective, it could simply be that the managers had already used up their holiday allocation.

Inside the Classroom

Throughout this period the scholarship exam, or eleven plus as it came to be known, was an important feature of school life. In both the boys' and girls' schools in the 1920s, 30s and 40s a decision would be taken early in the year as to which pupils should be entered for the scholarship. Generally it was about fifteen pupils in each school. The exam took place in March and pupils who had done well would then be invited for an oral interview at the school concerned. Usually this was Lydney Grammar; occasionally it was Monmouth. If successful, the pupil involved would be offered a free place. If they did not merit a full scholarship, they could be offered a half-scholarship, where they were offered a place if parents paid half the cost of the fees. Several pupils a year from Bream did gain a full scholarship. A similar number would be offered a half-scholarship but in most cases this would be declined for financial reasons.

During the war itself, evacuee children could be put in for the scholarship at Bream, but the exam papers would not be set or marked in Gloucestershire. They would be sent back for the pupils' own LEA to mark. Scripts from local pupils were sent to Gloucester for marking.

After the 1944 Act, education was reorganised. Secondary education became available for all and elementary education disappeared. Thus, in Bream, all children could now take the eleven plus scholarship exam in their last year at the newly created Bream Junior School. The result determined whether they went to grammar school or the new secondary modern. The half-scholarship place disappeared. In 1951, the first year of Bream Junior School, seven pupils passed the scholarship for entry to grammar school.

In the early 1950s the exam papers consisted of three English tests, two arithmetic tests and one intelligence test. Tests were taken under timed conditions. As a ten-year-old who sat those tests, I vividly remember the examiners' instructions 'pencils up' and 'pencils down.' I also remember being crammed for typical intelligence test questions such as 'Who is the father of the son of William Shakespeare?' and 'How many balls of string does it take to reach the moon?'

Other entrance examinations that were sat in Bream were for specific mining, engineering and commercial courses that were available at the Mining and Technical College at Cinderford.

The school curriculum continued to develop and undergo experiment. Outside speakers came to talk to children – one such annual visit was the Empire Lectures to Schools Programme. The number of educational outings, all subsidised by Gloucester, increased – as did trips to the cinema to see films such as *Tom Brown's Schooldays*' (1951),), *Robin Hood*' (1953), *The Coronation*' (1953) and *Scott of the Antarctic*' (1957). In the secondary modern school a full range of vocational courses was studied, some of which required specialist facilities – metalwork, woodwork, needlework and domestic science. General science appeared in the early 1950s and gardening became rural science. In 1958 governors agreed to buy a potter's wheel for the secondary modern school.

Before her retirement Miss Drabble attended courses on such exotic subjects as slipper making and lampshade making. Miss Wright became an expert in making soft toys. By 1953, needlework had been introduced in the junior school. By the late 1940s children were also receiving careers advice.

Sport in the secondary modern school took place when possible on the playground. The school playing field was officially the football ground near Bream Rugby Club. It was here that the inter-school sports were held in 1958. Sometimes also the tennis court and the sports field at the Cricket Club were used.

Performance was a major area of success at this time, particularly in Miss Drabble's school. Theatre groups came to perform plays inside school and outside in the open air. The schools always took part in country dance festivals and Forest of Dean eisteddfods.

The girls' school competed regularly at the Cheltenham Festival in both drama and music. The girls' choir in particular was famous throughout the county and beyond. In 1949 they were invited to audition for the BBC. The audition was successful. They were broadcast on the wireless (radio) as part of Uncle Mac's Children's Hour on 31 January 1950. Thirty-four girls conducted by Mrs V L Davies and accompanied by Mrs G Nowles sang seven songs at St Catherine's Hall, Bristol. They were 'on air' for seventeen minutes. Unfortunately, the BBC does not have a recording in its archive. On 28 February 1951 the choir did a pre-recording for the BBC at Lydney Town Hall and a similar event occurred on 31 January 1952. The recording was to feature in the BBC Junior Choir Light Series. It was truly remarkable that the choir of such a small Gloucestershire school could achieve such prominence.

Nowadays, schools have a constant battle to keep up-to-date with the technology of education and to train staff in its use. 'Twas ever thus. In 1951 the secondary modern staff had a demonstration of the Aldis film-strip projector as they struggled to come to terms with the advanced technology of film-strips. The secondary modern was well ahead of the field at the time – it had a wireless. Thus, at 11 a.m. on 8 February 1952 the whole school was gathered together in the hall to hear the proclamation of Princess Elizabeth as Queen Elizabeth II. One week later they gathered again, to hear the broadcast of George VI's funeral. They soon had a tape recorder as well. What a well-off school.

Across the road in the Church school (now the junior school) they used their 'Coronation money' to buy a wireless. The wireless was installed in 1955 and it had a Coronation plaque fixed to it. This may have made them bold. The following year they asked the LEA for a record player. What wanton extravagance! They were refused.

An aerial view of Bream infants and secondary modern school in the 1950s.
Photo courtesy of Phil Horsley

Domestic bliss. Willie and Lilian Watson in the garden of the school house c.1928. They had 2 daughters, Mary in the photograph and Joan born in 1930.
Photo courtesy of Joan Watson

Boys School, 1931. The staff are Willie Watson and Doris Worgan.
Photo courtesy of Joyce James

Miss Ivy Drabble. Headmistress of Bream Girls School and Bream Secondary Modern School 1927-58.
Taken from a photo kindly provided by Carole Butt

VE day tea-party at the end of the Second World War. The flag pole in the boys'
school playground can clearly be seen in the background.
Photo courtesy of Marlene Moore

The VE party at school, Friday
11 May 1945. Miss Burnham is
on the right of the photograph.
She was an evacuee teacher
from Essex who had arrived in
Bream in June 1940. She left
the village on 9 July 1945 with
the 4 remaining evacuee
children. Note the Hard-up
Tree on the left and the
signpost – still bare of its signs.
Photo courtesy of Patricia Dwight
(née McKinnell)

VE tea party. Is this a joyous occasion – or have too many cakes been eaten?
Photo courtesy of Tony and Brenda Preest

A further photo of the VE tea party. Adults from left are: unknown, unknown, Margaret Burdess, Mrs Morris and Mrs Watson.
Photo courtesy of Peter Richards

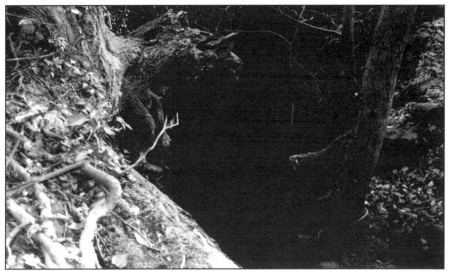

'The Joint'. The tree spanning the Joint where the accident happened in 1941 is in the foreground.

The entrance to the Joint.

The trip to London, Saturday 1 October, 1951.
Photo courtesy of Mrs E.M. Kear

The 'Galt' see-saw purchased by the Infant PTA in 1956.

Infant's school c.1952. This is the only picture I have seen that shows the 'white line' (the Berlin Wall). The infants doing their 'rolls' are on the 'wrong' side of the line.

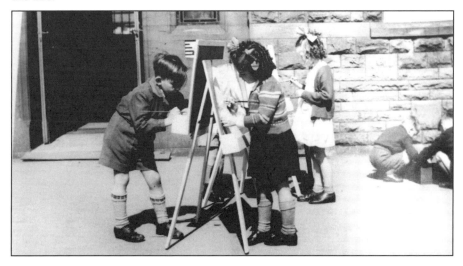

Infant art. Early 1950s

More infant pictures from the early 1950s

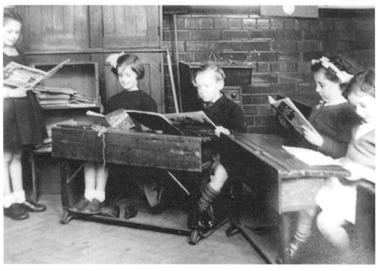

Infant milk monitors at work 1956.

Party time in the newly created Junior School c.1951. The vicar is the Revd Vernon. The picture was taken in the current Room 1 and the door to the old boys yard can clearly be seen on the back wall.
Photo courtesy of Roy Haviland

Infants school 1951. The headteacher in background is Miss Alford. From time to time the infants had a 'fair' in their playground. The boy in the distance is believed to have been 'sent out' from the fair for being naughty.   *Photo courtesy of Esme Pritchard*

Bream Girls School Choirs c.1947. The shields were won at the Forest of Dean Eisteddfod at Cinderford. The staff are Miss Arnold (music mistress) on left and Miss Drabble.   *Photo courtesy of Joyce James*

The BBC Choir of Bream Secondary Modern School. The photo was taken on the stage of Lydney Town Hall (where the recording was made) on 28 February, 1951. The girls were wearing turquoise blue skirts and white blouses. Mrs Knowles, conductress is on the left.
Photo courtesy of Jennifer Hancocks

Carnival Time, 1952
Photo courtesy of Jennifer Hancocks

CHAPTER EIGHT

1959–2006: All Change Again

Heads

Secondary Modern School	Junior School	Infant School
Mr J W H Stokes 1959–60	Kenneth Arthur Pritchard 1954–77	Cecily Leach 1955–69
Gordon Gwilliam 1960–73	Alan Cedric Garbutt 1977–86	Wilma Nash 1970–83
		Ann Coker 1983–85

Schools closed July1973 and the junior and infant schools amalgamated to form Bream Primary School

Bream Primary School
Roger Hughes 1986–89
Paul Woodward 1990–97
Carol Soble 1998–2000
Linda Banfield 2000–2002
Caroline Alty 2002–2004
Nick Stafford 2005–

The recent past and the writing of history are uncomfortable bedfellows. For one thing crucial information may not be available. Most public records are subject to a thirty-year closure rule. If records relate to sensitive issues they may be closed for even longer. Thus the census, a very personal set of records, is closed for a hundred years.

A further complication in writing about the recent past is that many of the participants are still alive. In respect of this book, this means that any account of recent years must of necessity be strictly factual, non-contentious, very circumspect and probably brief. Offence must be avoided. Thus, past pupils and staff, parents and grandparents may well have opinions about these years and stories to tell. That is fine but, understandably, they will not be included here unless I feel they are completely 'safe' and inoffensive. Far more dust needs to settle before the late twentieth-century history of the schools is subject to rigorous histori-cal scrutiny.

PREMISES AND ORGANISATION

Secondary Modern Closure?

Educational planning, as many of us can confirm, is not a precise science. Circumstances change, in some cases quite rapidly, and a decision taken on a school in one year can quickly become out-of-date.

This happened at Bream Secondary Modern School. The school had only been opened in January 1951 and yet by 1959 Gloucestershire were considering its closure. The problem was numbers. There were simply not enough pupils coming in to make the school viable. As originally planned, the school was to be a three-form entry but by 1959 that was revised to a two-form entry and a further reduction down to one-and-a-half was anticipated. In November 1959, the chair of Gloucestershire Education Committee, Major Birchall, and the Chief Education Officer, Mr Watkin, informed the school managers that the LEA wanted to close the school and transfer the pupils to the Lydney secondary modern schools. A special meeting of managers on 24 November 1959 voted in favour of the reorganisation plan by the fragile majority of five to four. This decision gave an uncertain mandate for closure – the chair of the managers, Dorothy Percival, had been absent from the meeting due to illness, and the right to vote of one of the managers who opted for closure was subsequently questioned and the said manager resigned.

In September 1960, the managers requested a Ministry inquiry into the closure plan. Meantime, the parents had become actively involved and sent a petition to the Ministry of Education, not against closure but against sending Bream children to Lydney schools. Their preferred option was Coleford/Berry Hill. Gloucester responded to this by offering a compromise of allocating three-fifths of Bream's children to Lydney and two-fifths to Coleford.

At this point the staff asked the managers if they could express their own views on the situation. Their particular concerns were that they had been kept in the dark about developments and they were also concerned about the loyalty of the managers to the school when they voted for its closure. The managers then rescinded their motion of November 1959 and supported the LEA plan of allocating children at age eleven to Coleford as well as Lydney.

In 1962 these proposals were again in the melting pot when the minister decided not to approve of the plan to close the school and the LEA in turn began to consider alternative plans, including building a new grammar school at Broadwell. The uncertainty prompted some parents to opt to send children to the Lydney secondary modern school even though they would have to pay the cost of transport. Such a decision had a further impact on the entry to the school, for in September 1964 there were only thirty-seven new entrants. The following year there were thirty-eight.

'Comprehensivisation'

By the mid-1960s the Labour Government was introducing comprehensive education throughout the country. Gloucestershire LEA now abandoned plans to reorganise the secondary modern schools in the south Forest. Instead the LEA presented two alternative plans for a comprehensive scheme in the area. The plans were presented to the managers by the LEA at a special meeting on 11 July 1966. Plan A involved two age eleven–eighteen comprehensive schools based at Lydney and Tidenham. Plan B would involve using the existing primaries for ages five–eight, using the secondary moderns as middle schools for ages nine–twelve and having one large upper school at Lydney to cater for age thirteen–eighteen year-olds.

Initially the managers favoured option B, because it would retain the existing buildings and possibly the staff, but as the national debate gathered pace, plan A, focussing on a primary/secondary break at the age of eleven, gathered popularity.

The die was finally cast in October 1970 when the managers received notice under Section 13 of the 1944 Act of the closure of Bream Secondary Modern School, Lydney Grammar School, Lydney Secondary School for Boys and Lydney Secondary School for Girls. A comprehensive school in Church Road. Lydney (subsequently Whitecross) would cater for 1,350, eleven–eighteen-year-olds and a comprehensive at Tidenham (subsequently Wyedean) would cater for some 450.

The newly reorganised schools were intended to be operational in September 1973. Inevitably, problems ensued. In 1971 Wyedean had been omitted from the building programme and no approach had been made to purchase the site in Beachley Road, Sedbury. The Secretary of State would not authorise phase one of building work to begin at Wyedean until April 1973. There was no way the school would be built by September of that year. The 'make-do-and-mend' solution to this problem was to house the first two years of Wyedean School at Lydney Secondary Modern School for the period September 1973 to July 1975. They could then transfer to a completed Wyedean in September 1975.

Thus Bream Secondary Modern School did finally close its doors in July 1973, its pupils and its staff transferring to Whitecross School. The school had only been in existence for twenty-two years and for most of that time its long-term future had been in doubt. Amazingly, the school put on a brave face and carried on as normal during these uncertain years. In 1959, a new woodwork room came into use. In September 1964, the school started its first ever fifth form with seventeen pupils staying on an extra year till they were sixteen years old. This resulted in further extension of premises – a new terrapin came on site to house the stayers. In September 1964, the school had 206 pupils on roll and a further terrapin was erected early in 1965 to enable the school to cope. Soon after this the headmaster and secretary relocated the office to the former needlework room. It remained there till the amalgamation of the infant and junior schools in 1986. The previous head's room, at the top of the stairs, became a staff room.

One can only marvel at the job done by the staff during these years. They lived with the constant threat of closure, they coped with change and they did the best possible job they could for the pupils under their charge.

On 26 June 1973 in a final act of defiance, a panoramic school photograph was taken. To my knowledge this is the only one ever taken of the secondary modern. The school finally closed one month later.

Vacant – One School

The closure of the secondary modern school had implications for the other two schools in the village at that time – the infants and the C of E junior schools. At a junior school managers' meeting as early as November 1963, ten years before closure of the secondary school, the head of the junior school had posed the crucial question. He asked his managers whether the juniors could relocate across the road if the secondary school were to close. The advantages were obvious – a newer building, larger premises and, above all, a corridor facilitating movement around the school.

Pending a decision on this the junior school continued as best it could in its current premises. In September 1965, with 143 pupils on roll, the managers officially declared the school 'full.' Any application to enrol in the school from out of the recognised catchment area, now had to be by letter to the managers. Other changes to the junior school premises at this time were the demolition of the flag pole on grounds of safety in 1965 and the connection of the toilets to the mains in 1966. This replaced the system whereby the toilets had been flushed from the school's rainwater tank.

In the early 1960s, the junior school managers had been trying to persuade the LEA to erect a 'youth hut' on the school site. The LEA could not afford to do this but in 1965-6 advocated another idea. They proposed using the recently abandoned Princess Royal site as a youth centre. The school managers were dismissive of the idea. They argued that the site was too remote and was already suffering vandalism. Nothing was done at either site.

In respect of the infant school the new staff room and toilets were finally installed in 1962. In 1970–71 a terrapin was brought onto the playground to relieve crowding in the school. The terrapin was in full use by the end of January 1971. Unfortunately, the installation contained one basic flaw that had to be corrected the following month. Initially there had been no wire-netting installed at the base of the structure, thus any number of infant balls went missing. A worse problem for the infant school arose later that year, when the roof began leaking. The managers' meeting on 23 September 1971 was told that remedial work had been carried out but the weather had been fine ever since and the effectiveness of the repairs had yet to be tested. During the meeting a heavy rain storm blew up. Cometh the hour, cometh the rain. The managers got wet and had to adjourn their meeting to a different room. One is tempted to ask whether it rained on the just or the unjust. In 1971 the school's first reference to pigeons occurs. They were apparently roosting in the infants' roof. The handyman closed off access to the roof but the birds still persisted to use the school site as their home. Possibly now it is descendants of those very same pigeons that plague the community centre.

At the beginning of 1972 the infants finally got total independence – it had installed its own separate telephone. The number still survives within the current school phone number. Originally in 1972 it had been Whitecroft 628.

As plans firmed up for the closure of the secondary modern school, the junior school started to think about moving. At a special meeting in October 1971, the managers formally agreed to transfer premises as soon as the buildings were available and the necessary adaptations had been made.

As far as the infants were concerned there were to be several changes as a result of the closure of the secondary school. The classroom that had been transferred to the girls' school was now returned. The secondary school canteen was to be taken over by the infant school. The terrapin was to have an extra bay fitted to serve as a staff room and the school was to undergo conversion to oil-fired central heating.

In September 1973, the junior school took over the main block of the secondary school. For a while, the juniors were to operate as a split-site school because the county could not afford the cost of converting the secondary school specialist rooms at one fell swoop. Only three out of seven classes were transferred in September 1973, two more classes followed in September 1974 and the remaining two in 1976.

The transfer of the junior school 1973–6 had two significant implications, one for the school itself and the other for the village as a whole. Regarding the former implication, the junior school and the infant school now occupied the same site. Where was the logic in having two separate heads and staff, two separate administrations and two separate schools? The case for amalgamation into one primary school was overwhelming. For the wider village the fact that, after over 100 years spent in the service of education, one of the principle buildings at the crossroads was now vacant and available for community use, was at once an opportunity and a challenge.

The Community Centre

The deed from the Crown to the archdeacon of Gloucester and the vicar of Bream in 1860, that led to the building of Bream National School, contained a restrictive covenant that if it ceased to be a school, the site was to revert to the Crown. If the building were to be used for general community use, that covenant would have to be annulled or released.

This was duly done by a Deed of Release dated 1 May, 1979 agreed between the Crown Estate Commissioners and the two trustees – Archdeacon of Gloucester (William Thomas Wardle)and Vicar of Bream (Philip Rees). The cost of releasing the covenant was £17,500, paid by Gloucestershire County Council. A month later, by a conveyance dated 5 June 1979, the trustees gave the buildings and land to the county council 'free of monetary consideration.'

Subsequently, the old school became a library and a youth and community centre. In 1980, a right of way was granted round the back of the building to facilitate potential movement between the community centre car park and the doctors' surgery. To my knowledge, this has never been used. In 1982, the school house was sold into private ownership and in 1985, land to the rear of the community centre was sold, it being deemed unnecessary to the centre's requirements.

For some twenty years the Bream Youth and Community Centre was run jointly by a local management committee and the county council. This was to change in the late 1990s when Gloucestershire County Council Education Committee decided to adopt a more flexible approach to youth work and to reduce considerably the number of fixed bases from which it was operating. At the same time, the county council itself operating on a remit of maximising the value of its assets, began to consider the sale of the Bream Community Centre site. Initial discussions on purchase or lease of the site by West Dean Parish Council stalled, and it did appear that the county council was intent on selling the site for housing development.

The thought of the demolition of a magnificent old building of which they were immensely proud provoked a massive outcry in the village. An action group was formed, a petition was signed by 2,000 people and on Friday 31 July 1998 over 200 people from Bream occupied the steps of Shire Hall to make their protest.

In the face of this the county council agreed to sell the site to the parish council in November 2000. This really was a victory for the community. With funding from the South West Regional Development Agency, the parish council then undertook a major refurbishment and redevelopment of the site. In 2005 further work was undertaken with the provision of a new parish office and toilet block. The building is now as it has been since 1862, a hive of activity and right at the centre of the community. The official reopening on 19 December 2005 was carried out by that distinguished citizen and elder statesman of Bream, John Hale. The Forest of Dean Male Voice Choir provided superb entertainment.

The Amalgamation of the Infant and Junior Schools, 1986

Even before the junior school moved across the road in 1973–6 to occupy the same site as the infant school, there had been some movement towards amalgamating the two schools. This was particularly evident in respect of the managers of both schools.

The infant school, since its beginning in 1907, had been part of the Forest of Dean Group of Council Schools, whose managing body met in Cinderford. There were some fifteen county primary schools in the group. The group had been in existence since 1903, as a result of the 1902 Act creating the Gloucestershire County Council Education Department. As an aside, it is interesting to note that most of the managers since 1903 had been men. Eliza Young, who had retired as headmistress of Bream Infants School in 1941, had been highly honoured to have been invited on to that august body. A lady from Bream was to break the mould even further at a group managers meeting on 3 February 1964. The lady was Councillor Marion Rees. In the absence of Mr Bevan, the chair, Mrs Rees chaired the meeting. At the end of the meeting Alderman J L Jones remarked that this was the first occasion in history that a woman had taken the chair at a Forest of Dean School Managers Group Meeting. He complimented Mrs Rees on her chairmanship. How times have changed – I hope – since 1964 when it then could be considered so remarkable for a woman to chair such a meeting. Marion was to serve Bream schools with distinction for many more years as a manager and then as a governor – including the role of chair.

The Church of England junior school had a different set of managers. For one thing they were not part of a group and for another they were closely connected to the Church and the vicar was usually the chair. In practice it was not unusual for a manager of the Forest of Dean Group to also serve as a manager of the junior school.

In 1969 the decision was taken to abandon the group system of managing Forest primary schools and set up a separate management body for each school. This was to come into effect in 1970. Logically, in Bream it would make sense if the same managing body was to administer the infant and junior schools, provided that the diocese, the two sets of managers and the local community were all in favour. They were. The new constitution specified two foundation managers to be nominated by the Church, two managers nominated by West Dean Parish Council and two managers nominated by the county council. The first meeting of the amalgamated management body occurred on 15 October 1970. The vicar, Reverend E C Musselwaite, was appointed chair. The managers agreed to meet at least once per term in each school with the appropriate head present and an agenda relating to that particular school only.

As this system evolved the managers eventually began to discuss both schools on the same afternoon, each meeting lasting forty-five minutes. Thus, one meeting would start at 2.30 p.m. with the infant head present and infant business being discussed. At 3.15 p.m. the infant head would be replaced by the junior head and the identical same managers would then discuss junior school business. In the interests of the genuine equality of schools the next time they met would begin with junior school business and so it would alternate. It is a mouth-watering thought that the entire business of the managers was conducted in just one-and-a-half hours per term. I have seen governors' meetings in the 1990s with nineteen items on the agenda of a meeting that lasted longer than three-and-a-half hours. I offer no comment on the length of today's meetings.

To anyone outside these two consecutive meetings' system there would seem to be an irrefutable case for amalgamation. When Ken Pritchard, the long-serving head of the junior school, announced he was retiring in 1977, the Chief Education Officer proposed the schools should amalgamate that September. There would be 280 pupils on roll, sufficient for a one-form entry primary school. Staff jobs would be protected. Managers were unanimous in rejecting this suggestion and were supported by parents when they were consulted in March 1977. Two into one was not going to go – yet. Both schools quite jealously guarded their independence even though they were on the same site. The white line across the playground ('The Berlin Wall'), which demarcated the schools continued and the corridor door between the two establishments was regularly locked. At one point, a notice appeared on the junior school staff toilet door 'This toilet is for junior staff only.'

The issue briefly reappeared in 1983 when Wilma Nash retired from the headship of the infant school but again nothing materialised.

It was a case of third time lucky for the LEA in 1985–6 and this time the situation was really opportune. The head of the infants, Ann Coker, was leaving in December 1985 and the head of the juniors, Alan Garbutt, was contemplating retirement. The opportunity for the LEA was too good to miss. In October 1985 the governors voted for merger. The following month the parents did likewise. What brought the change of heart? Had time and logic transformed local opinion? Or could it be a change of name for the managers? The Education Act of 1980 had decided that school managers were now to be called governors and their correspondent was to be known as their clerk. Could it be that the governors of 1985 were wiser than the managers of 1977? It is an interesting speculation along the lines of 'what's in a name'? In fact the managers of 1977 were broadly the governors of 1985.

The new school, Bream Church of England Primary School, opened on 2 September 1986. There were 214 children and, apart from the new head, Roger Hughes, eight full-time staff. The vicar, Philip Rees, was chair of governors. A new monthly newsletter began. In 1987, as a result of the 1986 Education Act, the governors began that hardy annual presentation 'The governors' report to parents.' In the summer of 1987 the school staff and parents had a major confrontation with the LEA. At the time of the merger, Gloucester had given an assurance that 'no child will suffer as a result of the amalgamation.' There was understandable fury in Bream when the staffing complement was reduced from eight full time staff to seven with effect from July 1987. A parents' group visited Shire Hall on 10 June and LEA staff braved a very hostile meeting in school on 25 June. All to no avail. The two sides disagreed and differed.

Inevitably premises changed following amalgamation. The HORSA building was demolished to be replaced in 1993 by a new Elliott Medway (prefabricated) classroom. A few years later, a grant of £400,000 enabled a major extension of the school to take place – a new hall, kitchen, toilets and two classrooms. The extension was formally opened by Secretary of State, David Milliband on 1 April 2004.

STAFF

Infant School Heads

Of the two candidates interviewed for the infant headship in December 1954, Cecily Leach was the unanimous choice of the ten managers present. She took up her post at the start of the summer term in 1955, the school having had a supply head from Christmas to Easter.

When I started work on this book in 2004, I was fortunate to interview Cecily some months before she died at the ripe old age of ninety-five. She was a delightful lady and a very good head. The school was inspected in 1958 and it is quite frankly one of the best HMI reports I have read. Accompanying the report was a lovely letter from Mr H J Beddington[9],

---

[9] This was Harry Beddington who was also a favourite Forest entertainer with his stories and verse in Forest dialect. He went on to publish some wonderful books including the Forest of Dean classic *Forest Humour*.

correspondent in the Education Office at Cinderford, which begins 'Dear Mrs Leach, Congratulations on a very excellent report. . . '

Cecily had been born in Yorkley in 1908. Her father was head of Pillowell Boys School. During the Second World War she taught in London. After the war she worked at Blakeney School before coming to Bream in 1955. She retired at Christmas 1968.

Cecily's success at Bream can be summed up by three anecdotes. When I met her, thirty-five years after her retirement, she said to me quite simply 'I loved my school.' She also told me about an aggressive mother who did not hesitate to come into the school to complain in no uncertain terms. On one occasion she was going to telephone her complaint to the Education Office. Cecily invited her to use the school phone. Somewhat taken aback the mum declined. With no residual animosity, Cecily summed the mum up: 'She was a sweetheart really. She had the interest of her child at heart.' Cecily also told me how it was in her class prior to going home time on a Friday afternoon. The sweets were given out to settle the children down, she read them a story and they then went happily home.

The search for a successor to Cecily was difficult. The initial advertisement did not, in the LEA's view, produce any candidates of sufficient quality. They re-advertised. Six candidates were invited for interview in January 1969. Of the six candidates two withdrew by letter, one telephoned that her car had broken down on the way, one did not appear and apparently sent no message. This left only two candidates, neither of whom was considered suitable. Miss Wilma Nash, the senior mistress, was asked to take temporary charge of the school. In June, two further candidates were interviewed and again managers felt neither was suitable. They asked that Miss Nash be appointed. In reply, the LEA asked Miss Nash to 'continue indefinitely.'

This ridiculous situation continued. At the end of 1971 the managers wrote again to point out that Miss Nash had been 'acting head' for three years and that their wish was that she should be made permanent. The LEA replied that the only alternative to the present situation was to advertise the post. The managers decided to let 'sleeping dogs lie.' Wilma Nash thus became head of Bream Infants by default, some three-and-a-half years after she had started doing the job temporarily.

Miss Wilma H E Nash finally retired from Bream Infants in July 1983. She had started at the school in 1951 and had been head since 1969. As Cecily Leach had done, she ran a happy and successful school. Her passing has left behind a fascinating controversy. On the window-sill in the school there was a jar of soapy water, labelled as such and intended as a deterrent for infants who might use bad language. Was it ever used? There is the mystery. Several adults I have spoken to think not. Among the children, however, there is an as yet unconfirmed report that it might have been used on a little boy called Chalky White. Who knows? It will all come out in the wash.

Ann Coker became the head of the infant school in September 1983. At the time there were only seventy-four children on roll. In December of that year Mrs Adams retired as deputy head and was replaced by Val Pittaway. The following December Mrs Wildin, the secretary, retired and was replaced by Jane Murrell. In December 1985, Ann Coker left the school for a promotion to be General Adviser in Derbyshire. Val Pittaway became acting head until amalgamation in September 1986, when she became deputy head of the new primary school before going on to a headship of her own at Coalway infants.

Junior School Heads

The head of the junior school, following Willie Watson's retirement, was Kenneth Arthur Pritchard who was to serve the school with distinction for twenty-three years. By a quirk of fate, he very nearly did not get the job. Willie Watson gave formal notice of his retirement to the Church school managers over six months before he finally left to give them ample opportunity to appoint a successor. First time round, Ken Pritchard did not even apply. Three candidates were interviewed by the managers and Miss Armson of Dursley Primary School was selected. She subsequently declined the post and the managers had to start the selection process all over again. This time Ken Pritchard, head of Pillowell School, did apply and was selected from an interview field comprising five candidates. At his interview it was made clear that the occupation of the school house was not a condition of his appointment. For a term, the school had a supply head and Ken Pritchard officially took up post on 3 May 1954.

Ken Pritchard's impact on the school was dramatic. Of the pupils in the top class who had taken the eleven plus before his arrival only five went to grammar school. In his second full year in charge, 1955–6, eighteen went to grammar school. Recently, I asked Mrs Audrey Cooke (née McDowell), for her recollections of school life under Ken Pritchard. Audrey had been one of the staff in the late 1950s and early 1960s. Her abiding memory was of a happy school. She particularly remembered Ken Pritchard's desire to give Forest children experience of the world outside the Forest and his enthusiasm for school visits. On one trip to London he apparently had a crocodile of no fewer than eighty-nine children. Another trip was to Bournemouth by train, three hours to get there, two hours in Bournemouth and then three hours to get home.

Lady Edna Healey was a dear friend of Ken. She has submitted the following recollections of Ken for this book:

I don't know when it was I first met Ken but it must have been in Sunday school in 1924. He and his family were part of our Baptist Chapel childhood. His mother had great sympathy with those in distress and always went to visit and, as she used to say 'to weep with them.' His father, like Ken himself, was a true Forester. His sister, Flossie, was my Sunday school teacher and a friend of our family all her life.

Then Ken and his wife, Gwen, came to live in Coleford next door to my sister, Doreen, and once again, they were an important part of the pattern of my life. He met his wife in the Army. It's difficult to imagine Ken as a conventional soldier. He must have often puzzled his Sergeant Major: ingenious, doubtless with clever wheezes for avoiding unnecessary trouble, but brave he certainly would have been.

It was a very happy marriage, Gwen made a perfect wife for an unusual man. They were model parents encouraging their two sons through school homework and universities and had the reward of seeing them prosper in successful careers. When I stayed with my sister I was always glad to see Ken, admire his gardening prowess and hear of his golfing enthusiasms. I sorely miss them both when I come to Coleford.

But I best remember Ken as a young man in our sixth form classroom at Bell's Grammar school. His seat was in the front by the window – wide open in summer – and outside, a row of scented pinks and a distant view of the Welsh hills. Suddenly between lessons that rich Forest burr would break out with *'Out Through the Windy, Borge.'* He would throw his neighbour's ruler outside into the flowerbed and Borge would be out and back again before the next teacher came. 'Out through the windy, Borge' has become part of our family language for a quick exit. It must be explained that the Borge in question was Kenneth Butler. But in those days Ken Pritchard liked to change names. In our mad little sixth form community we often knew the boys by their fathers' names. So Ken

Butler was George Butler but then Ken Pritchard would turn the initials around and George Butler became 'Borge Gutler.'

How simple and dotty our fun was in those days. But it was interesting that we always knew the fathers' names. We tapped deep roots in the Forest and never forgot our inheritance. The father's surname might also indicate his occupation. For example, most James's were called 'Chopper James' and the nickname was handed down from father to son.

I am sorry that I never went to see him at his school in Bream but I know how much the school meant to him, and the pupils today can be very proud that they had so original a character for their headmaster.'

According to Albert Weagher, one of his staff, Ken had been an excellent cricketer in his day. Apparently he was known by the nickname 'Flop' because his hair came down over his eye when he was bowling. Albert also recalled that he served eight years and one term under Ken Pritchard and attended only three staff meetings during that time. That fact would very much endear Ken to today's teaching profession.

Having seen the entire junior school across the road by September 1976, Ken Pritchard retired the following summer in August 1977. His successor, Alan Garbutt from Evesham, did not take up post until January 1978. In the meantime, Mrs Marfell, the deputy, became acting head for a term, with Ray Richards as acting deputy. By the autumn term of 1980, Mrs Marfell who had reverted to deputy was away on long-term sickness. Her place was taken by a young teacher from Dinglewell School in Gloucester, Dave Thorley. Mrs Marfell retired on health grounds in July 1981.

Alan Cedric Garbutt retired as the last head of Bream Junior School in July 1986. Ray Richards retired at the same time after twenty-nine years at Bream. Recently she told me a nice story about when she was interviewed at Bream. After the interview she met her husband Lyn in the bar of the Feathers Hotel in Lydney. Someone at the bar overhead her telling her husband that she had got the job at Bream School. With a horrified look on his face he advised Ray to be very careful 'There's some queer buggers up there'!

Primary School Heads

Interviews for the headship of the merged schools were held on 2 April 1986. Roger Hughes from Hamble Primary School in Southampton was appointed. The historic first day of the new school was Tuesday 2 September 1986. As well as Roger, the staff were as follows:

Class	Teacher	Level	Children
1	Mrs H. Wood	Reception	22
2	Mrs D. Witt	Reception/Middle Infant	7/17
3	Mrs M Edwards	Middle/Top Infant	18/8
4	Mrs V Pittaway	Top Infant	28
5	Mrs C. Hendy	Top Infant/1st year Junior	6/21
6	Mr G Bevan	2nd Year Junior	24
7	Mr A Kear	3rd Year Junior	29
8	Mrs S Thompson	4th year Junior	34
		Total	214

The amalgamation of two separate schools is a huge task. Staff, premises and systems all needed to be integrated as quickly as possible and with no diminution of standards and an acceptance of changes that were coming in. A challenging time to be a head. A challenging time to be on the staff of Bream Primary School. As Roger himself wrote specifically about the introduction of the National Curriculum in 1989, 'There is an awful lot to learn. I hope the staff can take it in. The problem is the huge volume and fast pace of change.' Staff today would give a heartfelt 'Amen' to that sentiment. If anything, the pace of change has accelerated since those days.

All the challenges of amalgamation were resolved and comparatively seamlessly. Challenges such as in class 5. The previous infant school had closed at 3 p.m. The previous junior school had closed at 3.25 p.m. Class 5 was now a mixed infant and junior class. As an interim measure, permission had to be sought from six infant parents to keep their children till 3.25 p.m. In the long term, the school day had to be discussed with parents, staff, governors and Shire Hall. The outcome – as we now know was, and still is, a closure at 3.10 p.m.

Roger's successful stewardship of Bream School saw the introduction of school uniform, a new PTA and the adoption of Local Management of Schools (LMS) and the National Curriculum.

In March 1989, deputy head Val Pittaway left to be head of Coalway Infants School and Linda Banfield, who was teaching at Coalway infants, took her place. In December 1989, Roger Hughes himself left the school to take up a headship at a larger school near Torquay in Devon.

The new head, Paul Woodward, did not take up post until 23 April 1990. Linda Banfield meantime was acting head from January to April. Paul is – to-date – the longest serving head of Bream Primary School, from April 1990 to July 1997. During that time he successfully led the school through two inspections. In September 1990–91, his first full year, the practice began of calling classes by the names of trees: Holly (reception class), Sycamore, Rowan, Beech, Silver Birch, Elm, Cedar and Oak.

Paul also saved the school a fortune by somehow finding time to undertake many repair jobs around the school that otherwise would have been contracted out. When in that role, he was known by himself and his staff as Gilbert. 'Looks like a job for Gilbert' was a frequent cry from those years.

Paul left to go to St White's Cinderford in the summer of 1997. The school then had a succession of short-term heads, all of whom made their contribution to the school. When Paul left, Adrian Osborne was acting head for a year, 1997–8. Carol Soble was head 1998–2000. Linda Banfield, previously deputy head, was head from 2000 – 2002. On her retirement the deputy, Caroline Alty, was head from 2002 to 2004. When Caroline left teaching in December 2004, her deputy, Melanie Davies was acting head for a term pending the arrival of the new head, Nick Stafford, in April 2005.

The turnover of heads at Bream in the last twenty years has been truly rapid. Perhaps this reflects a national trend, whereby after three years one hits 'Beecher's Brook.' Certainly the days of heads staying at a Bream school until they retired seem to have long since gone. Another recent national trend that is reflected in events at Bream School is the lack of applicants for head and deputy head vacancies. When Linda Banfield was appointed deputy head as recently as 1989, there were twenty-four applicants for the position. That would not happen now. There would be far fewer.

Secondary Modern School Heads

Ivy Drabble was due to retire in December 1958. Five applicants were interviewed for the headship on 1 October. Mr J W H Stokes, Assistant Master at Lydney Grammar School, was chosen unanimously. One would assume he felt flattered and elated to have been chosen. His first headship. How he would have felt the following month when the managers voted 5–4 to close the school and transfer its pupils to Lydney is any-body's guess. He was committed to leaving a permanent and secure job in Lydney for a future at Bream that looked like being no future at all. In fact, all of this happened before he had even started. He was not due to begin at Bream till 1 January 1959.

It may have been conceivable that he was unaware of the closure decision, but subsequent events certainly indicate that he did know. He began applying for headships elsewhere and was successful in gaining a post at Taunton just over a year after he had started at Bream. He left mid-term on 30 June 1960, a bare eighteen months after taking up post. From the facts as known, he would be entitled to feel badly let down.

The deputy head, Gordon Gwilliam, was given the responsibility of acting head with effect from 1 July 1960. The phrase used by the manag-ers was 'for the time being.' At that point nobody knew for how long the school would be open. Two years later he was still acting head and the managers wrote to the LEA to ask if he could at least be made temporary head. Gloucester said no. The managers asked again in April 1963, arguing that to have an acting head for three years was having a detrimental effect on both Gordon Gwilliam's and the school's status. Given the uncertain future of the school, the LEA would not consent to a permanent ap-pointment. They did however eventually relent somewhat and agreed to advertise a temporary headship for Bream Secondary School. Four candidates were interviewed in January 1964. The selection panel of twelve unanimously chose Gordon Gwilliam to be temporary head of Bream Secondary School. No great surprises there. He had after all been acting head for nearly four years. Had he been there another twenty years he may have got the job permanently. Who knows?

One cannot but admire Gordon Gwilliam's huge loyalty to the school. He was to continue as head (presumably temporary) until the school did finally close in July 1973. He then became head of the upper school at Whitecross. While at Bream he had been heavily involved in school sport and had a reputation as an excellent footballer in his younger days.

Standards of Health

The health of children continued to improve. By the beginning of this period the child killers of the past were all included in an inoculations programme in schools. Infections can still go the rounds in school but are usually restricted to more minor illnesses such as colds and influenza.

As children's health improved the annual checks in schools became unnecessary and were replaced by a referral system. This has enabled the Schools Medical Service to diversify somewhat, rather than concentrate on a universal 'basic health' programme. For example, included within the service from the 1960s was the referral system to educational psychologists.

There may have been quite a time between referral and consultation but at least the service was there. Health issues themselves also have become part of the curriculum and are currently part of the Government's 'Every Child Matters' initiative in schools. An early example of a curriculum approach to health occurred in the early 1960s at Bream Secondary School. Before they left school every child had to watch the film *'Smoking and Health'* and have a talk from a doctor – Doctor Hunt. In the 1950s, no school would have tackled smoking as an issue. By the 1960s there was a growing recognition of the possible dangers attendant on smoking and schools were one of the messengers for that campaign.

As part of the improving health support for children, the Forest of Dean Group Managers faced a dilemma in 1963. Recently developed in first aid was the concept of the 'kiss of life.' At the time, there were some ethical questions about whether it was right and proper to allow the treatment to be done. Managers decided that it was. Then there was the training issue. West Gloucestershire only had one dummy on which staff could be trained. The issue then was where the dummy would be located. The agreed answer was the education office in Cinderford.

In the 1960s and early 1970s school meals continued to be cooked on both sides of the road. There was still the occasional 'issue' in respect of the junior school kitchen. In 1961 the county auditor was critical of the record keeping and, in 1967, the area organiser was not happy when she thought that an advertised hot roast may have been cooked the previous day.

When the junior school moved across the road to the secondary modern school site, the old kitchen and dining room were completely refurbished. They were 'handed over' in March 1976. Soon after, there was a vacancy for a new cook supervisor. This led to one of those periodic Bream versus LEA conflicts. The LEA was anxious to redeploy a cook from another school. Bream managers were having none of this interference. They told the LEA that their candidate would be considered along with any other applicants. In fact, the LEA candidate was not even interviewed. The job was given to Rose Clements.

With both schools now on the same site it made sense to rationalise cooking arrangements. In 1981 the infant kitchen was closed. They still ate separately from the juniors, their dinner being transported across the playground (and across the white line) on a heated trolley.

The school meals continue to be cooked on site as they have been for over sixty years, but now, in 2007, they are cooked in the new kitchen which replaced that of 1976 and are eaten in the new hall.

Inevitably, children continued to be vulnerable to accidents. In 1963 Sheila Gifford continued the infant school tradition of getting a bead up her nose. The bead was removed at Lydney hospital. Early in 1974 the junior school experienced something that could have been very serious. When the children were outside at playtime, two dogs entered the school yard. Six children were bitten. The police were called and one of the dogs was subsequently put down. In 1975, a ten-year-old junior girl was knocked down in Parkend Road. She broke her hip.

In one sense this had been an accident waiting to happen. For years teachers and parents had been concerned about the increase of traffic and the safety of children around the school sites. As early as 1964 the infant school PTA had asked the headmistress, Mrs Leach, to raise with the managers the need for a road safety warden. The Road Safety Organiser visited the site, observed that there was good visibility on the crossroads and stated that the amount of traffic using the roads did not justify the LEA employing a warden. In reply, the managers pointed out there were three schools in Bream, very close to each other, and it was very busy at the beginning and end of the school day. The LEA did not change their mind.

In 1968 it was the turn of the junior school managers to have a go. They pointed out that, despite the secondary modern school building a staff car park at the rear of the premises, it was not being properly used and there were still cars parking by the gates and it was dangerous for the children. They asked that school signs be put up and yellow 'no parking' lines be painted. The LEA answer was no. The managers replied that they would not be held responsible if there was an accident.

In 1971 the LEA did concede. A road safety warden was appointed to do 'six-and-two-thirds' hours per week on the crossroads. The first warden was Marina Lambert. In respect of the 'Lollipop Lady' at Bream, the landmark date was 24 September 1979 when Jean Crockett started work as School Crossing Patrol (SCP). I wonder how many children Jean has escorted across the road since? In 1993 Jean was awarded the title of 'Gloucestershire Lollipop Lady of the Year' – a much deserved award. As far as the pupils and parents are concerned Jean has deserved such an award every year since 1979.

When the ten-year-old girl was knocked down in 1975, the junior school managers demanded action by the LEA. A barrier was then erected to stop any children going straight from the playground into the road. School signs and 'no parking' zigzag lines were also installed. The barrier later had to be moved across the road in 1978 to locate it opposite Blue Rock Crescent and where the junior school pedestrian gate now was.

Was all now well with parking by the schools and road safety issues? No it was not. Miss Nash reported to the infant school governors in 1980 that parents were still parking outside the gates and that the 'no parking' signs had been vandalised. Recently the area has been designated as a school safety zone with a 20 mph speed limit.

Holidays

The general school holiday pattern of three terms with significant holidays at Christmas and Easter, three half-term holidays and six weeks in summer has continued for much of the last fifty years with minor modifications. One modification was the introduction of an extra bank holiday – May Day – in the 1970s. Usually the half-term holidays were two or at most three days in October and February but by 1981 they had become a week in length. For one year in 1972, the February half-term was extended from two days to a week due to a national emergency. It was the time of the fuel crisis and the 'Three Day Week.'

In total, children now attend school for 190 days per year. Staff are often in school during their holidays anyway but on some occasions are there as a result of formalised in-service training days. These consist of five in total and because they were introduced by Secretary of State, Kenneth Baker, they were known as 'Baker Days.' In the profession at the time (the late 1980s) they were referred to as 'Bidets.'

Recently the authorities have begun to amend the three-term pattern in favour of a six term system. The problem with the traditional three terms has been that Easter is, in the Christian calendar, a moveable feast. Traditionally it is held on the Sunday after the first full moon following the spring equinox (21 March) thus it can be in March or in April. If Easter is early then the traditional three school terms could not be of equal length.

In the new six-term model, if Easter is in March, as it is in 2008, then the school will just be closed for the two bank holidays over Easter – Good Friday and Easter Monday. Interestingly, this has similarities with the situation at Bream schools in the 1860s. Then, the only time off for the children at Easter was on Good Friday – after they had attended a church service.

As always royal occasions would trigger a school holiday. The schools closed twice in May 1960, once for the marriage of Princess Margaret and secondly for the birth of Prince Andrew. The Queen's Silver Wedding on 20 November 1972 and Princess Anne's Wedding on 14 November 1973 were also school holidays.

Day outings for children continued in all three schools as regular events. As well as whole school outings, individual classes continued to attend more local events to do with music, drama, vocational education and sport. Extended outings began in the 1960s in both the secondary modern and junior schools. To my knowledge the first secondary modern residential was in March 1966, when twelve boys and three teachers (Mr Booth, Mr Jenkyns and Mr Griffiths) went on an Outward Bound visit to Snowdonia. In 1968, Steve Booth led a secondary school skiing holiday in Switzerland. This was so successful it became an annual event. The first junior residential, as far as I know, was on 30 January to 3 February 1967, when Ken Pritchard and Ray Richards took a party of children to Seven Springs for the week. Two years later, Ken Pritchard took eleven children on an educational cruise on the *SS Uganda*. In 1982, Dave Thorley and Ray Richards took some juniors on a three-day visit to Winchester. Later in the 1980s the residential trip went annually to London and, amidst great excitement, included a West End show. The current pattern of residentials for juniors – Craven Arms in Shropshire – began on 1 June 1989 when thirty children were taken for a week. The cost was £95 per head.

In the early part of this period of time, half-day attendance holidays still occurred although they no longer exist now. Ken Pritchard had a creative idea in the junior school for attendance holidays. He would put two half-days together and award the whole school a Friday off in December for Christmas shopping. The Sunday school treat holiday had disappeared by now but elections continued to provoke a school closure, even more so, when European elections were held after Britain joined the Common Market.

Inevitably, bad weather continued to close the school. Early in January 1963, the infants school was closed for two days because of frozen pipes. Later that month both infants and secondary modern schools had to close from 23 January to 4 February because there was no fuel to run the boilers. Fuel had originally been ordered on 12 December, but poor road conditions made fuel supplies unreliable. Increasingly desperate requests for anthracite fuel were made. When the fuel did run out the heating system had to be drained completely to prevent frozen pipes. When anthracite was finally delivered on 31 January, it was so frozen it was very difficult to use in the boilers. The frozen fuel was putting out the fires. Eventually the boilers were lit successfully and the needlework room was used as a fuel thawing and drying area.

The worst conditions since 1947 occurred in January 1982, when the village was cut off and the infant and junior schools were closed for a week. Other bad weather closures occurred (and still do) from time to time. One such in 1996 raised an interesting problem. The school was closed on Tuesday 6 February because of snow. A notice was put on the gate to inform parents that it would reopen on Wednesday. Unfortunately someone had changed the notice to read that the school was closed until Monday 12 February. Consequently only half the school turned up on the Wednesday. It is amazing the lengths the staff will go to in order to avoid school! That week's *Forester*, with a true journalistic eye for a pun, ran the story under the headline 'Snow Joke'!

Perhaps the most unexpected holiday during this period occurred on the occasion of a 700th and 750th anniversary on 25 June 1965. I wonder if any of today's pupils would know what the holiday was commemorating? It was the 700th anniversary of Simon de Monfort's Parliament and the 750th anniversary of Magna Carta.

Children and their Doings

Despite the fact that the schools are in a prominent position right at the heart of the village, they have always been prone to petty burglary and some vandalism. Usually there is no cash to steal in school anyway. In 1983 when the junior school was broken into, 25p was stolen. In 1980 both infant and junior schools were broken into. £15, a calculator and 2 lb of bacon was taken. In terms of out-of-the-ordinary break-ins, one in July 1966 is worthy of note. The thieves broke into the secondary modern school kitchen and cooked themselves a plate of liver and eggs.

Given the nature of children, out-of-the-ordinary behaviour will always occur. In 1968, a boy in the secondary modern school was suspended for assaulting not just one, but two, members of staff. The managers logged the reason for his suspension as being 'continuous truculent behaviour.' Truculent seems an unusual word to use to describe an assault. In 1967, infant staff were surprised to see some of the secondary modern school-boys on the school roof. Nobody had thought to extend the playground white line over the tiles of the roof so it could have been an interesting hypothetical legal question as to which school's jurisdiction they were within. Were they trespassing? Whether they were or they were not, I am sure they were suitably dealt with by Gordon Gwilliam, the secondary school head.

Problems with the youth club continued even though they had been moved from the infant school to the secondary school, where it was felt the furniture and fittings would be more suitable. In 1961, there were school complaints when there was damage to the corridor lights (truculent horseplay?) More seriously, in April 1964, the locked corridor door separating the two schools had been forced. When infant school staff arrived the following morning they found matches, cigarette ends and apple cores littering their staff room. Obviously the infant staff room was well away from the prying eyes of the youth club adult supervisor. To prove youth work can go well, in October 1968, the secondary school was hired by the Bishop of Bristol's Youth Committee for a weekend of expeditions into the Forest. All was fine. In 1972, the junior school across the road was also successfully hosting a Church young people's club.

The senior Christmas party at the secondary school by 1964 had become a dance with a live dance band – it was after all the 'swinging sixties.' The dance became a regular event and by 1968 had become so popular that a Valentine's dance had developed as well.

A noteworthy success for the junior school in 1985 occurred when Sarah Yeates and Keith Wildin were selected to take part in the television play by Dennis Potter, *The Singing Detective*.

Hilary Wood first taught at Bream on a temporary contract in 1966. Later she returned to Bream and became a specialist reception teacher until her retirement in 1995. In the reception class Mrs Wood was often called Mrs Ood. She was also called Mrs Block. Her most charming moment came after she had been explaining something to her class. One little boy then asked in wide-eyed wonder 'Mrs Wood, how do you know all that?'

Parents and their Doings

Over the last fifty years, the partnership between parents and schools has continued to develop. In today's jargon parents are key 'stakeholders' in the school and, without their full involvement and co-operation, it is difficult to see how a school could function properly. It was not always so. In the early years of this period some heads took the view that parental involvement stopped at the school gate. Home was home and school was school and never the twain should meet. Such heads would not have

PTAs. That was to invite possible interference on what were regarded as matters that were properly the domain of the profession. A brief termly report and a signed tear-off slip to acknowledge receipt followed by an annual parents' evening was, in some establishments, the limit of parental involvement.

In the 1950s and 1960s Bream schools did not always have PTAs. To flourish, they needed the active support of a head and bottomless enthusiasm from sufficient parents to fulfil the key committee functions of the organisation. When they were in existence their role could be pivotal. For example, it was the AGM of the infant school PTA that started the campaign for a road safety warden in 1964. Later, as key personnel left, the organisation lapsed only to be reformed in 1972. In the early 1970s one of the managers asked, since there was a successful PTA in the infant school, why was there not a comparable group in the junior school? There soon was and the junior PTA was actively engaged on what was probably the most ambitious PTA project in the history of the schools to date – funding a swimming pool. The decision to fund a pool was taken early in 1974 with a target completion date of September 1975. By September 1974, £2,300 had been raised, of which £1,112 was from public subscription. The pool was opened in time for the summer term 1976. 'Swimming buses' down to Lydney pool could now be abandoned.

An agreement was reached with the LEA in 1979 whereby the county council took over the maintenance of the pool and its heating costs for eight weeks and the PTA received a grant from them of £400 to fund a new liner. Thereafter, every May, an intriguing sight could be seen in the pool area – a team of wet and bedraggled parents and staff armed with buckets and mops and wearing wellingtons, clearing out the pool ready for that summer's use. Reluctantly, owing to structural deterioration, the governors had to take the decision in 2005 to dismantle the pool. The area is now transformed into a beautiful environmental area, courtesy of funding from the Friends of the school (once the PTA and now, since 2000, a registered charity under the name of 'The Friends of Bream School PTA').

One of the chief fundraisers for the Friends over the last twenty-five years has been the fête. In the 1980s this was held on the playground, but from 1991 has been held on the Sports club field. It seems I owe an apology for the 1991 fête. Paul Woodward's record of the event reads 'The fête was opened by Ian Hendy and down came the rain.' My profound apologies. In fact Paul went on to describe the event as an amazing success that raised over £400. The fête has continued on the sports field ever since and nowadays would expect to raise in excess of £3,000.

Maintaining the momentum of a PTA can be a thankless task. To misquote Churchill, much can be owed by so many to so very few. PTA AGMs can be poorly attended and sometimes staff can nearly outnumber parents. Various inducements have been tried – holding meetings at the Montague (in 1993) or at the Rising Sun, but there is no magic formula that will guarantee a solution to the perennial problem of recruitment. That said, when helpers are needed – as at the fête – helpers are always there.

Events can sometimes have a downside – quite apart from the weather. In 1979, at a playground junior fête, the infant school had been left open to increase the indoor facilities available. The PTA subsequently received a letter from the infant school complaining of obscene writing on blackboards, furniture overturned and toilets left in a filthy state. The infant school was locked for subsequent junior fêtes. In 1992, the PTA helped organise the Country Dance Festival on the sports field. A crowd of 1,500 was expected, but there was a last minute controversy over whether the event should proceed because of possible damage to the cricket square.

Parents now, quite rightly, have considerable responsibilities and influence in school. Since 1986 parents have been represented on the Board of Governors. The current instrument of government for the governing body requires there to be fifteen governors for Bream School. No fewer than five of those governors are parents, the largest group on the committee. When governors appoint a head or deputy the parent governors are always represented on the selection panel. Parents are in the school as helpers in some capacity or other every day. Via the Friends, an enormous sum of money is raised every year to benefit the school. The role played by parents today in the success of the school is enormous.

Occasionally, as in all good marriages, there are spats. It has been known for individual parents to complain to Shire Hall. It has also been known too, for individual parents, possibly in the heat of the moment, to threaten legal action. Such instances are rare. By and large the relationship between parents and school at Bream is harmonious and productive.

School Links with the Community

The school continues to be at the heart of the community. Any stranger to the village would be surprised by the activity around the school at 8.45 a.m. and 3 p.m. The community centre, while no longer a school, still contributes enormously to the service of the school in its role as a car park. The meeting of parents and grandparents at the school gate, particularly at 3 p.m. is impressive. This, I am convinced, is one of the heartbeats of the village, a central part of the village grapevine and the source of all knowledge on every local topic under the sun. Long may it flourish.

As previously, the school sites at the village centre are the focus of the community. In a crisis this is where the village meets. In 2006 when news broke of the threatened closure of the Dilke and Lydney hospitals the 'Save our Hospitals' meeting was held at the community centre (the old school) with overflow being at the primary school (the new school).

Any number of organisations have continued to use the schools for a wide variety of activities. In the 1960s the secondary modern school hosted a variety of evening classes – woodwork, needlework, pottery and keep fit. The Horticultural Society used the hall for its Chrysanthemum Show, the school for its meetings and the playground to crown its Carnival Queen in 1965, its centenary year. The choir, Brownies, Darby and Joan, youth clubs, West Dean Parish Council, Mothers' Union and various political party associations have all used the schools at different times.

The schools have also been involved in community initiatives. When the Cenotaph needed restoration in 1970 the restoration committee met in the secondary modern school and the pupils took part in a sponsored walk that raised a substantial £60 towards the project. Similarly, when the monument needed further work in 2000 the school was heavily involved. On 10 November 2000 the children did a sponsored silence and raised over £700 for the restoration fund. On Friday 20 September 2002, the school processed behind Bream Band up the High Street to take part in the Cenotaph Re-dedication Parade and Ceremony with the Lord Lieutenant and the Royal Gloucestershire, Berkshire and Wiltshire Regiment. The children's rendition of *'Good-bye-ee'* and *'We'll Meet Again'* captured many hearts. In October 2005 the school planted the Nelson Oak to help commemorate the 200th anniversary of the Battle of Trafalgar.

The next major community event the school will be involved in is their own – the celebration of the centenary of their current building.

Links with the Church

Ever since Henry Poole enrolled Bream School into the National Society in 1819, the clergy of Bream have occupied a central role in the development of education in the village. When the infant and junior schools amalgamated in 1986, it was Reverend Philip Rees who was chair of the governors. The most recent vicar, Reverend Alistair Kendall, was chair for seven years till 2004.

As a voluntary controlled school the constitution of the governing body requires the vicar of Bream to be an ex-officio member of the governing body. The constitution requires two other foundation governors which ensures that the Church has a voice in every decision made by the governors. It is customary for at least one of the foundation governors to be involved in any selection panel for senior staff of the school.

Ever since education began in the village schoolchildren have attended services in Bream church. That custom continues to this day. The secondary modern school began a tradition of an annual carol service in 1966 which was followed until the school closed. The present school continues to attend the parish church and the Methodist chapel and both the vicar and Methodist minister regularly take assembly in school.

In the past, the school's facilities have been used for specific Church events. The hall has been used for Church bazaars and fêtes. In July 1992 the swimming pool was even used by the Church – for baptisms.

Inside the Classroom

In the secondary modern school pupils continued to have opportunities to transfer elsewhere for their education even though they had 'failed' the eleven plus. It was possible – via examination – to transfer to Cinderford Technical College or to take a thirteen plus exam to gain a place at Lydney Grammar School or the technical stream of East Dean Grammar School.

In 1962, a new examination was created for pupils in secondary modern schools in the Forest. This was the Forest of Dean Secondary Modern School Certificate. Twenty-four pupils sat this exam in May 1962 at Bream and all twenty-four successfully gained the certificate.

In 1964, the secondary school curriculum developed further when the school introduced its first ever fifth form. Pupils who stayed on had the perk of golf lessons from the professional at Monmouth. There were also staff coming into school from the technical college in Cinderford to teach commerce to the fifth form girls and engineering drawing to the boys. Towards the end of their fifth year the students took part in an 'Insight into Industry' scheme and had two weeks' trial employment or work experience outside of school to prepare them for the world of work.

The first fifth form cohort at Bream were the guinea pigs for a new exam, the Certificate of Secondary Education (CSE). A Grade 1 CSE was regarded as the equivalent of a pass grade at GCE Ordinary Level. In

1965 the school entered pupils in seventy-six subjects, of whom ten (14.3 per cent) were passed at Grade 1. Other good result years were 1971 and 1972. In 1971, thirteen pupils gained eighty-six pass grades, twenty-five of them at Grade 1. In 1972, five boys gained forty-three passes, seventeen of which were at Grade 1. Not all pupils stayed on to do exams. In the 1960s and 1970s many were Easter leavers who had left school before the exam season started.

The secondary modern at Bream was a busy school that provided varied opportunities for its pupils outside the narrow confines of the curriculum. In 1954, the first school magazine was published. It cost 1s. 6d. per copy and the school incurred a loss of £10 on the print-run. The magazine lapsed until it was revived by Mr Stokes in 1960. Gordon Gwilliam again revived it in 1962 and it may well then have become an annual event until the closure of the school. In the early 1960s the Commonwealth Lecturers continued to visit as did a wide variety of other speakers. For a time, the police delivered a series of lectures. Typically for the girls, in 1966 there was a visiting lecturer on feminine hygiene, followed a few days later by a demonstration conducted by a Ponds beauty consultant. In 1962 the school hosted its first fashion show where the girls modelled clothes they had made in class that year.

In competition against other schools, the Forest music and the country dance festivals continued. The school also took part in road safety quizzes and the inter-school Bible quiz.

In the junior school, the arrival of Alan Garbutt as head in 1977 saw the introduction of the teaching of French to the top class. It lapsed on his departure but has recently been reintroduced into the curriculum. It is hardly surprising that as some new initiatives arrive in education, staff with long memories may react with a 'been there and done that' attitude.

In the 1980s 'block' activities became popular. Thus, in March 1985 the junior school had a reading week. The following year they had a maths week. In 1989, however, the primary school was completely taken up with the national curriculum followed by the literacy hour and the numeracy hour. Now, many would argue that the primary curriculum is more restrictive and prescriptive than it has ever been. While it is important to educate children for the adult world they will face, we must also be very careful we do not take the fun out of education.

One fun thing that happened at the primary school in June 1990 was when a helicopter landed on the school field. This was as a result of a school project on flight. The helicopter then took an aerial photo of the school which retailed at £6.95. How exciting that must have been for the children.

Thankfully ,there are still many opportunities for children to enjoy education. Circle time was trialled in class in 1992 and has been with us ever since. Summer shows, nativity plays and pantomimes are real opportunities to enjoy – and excel. John Isaacs, Primary School Adviser for Gloucestershire, wrote of Bream Junior School's concert in July 1981 'It was quite one of the best school concerts that I have ever seen.' Believe me there have been others before and since of comparable standard.

Any number of visitors come into Bream Primary School with interesting shows and ideas. A typically fascinating assembly was in December 1990 when Mrs Staley, the Methodist minister who was visiting from the USA, brought an American bear into assembly. Mrs Staley explained to the children that the bear did not know anything about Christmas and she had brought the bear to school to find out what it was about. Sometimes, musicians from other countries come to entertain and work with the children – as do theatre groups. The child that is rampant in me would have loved to have seen the Pandemonium Theatre Company perform *'Mugglewumps and Marshwiggles'* in 1986.

The rate of technological change in teaching has continued to accelerate. In February 1958, the infant school purchased a Fordigraph 100 duplicator. A demonstration was arranged to enable staff to come to terms with the infernal machine. In 1962 a new record player arrived and in 1965 an Aldis projector. In 1968, the secondary modern school's first trip abroad was actually filmed. Gordon Gwilliam wrote that this was the school's first attempt at film making. Apparently it was very successful and was shown to parents on return. I wonder if a copy has survived? In 1970 the secondary school acquired an epidiascope[10] – the wonder of wonders at the time. In 1982 the infant school bought a colour television and got rid of their black-and-white set; and video had already arrived. Finally, in 1984 in the junior school a special parents' evening was arranged. The attendance rate was over 80 per cent. There was a display of educational equipment. Part of that display was just one computer and children were just learning how to use it. Today the school has thirty-four computers.

I suspect Bream schools have always done well at sport. Yet there have never been playing fields actually on the site of any of the schools and that makes their sporting success all the more remarkable.

In the early 1950s the secondary modern school had high hopes of the proposed High Beech site which would have provided ample playing

---

[10] An epidiascope is a predecessor to the overhead projector. Bright light, mirrors, prisms and lenses are used to display an image of an opaque material onto a screen.

fields. When that plan was abandoned in 1952, the managers had to seek alternative sites. The Cricket Club was one possibility. Another was the possibility of purchasing the rugby field. A third was to rent the field next to the rugby field which was owned by Mrs Cooke and used by Bream Amateur Football Club. The third option was chosen. The school became a tenant of Mrs Cooke and in turn sub-let to the football club for £15 per annum. As part of the arrangement, the school was allowed to use the football club changing rooms. In 1960 the football club was given permission to erect a spectator stand on the ground.

There were inevitably problems with animals. The managers' minutes for February 1958 state that the field had been 'invaded' by pigs. Having solved the pig issue the next meeting discussed the fact that Mr Jones' sheep were now on the field.

The lack of playing fields was also a problem for the junior school across the road. In 1968 the LEA proposed that they could purchase a two-acre site near to the school for playing field facilities if the managers approved. The managers did. It took quite some time however for the proposal to become fact. Five years later terms had been agreed on the 2¼ acre site but it had not yet been seeded. For a number of years the junior school had been using the secondary school field for matches. The lease on that field was extended till 1975, even though the secondary school had closed in 1973, just to give the juniors a green field site. Finally the managers received a letter in September 1974 from the LEA, to advise that the field off Highbury Road had its goalposts up and was now ready for use. It has been in use ever since.

There have, however, been problems even with this playing field site. In 1978 there were complaints from staff about broken bottles and dog excrement on the field. Later that year it was noticed that sheep had been found on the field and – with the fencing intact – nobody knew how they could possibly have got in. The gate was then fitted with a sheep-proof padlock. A few months later the fencing somehow got broken and the sheep were in again.

Over the last twenty-five years the school has built up a formidable record of sporting achievement. The children of this village are naturally keen on sport but a lot of the recent success has to be down to Andy Kear and the team of teacher and parental coaches who have helped out with the football, netball and other sports' teams over the years. I do not know how many Bream School runners have been Gloucestershire cross-county champions, how many Bream children have represented the County at sport, or how many Wildin Cups or Forest netball tournaments the school has won. The list could go on and on. The enthusiasm and commitment of Bream children to sport can be summed up by one six-year-old infant who recently asked Andy 'Mr Kear, when can I play for the school football team?'

But the success of Bream School is about more than sport. It is a happy school; a busy school; a supportive school. In April 1993 *The Citizen* newspaper summarised a recent (1992) HMI report with the following sentence, 'Bream School is a friendly, welcoming community with a strong corporate identity.'

It has been so for a very long time.

Friday 31 July, 1998. A community up in arms. The demonstration against the sale of the Community Centre for housing development, on the steps of Shire Hall.

1 April, 2004. The official opening of the new buildings. From left: John Hale (LEA Governor), Diana Organ MP, Caroline Alty (Head), John Elliott (Parent Governor), Revd Alistair Kendall (Chair of Governors), David Miliband (Secretary of State) Liz Cann (Staff Governor) and Ian Hendy (Community Governor). *Photo courtesy of John Hale*

The original gates in 2006, just prior to their replacement.

Infant Staff mid 1960s. From left Joyce Beach, Wilma Nash, Muriel Edwards and Cecily Leach (Headmistress, 1955-69)

Top class leavers in 1982 with Mrs Ray Richards (class teacher) and David Thorley (Deputy Head). The backcloth is the wall that had recently been painted by students from Cheltenham Art College.
Photo courtesy of Bream School

The school meals service has been in operation in Bream Schools in 1926 and continuously since 1943. This is one representative team of the canteen staff in 1961 in the Junior School.

From the left Mrs Saunders, Mrs Bath (cook) and Mrs Allen. *Photo courtesy of Diane O'Dell*

20 September, 2002. The re-dedication of Bream Cenotaph. The school in procession behind Bream Band.

20 September, 2002. During the re-dedication service.

Friday 21 October 2005. The School Council plant the Nelson Oak on the site of the Hard-up Tree.

1959 domestic science class show their Christmas cakes. This photo was on Miss Parry's wall. *Photo courtesy of Esme Pritchard*

One of the early great teams of the 'Andy Kear era'. There have been many successful teams of boys and girls, in many different sports over the years at Bream schools. *Photo courtesy of Bream School*

Another successful team. The staff in 1991. There have been countless other successful staff teams – before and since. *Photo courtesy of Bream School*

Life in a village school – the Browns, Harries and Baldwins. When this photograph was taken all eight were in school at the same time. They are all either brothers or sisters or first cousins. Back row from left: Richard Brown, Gavin Harries, Daniel Baldwin and Shane Baldwin. Front row: Andrew Brown, Nicola Harries, Megan Harries and Jonathan Baldwin.
Photo courtesy of Nicola Harries

Life in a village school – Four generations through Bream schools. Maud Randall (right) 1923-32, David O'Dell 1945-51, Janet Ray 1973-79 and Daniel Ray 2003 to present. *Photo courtesy of the family*

CHAPTER NINE

2007

This chapter contains the work of Bream school children, produced in the spring of 2007. It begins with the thoughts of the oldest class, Willow, and then moves sequentially to Oak, Cedar, Elm, Beech, Rowan and finally Holly, the reception class.

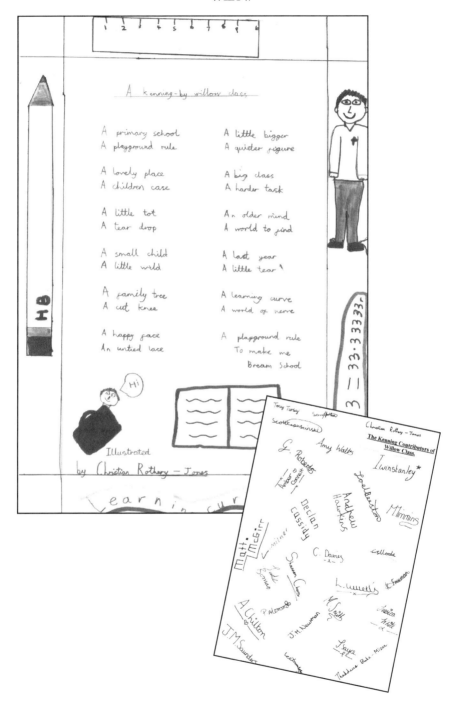

A kenning - by willow class

A primary school
A playground rule

A lovely place
A children case

A little tot
A tear drop

A small child
A little wild

A family tree
A cut knee

A happy face
An untied lace

A little bigger
A quieter figure

A big class
A harder task

An older mind
A world to find

A last year
A little tear

A learning curve
A world of nerve

A playground rule
To make me
Bream School

Illustrated
by Christian Rothery - Jones

Hi

Learning curve

The Kenning Contributors of Willow Class.

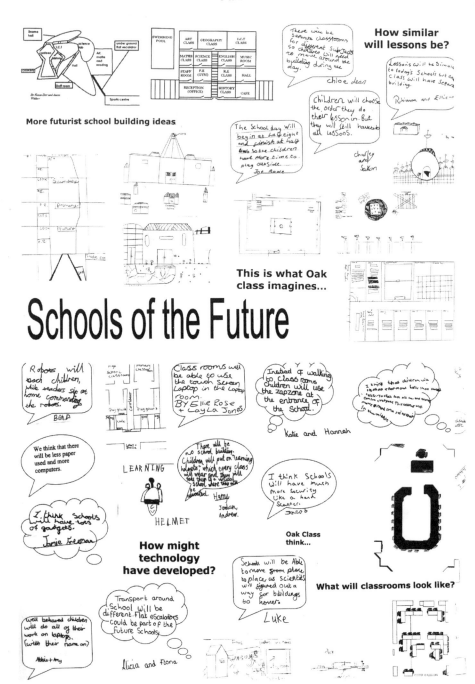

Schools of the Future

More futurist school building ideas

This is what Oak class imagines...

How similar will lessons be?

How might technology have developed?

Oak Class think...

What will classrooms look like?

What will Bream School be like in another 100 years?

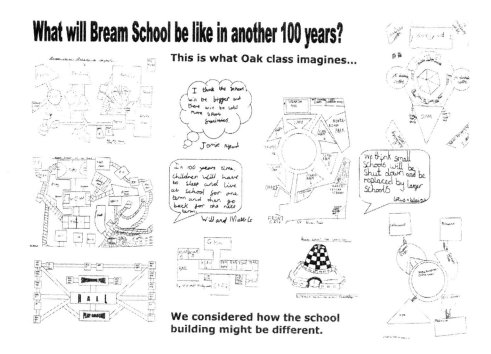

This is what Oak class imagines...

We considered how the school building might be different.

Addendum: A setting error meant that this picture was missing from the Oak class contribution
Here it is as an addendum to this first edition of *Meet at the Schools*..

Cedar

Cedar class would like you to meet the staff at Bream CE Primary School. 2007

mr Stafford is the head teacher and does paper work in his office.
JOSH Skidmore

Joe Whittington

Mrs McLaughlin works one day a week. She is always happy.

Liam Rutter

Daniel Ray

JACK Vaughan

Mrs Kear does a lot of work on the concert and is really good on the Piano.

Rhiannon Jones

MRS DUNFORD

She helps teach country dancing on mondays and in charge of the Year 2 Class
Liam Brady

Mrs Kibble does first aid. She bandaged my leg when I fell over.

Billy Biddle

Taela Cutmore

Mrs J Watton teaches the youngest children and shows us how to do country dancing.

Ciaran Bowden

Alicia Brazier

MRS COOK

She is very kind and helps us with words We get stuck on
Adam Arkell

Tommy Brett

Mrs Martin is quite a new teacher here. she is deputy head of the School.

Mark Franklin

Ryan Cassidy

Mrs Blake-Mizen is a sweet caring lady with lots of good ideas.

Emily Perrett

Beth Watts

Miss Harris works in the infant classes and a very caring person.
Naomi Davies
Hugh Spencer

Mrs Martin helps in lots of classes and is really kind.
Beth Watts

Reuben Elliott

miss Jeavons helps me with maths and is a very good teacher.
Lee morgan
Naomi Davies

Keely Hughes

mrs Clapp is very patient and helps us with our writing.
Damian Baggs

MRS. WALLER
She is clever, funny and very kind and helps in lots of classes.
Sam Brough
Josh Skidmore

Mr Kew is in charge of PE and is good at sport.
Sean Brett

Kyle Brain

mrs spencer is very kind and helpful and teaches year children.
Alex. Rennie
Alexis Rothery-Jones

Emily Perrett

Sean Griffiths

mrs turner is our class teacher she is very good at her science and at doing aerobics. Everybody loves her.

Mrs Hann smiles and laughs a lot and helps me with my maths.
Oliver Lewis

Tayah Allen

mrs marshall teaches maths to some of us and is a very caring person
Callum Rogers

Cedar class would like you to meet the staff at Bream CE Primary School. 2007

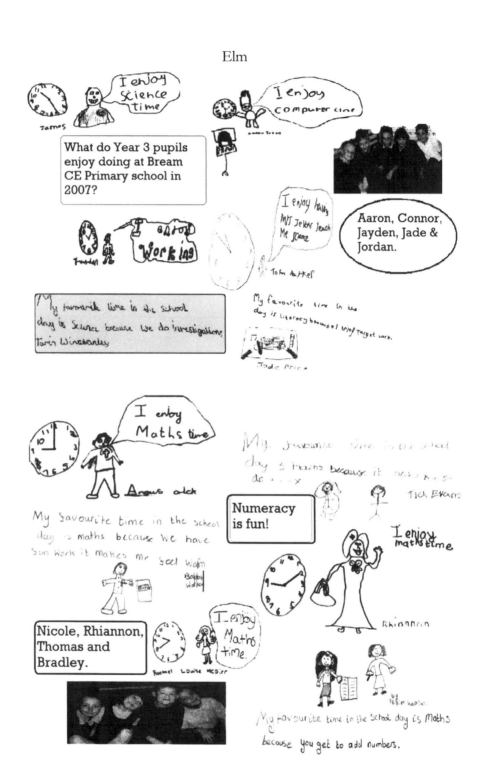

What do Year 3 pupils enjoy doing at Bream CE Primary school in 2007?

Aaron, Connor, Jayden, Jade & Jordan.

Numeracy is fun!

Nicole, Rhiannon, Thomas and Bradley.

Investigating artefacts and creating our own artistic items is time well spent!

Samuel, Zac, Tia and Morgan

Time for sport and leisure.

Bradley, James, Angus, George and Lauryn.

Tea, Maisy, Tarin, Ben & Joshua.

Jacob, Samuel, Bobbie & Yesim.

In 2007 Year 3s can sing and tell stories in French.

Rachael, Holly, Jessica & Tom.

In 2007 collective worship and meeting with the community is an enjoyable activity.

1907   Bream Primary School   2007

I wonder!

Left margin (top to bottom): Jamie, Emma, Ryan

Right margin (top to bottom): Harryson, Charlie, Harra, Micky, Georgia, Keely, Arron, Jade, Chloes, Aalon.P

In our classroom we have brightly coloured tables and chairs.
In our classroom we have central heating to keep us warm.
We use paper, pencils and pens.
I wonder!
Today in class we have books, puzzles and games.
In school we have science lessons.
Science books, interesting facts and information
I wonder!

Left margin: Caitlin

At school we use laptops, computers and smart boards.
We use the internet and knowledge box.
Today we watch video's and listen to CD's.

Left margin: Luke, Ellie

I wonder!
In school we learn to read and write.
Today we use capital letters and full stops.
We learn to count, add, subtract, times and divide
I wonder!
In school we do P.E.
we use the large apparatus and play tennis.

Left margin: John

we play football and have races.
I wonder!
In school we have a school council.
Two members from each class.

Left margin: Gayla

we make the school a better place.
I wonder!
Today i have stickers in my sticker book.
Swiming certificates and trophy's.
SPORTS awards and medals.

Left margin: Emily

I wonder!
At school we all love playtimes.
Skipping ropes, stilts and hoops.
hear the bell, stop. quick, Line up.

Left margin: Osydd

I wonder!
Today we have after school clubs.
Dancing, sport, art, and music.

Left margin: Ethan O

Have enjoy yourselfs.
I wonder what it was like 100 years ago?

Holly

CHAPTER TEN

Postscript on the Future

As part of the centenary celebrations in 2007, Bream children will be experiencing what it was like in school in 1907. It is fascinating to speculate on how it will be in 2107 and how – even if – the 200th anniversary will be celebrated.

I bow out before the last word.

Ian Hendy

Bream Primary School 2107

Say, will the oak trees still be standing
Around that grey and red-roofed building?
And will Bream's children as before
Come running, chattering through the door?
Will there be learning still to find
And precious blossoming of the mind?
Will teachers still be there to see
Or lost to new technology?
Will gathering parents content to be
At the gate at ten past three
To meet and greet, discuss the day
And finally wend homeward way?
Will education have a case
To be continued in this place?
Or will there be some different rules?
And will we still 'Meet at the Schools'?

Cath Hendy
(With apologies to Rupert Brooke)

References

Extensive use has been made of indexes of births, marriages and deaths, census returns, trade directories, the *Victoria County History* and log books of the schools.

In some cases references used are named in the text. Otherwise they are listed below.

Chapter one: 1907: A very handsome pile of buildings . . .'

1.   The Public Record Office   ED21/6048
                                         ED7/35/347A
                                         ED21/6047

2.. The Gloucestershire Record Office
                                         Education Committee Minutes 1907
                                         Gloucester Journal Nov 2 1907
                                         SM85/1 M1 and M2
                                         D9096/F3/365

Chapters two and three 1700–1862: A £50 Acorn and an 'Indefatigable Clergyman' and 1862: The Wonderful Work of Witherby and White

1 The Public Record Office   ED7/35
                                     ED103/42
                                     ED49/10628

2. The Gloucestershire Record Office D2186/94
                                     D9096/F3/17
                                     P57/CH1/1 and 2
                                     P57/CH1/3
                                     Wills of Mary Gough and Henry Poole
                                     Glos. Notes and Queries Vol. i p 292–3

3. Lambeth Palace Library. No 345.

4. Other.   *Bible Christians of the Forest of Dean* – George E. Lawrence.
              Personalities of the Forest of Dean – H.G. Nicholls (1863).
              Children's Employment Commission 1842. Report on the Forest of Dean by Elijah
              Waring (Picks Publishing,1998).
              Education in Gloucestershire, A Short History. (Published by Glos. C. C. 1954)

Chapters four and five: 1862–1907: The Big Picture and At the Chalk Face

1. The Public Record Office   C54/16664 F3/17

2. The Gloucestershire Record Office AE/R4/347
                                     D9096/F3/ 411, 412, 413, 414

K521/18
K526/1
EL567/F3/3
SM85/1/M1,M2

3. Lambeth Palace Library. No 348
4.   Other. Deed re. 'Cherries' Courtesy of Jane Hardman
          Information from Ida James re. Jasmine House. Courtesy of Paul James.

Chapters six, seven and eight – 1907–27: On to the Next Crisis, 1927–58: All Change ,1959–2006: All Change Again
1. The Public Record Office   ED21/51956 and 51957 and 6046 – 6048
                                ED21/29006 and 29007
                                ED70/885
                                ED161/5864
                                F3/18
                                D9096/F3/18

2. The Gloucestershire Record Office SM57/1/M1
                                SM57/2/M1 and M2
                                SM57/3/M1,M2,M3
                                SM57/4/M1
                                SM85/1M3 –M17
                                S57/2/1–9
                                S57/1/1–3
                                S57/2/1–2

3. Lambeth Palace Library No 348
4. Other.   Deeds of Community Centre held by Solicitors to South West Regional
          Development Agency

Index